THE LIBRARY

ST. MARY'S COLLEGE OF MARYLAND
ST. MARY'S CITY, MARYLAND 20686

REGULATION UNDER INCREASING COMPETITION

Topics in Regulatory Economics and Policy Series

Michael A. Crew, Editor

Graduate School of Management
Rutgers University
Newark, New Jersey, U.S.A.

Previously published books in the series:

REGULATION UNDER INCREASING COMPETITION

edited by

Michael A. Crew

Center for Research in Regulated Industries
Graduate School of Management
Rutgers University
Newark, New Jersey, U.S.A.

Kluwer Academic Publishers
Boston/Dordrecht/London

Distributors for North, Central and South America:
Kluwer Academic Publishers
101 Philip Drive
Assinippi Park
Norwell, Massachusetts 02061 USA
Telephone (781) 871-6600
Fax (781) 871-6528
E-Mail <kluwer@wkap.com>

Distributors for all other countries:
Kluwer Academic Publishers Group
Distribution Centre
Post Office Box 322
3300 AH Dordrecht, THE NETHERLANDS
Telephone 31 78 6392 392
Fax 31 78 6546 474
E-Mail <orderdept@wkap.nl>

 Electronic Services <http://www.wkap.nl>

Library of Congress Cataloging-in-Publication Data

A C.I.P. Catalogue record for this book is available
from the Library of Congress.

Copyright © 1999 by Kluwer Academic Publishers.

All rights reserved. No part of this publication may be reproduced, stored in a retrieval system or transmitted in any form or by any means, mechanical, photo-copying, recording, or otherwise, without the prior written permission of the publisher, Kluwer Academic Publishers, 101 Philip Drive, Assinippi Park, Norwell, Massachusetts 02061

Printed on acid-free paper.

Printed in the United States of America

This book is dedicated to Horace J. De Podwin, distinguished economist, dean, and colleague.

CONTENTS

AUTHORS AND DISCUSSANTS

Christopher T. Babb, Manager—Network Modeling, NECA

Mark C. Beyer, Manager, Office of the Economist, NJ Board of Public Utilities

Joel Brainard, Chief of Regulatory Research, New York State Department of Public Service

Timothy J. Brennan, Professor of Policy Sciences and Economics, University of Maryland—Balitmore County

Janie Chermak, Assistant Professor of Economics, University of New Mexico

Michael A. Crew, Professor of Economics and Director of the Center for Research in Regulated Industries, Rutgers University

Stephen M. Friedlander, Manager, Law and Government Affairs, AT&T

Jiong Gong, Member of Technical Staff, Bell Communications Research

Yoonyoung Kang, Fellow, Energy and Environmental Policy Division, Korea Energy Economics Institute

Paul R. Kleindorfer, Universal Furniture Professor of Economics and Decision Sciences, Wharton School, University of Pennsylvania

Robert Levin, Senior Vice President, New York Mercantile Exchange

Colin J. Loxley, Director—Resource Planning, PSE&G

John Mayo, Professor of Economics, Georgetown University

Glenn Meyers, Senior Consultant, Economic Studies

Richard A. Michelfelder, Vice President—Marketing and New Business Development, Comverge Technologies

William R. Moore, Independant Consultant; formerly Government Affairs Director, AT&T

John R. Norsworthy, Professor of Economics & Management, Rensselaer Polytechnic Institute

Robert H. Patrick, Associate Professor of Economics, Rutgers University

Carl Pechman, Director, Law and Economics Consulting Group

Mark Reeder, Chief of Regulatory Economics, New York State Department of Public Service

Michael Salinger, Visiting Professor, Sloan School of Management, MIT, and Associate Professor of Economics, Boston University

Joseph C. Schuh, Rutgers University

Richard E. Schuler, Jr., Associate Economist, New York State Department of Public Service

Richard Simnett, Director, Strategic Alternatives Analysis, Bell Communications Research

Menahem Spiegel, Associate Professor of Economics, Rutgers University

Diana H. Tsai, National Sun Yat-Sen University

Frank A. Wolak, Associate Professor of Economics, Stanford University

PREFACE AND ACKNOWLEDGEMENTS

This book is a result of two seminars held at Rutgers—The State University of New Jersey on October 24, 1997, and May 1, 1998, entitled "Regulation under Increasing Competition." Twenty previous seminars in the same series resulted in *Problems in Public Utility Economics and Regulation* (Lexington Books, 1979), *Issues in Public Utility Economics and Regulation* (Lexington Books, 1980), *Regulatory Reform and Public Utilities* (Lexington Books, 1982), *Analyzing the Impact of Regulatory Change* (Lexington Books, 1985), *Regulating Utilities in an Era of Deregulation* (Macmillan Press, 1987), *Deregulation and Diversification of Utilities* (Kluwer Academic Publishers, 1989), *Competition and the Regulation of Utilities* (Kluwer Academic Publishers, 1991), *Economic Innovations in Public Utility Regulation* (Kluwer Academic Publishers, 1992), *Incentive Regulation for Public Utilities* (Kluwer Academic Publishers, 1994), and *Pricing and Regulatory Innovations under Increasing Competition* (Kluwer Academic Publishers, 1996).

Like the previous seminars, these seminars received financial support from leading utilities. The views expressed, of course, are those of the authors and do not necessarily reflect the views of the sponsoring companies. AT&T, Atlantic Electric Company, Bell Atlantic (and, separately, NYNEX in 1997), Elizabethtown Gas Company, GPU, New Jersey-American Water Company, Orange & Rockland Utilities, Public Service Electric and Gas Company, Sprint, and United Water Company provided funding for the seminars. Company managers freely gave their time and advice and, on several occasions, provided information about their industries. I especially thank, Lawrence Cole, Frank Delany, Alan Friedman, Gary Gatyas, John Graham, Frank Gumper, Robert Iacullo, Patricia Keefe, Daniel Kelleher, Steve Levinson, Dennis Lombardi, Joel Lubin, Colleen McCloskey, Arthur McGrath, Richard Michelfelder, Don Myers, Lou Peoples, R.S. Plenderleith, Richard Perniciaro, and Joseph Schuh. Horace J. DePodwin, Dean Emeritus, Graduate School of Management, Rutgers University, and President, Economic Studies, Inc. was the keynote speaker at the Seminar on October 27. Fred Grygiel, Chief Economist, New Jersey Board of Public Utilities, was the keynote speaker at the Seminar on May 1. Horace's and Fred's interest in the program, which originated with the first Research Seminar in 1978, has continued ever since and has been a major factor in the success of the program. Both have been extremely helpful to me with their advice over the years, and both were highly instrumental in getting the program off the ground.

Many thanks are owed to the distinguished speakers and discussants, listed on pages vii and viii, for their cooperation in making the seminars and this book possible. Most of them worked very hard in achieving deadlines, without which the speedy publication of this book would have been impossible.

I would especially like to thank Linda Brennan, Assistant Director of the Center for Research in Regulated Industries. Not only did Linda provide able editorial and research program assistance, but she also produced the camera-ready copy for this book.

Finally, I would like to thank Paul Kleindorfer for standing in for me as Chairman of the proceedings on May 1, 1998—the only occasion over the last twenty years or so on which I was prevented from attending. Paul has been associated with the program from the very beginning, having authored and presented many papers and been a source of numerous stimulating comments. I am delighted to acknowledge his contribution over the years.

MICHAEL A. CREW

1

REGULATORY GOVERNANCE AND COMPETITIVE ENTRY[1]

Michael A. Crew
Paul R. Kleindorfer

Regulation of network industries, notably, telecommunications, electricity, gas and postal service, has changed significantly in recent years and has become increasingly complex. Although 1984, with the divestiture by AT&T of its operating companies, was seen as a landmark event, the process had begun several years earlier when competition in the long-distance market was first allowed on a small scale. The entry by MCI into long distance was initially minuscule. However, the camel's nose was under the tent, and, despite valiant efforts by an exceedingly accomplished and regulatory-oriented AT&T management, the battle and the war were lost. AT&T and regulation would never be the same again. Not only was AT&T affected, but the impact was also felt on other industries formerly subject to traditional cost-of-service regulation. Allowing entry into regulated monopolies undermines the traditional structure of these industries and of regulation itself. The problem is that regulators and companies, to say nothing of regulatory economists, were flying blind. Once entry was allowed, the consequences were not clearly foreseen. The contradictions created are still to be resolved.

In this paper, we will argue that traditional and current regulation are inefficient governance structures for the regulation of natural monopoly under the conditions of competitive entry faced today. Existing institutions face internal conflict, making it unlikely that they will be able to reconcile a number of conflicting objectives that they face. This paper will examine the nature of regulatory governance structures under entry. The approach will draw on the approach of comparative institutional analysis pioneered by Oliver Williamson (1980) and employed by Crew and Kleindorfer (1987). As we will demonstrate, the approach to regulatory governance is not as clear and transparent as it was in the days of a traditionally regulated monopolist. Similarly, the objectives of regulation are less transparent.

---

1   We would like to thank Mark Beyer, Janie Chermak, Andrew German, Jiong Gong, Jonathan Lesser, Steve Levinson, Roger Sherman, and Anton van der Lande for helpful comments.

Thus, regulation has becomes more complex and less focused. To make the process more transparent, we will argue that regulation needs to be directed at the residual natural monopoly or that part of the industry that should remain subject to regulation. In electric power, for example, the residual monopoly consists of the wires used in transmission and distribution. In gas, it would be the distribution pipes and ancillary equipment. In postal service, there is a powerful case for considering local delivery as the residual monopoly. Our approach will throw light on current examples of where regulation may not be achieving its objectives or may be inefficient. Areas of concern include the regulatory changes taking place as a consequence of the Telecommunications Act of 1996 and the Energy Policy Act of 1992.

The paper is divided into four sections. Section 1 provides some of the origins, a statement of the problem, and an outline of the proposed solution. Section 2 provides a detailed examination of the changes in regulatory governance and in industry structure needed to address the problem in sunk or fixed network industries.[2] Section 3 discusses the application to postal service. We consider that this warrants a separate treatment because postal service has some significantly different characteristics from traditional public utilities. Section 4 is by way of summary, conclusions, and implications.

1. Origins, Statement of the Problem, and Proposed Solution

Traditionally regulated monopoly was exactly what it appeared to be. It consisted of a single firm supplying the entire market. The regulator did make adjustments from time to time, but these were generally predictable. As Goldberg (1976, 427) argued "Regulation can be viewed as an implicit administered contract..." He argued further that such administered contracts are likely to be efficient relative to some alternatives in situations where assets are long-lived and specific. Indeed, it is these elements that place a burden on the monopoly regulator. He has to act as a neutral referee. He has to balance the interests of consumers and the regulated firm. The consumer would always like to see lower prices. In view of the high level of asset specificity, it would always be possible for the regulator to under-price the services of the regulated firm with little likelihood of dire consequences at least for some time. Unlike the competitive firm, the regulated firm could not just take his marbles and leave, as most of his assets had only their existing use. Wires, poles, conduits, trenches, pipes, and manholes have little value and sometimes a negative value outside their existing uses. For many years, regulation functioned by maintaining the current supplier's monopoly with entry barred and the consumer paying a price that was determined to be reasonable by the regulatory commission. Goldberg's characterization of the regulator administering an on-going and complex contract describes in a few words the nature of regulation. Indeed, because

---

2   Fixed network industries are those with physical connections, namely, electricity, telephone, gas, water, and CATV.

regulation is an administered contract, it had the primary virtue of being flexible. This flexibility inherent in the administered contract worked well as long as the shocks to the system were not too great. The rapid increase in fuel prices were a major shock in the 1970s to the energy industries, but regulators were mostly able to make adjustments for this in the form of fuel adjustment clauses. However, permitting competitive entry was probably too big an event for the system to handle, as it undermined one of the fundamental tenets of regulation. The effects were also insidious in that entry did not occur instantaneously and its effects were gradual. Just because an independent generator set up shop did not mean that the lights went out. This lulled regulators and companies into a sense that nothing bad would happen if they operated in a business as usual mode. Some accommodations to the new situation were made, including allowing the regulated firm more pricing flexibility. Under traditional regulation, prices were set based upon the cost of service and the firm could not change prices without permission of the regulator. Similarly, if it made profits in excess of the amount allowed, it was subject to a rate case and adjustment in rates. Under current regulation, at least where the firm is regulated by price-cap regulation,[3] it is allowed some freedom in setting prices within the constraints of a price-cap formula. The regulator still administers a contract between it and the regulated firm, but the contract is less transparent. The regulator exercises less control over prices but may have to become more concerned over such issues as service quality and the terms and conditions under which entry takes place, including the price paid by competitors for inputs supplied by the regulated firm. Probably the biggest change, as a result of allowing entry, is that the regulator now has to deal with not only the regulated firm but also a number of competitors. Frequently, these competitors are unregulated, but they may stand to gain considerable financial advantages by influencing the regulator's treatment of the regulated firm.

The problem regulators and the industry face is perhaps nowhere better illustrated than in the case of telecommunications. Until the 1970s, telecommunications had been a highly successful and stable industry. It was regulated based upon the traditional argument for regulated monopoly, namely, natural monopoly. Because of overwhelming scale economies there were some markets where one firm was the natural result of allowing unfettered market forces. Traditional regulation attempted to retain the benefits arising from the scale economies, while at the same time preventing monopoly exploitation. For many years, with few detractors, notably Posner (1969; 1975), it was argued that regulation was indispensable in such situations. With a gradual change in this perception, firms selectively entered the business of the regulated firm. For example, MCI only entered the long-distance part of the business of the former AT&T. This immediately raised issues on the terms under which access to AT&T's local companies should be provided. Amid claims of discrimination and other antitrust violations AT&T settled its suit

---

3   For a recent discussion on the effects and operations of price caps see the Special Issue of the *Journal of Regulatory Economics*, May 1996.

with the Justice Department by divesting itself of its local companies, the Regional Bell Operating Companies (RBOCs). This structure of AT&T providing long-distance service and RBOCs providing local service continued for several years. However, the RBOCs wanted to enter long-distance markets and the long-distance carriers wished to get into local service. The Telecommunications Act of 1996 aimed at opening up local service to allow long-distance companies to provide local service and allowing the RBOCs into long distance. *Prima facie*, this seemed to be a clear *quid pro quo*. However, it did not work out quite as intended because of asymmetries in the situation faced by the sides. It would be relatively easy for the RBOCs to supply long-distance service. They could lease facilities from a choice of long-distance carriers, build their own facilities, or much more likely employ a combination of both strategies. However, allowing long-distance carriers in local service was much more complicated because, at least in the case of residential wireline service, there is little scope for more than one supplier.[4] The RBOCs were monopoly suppliers of the inputs required if the long-distance companies were to enter the local market. Thus, the price and the terms of entry by long-distance companies were subject to arbitration by state regulators. The process turned out to be expensive and very little entry has currently taken place into local service. Indeed, the two largest long-distance carriers have shelved, or at least significantly curtailed, their efforts at entry into local service by these means.[5]

This situation in telecommunications illustrates, not surprisingly, that the path to competition in network industries is a rocky one. This is largely because the existing regulatory governance structures, while flexible and evolving, may be failing to address critical aspects of the current situation. In particular, they may not be coming to terms with the role of competitive entry and the notion that regulation may have a different role under competitive entry. In addition to the traditional role of consumer protection, regulation may have to be concerned with enforcing, for example, universal service obligations and with protecting competition from the power of the incumbent, while avoiding severely disadvantageous treatment of the incumbent. The regulator, thus, faces a number of conflicting objectives not the least troubling of which is the continued desire by politicians to maintain some of the cross subsidies that were part of traditional regulation and perhaps add additional ones.

Our proposed solution to these problems derives from the nature of the technology and markets of network industries. These industries involve two basic functions: production of the commodity and delivery of the commodity. With the opening up of traditional network industries to competition, it has become apparent that the natural monopoly argument generally applies to delivery rather than

---

4   It is not to say that absolutely no alternatives exist. Residential subscribers could consider wireless systems. However, the prices have not yet become sufficiently attractive that most subscribers would find them attractive for their residential service, except perhaps in some isolated location where installing a wireline would be very unattractive.

5   AT&T has shelved its efforts and has announced its intention to merge with TCI as an alternative route to local competion. Similarly, MCI is merging with WorldCom.

production. Our basic proposal is that the core monopoly of the regulated business be clearly separated from all other parts of the business and this core should become the primary focus of regulation. The non-core parts of the business should be driven primarily by competition, with the sole role of the regulator in this non-core areas to assure rapid and unconstrained entry. For example, the gas industry has unbundled production, transportation, and distribution of gas and has encouraged the entry of brokers and other financial intermediaries to set up delivery and risk management contracts. This has assured that there is competition in the production of the commodity, natural gas, while the transportation and delivery of gas (which may be regarded as the core monopoly functions of this industry) are usually performed by a monopoly. The electric utility industry has traditionally been organized as a vertically integrated industry, where the utility generates, transmits, and distributes power to the final consumer. There was always some on-site generation where large process industries generated electricity mostly for their own use. With the Public Utilities Regulatory Policies Act of 1978, and the Energy Policy Act of 1992, other companies have entered the generation business. The Modification of Final Judgment recognized the importance of severing the more competitive long-distance business from the monopolistic local business by divesting local into seven RBOCs and leaving AT&T with long distance, equipment manufacturing, computers, information services, and Bell Laboratories. This structure, however, did not draw a bright line between competition and monopoly. The RBOCs were not solely monopolistic businesses. They operated the Yellow Pages advertising and quickly faced competition in their intraLATA toll markets. Some of their access business was also under attack, particularly in the case of their larger customers.

Despite the increased competition, the RBOCs were extremely successful following the Divestiture. They were successful both in their traditional monopoly markets and also in the competitive arena. They benefited considerably from changes in technology with rapid growth in all usage, access, and lines. As a result, they began to look less like the monopolistic providers of access and local service than they had at Divestiture and, as a result, became increasingly eager to enter the long-distance and information markets. The Telecommunications Act set up a process to allow this, taking the RBOCs further away from their monopoly roots. As yet, they have not entered the long-distance market nor have the inter-exchange carriers made any significant entry into the local markets. In view of the disappointing performance at bringing about increased competition in both local and long-distance service, the alternative of paring down to the core of the monopoly may have several advantages from a competitive point of view.

Given these problems, the idea of redefining the monopoly and concentrating the regulation there warrants consideration. The initial step would be to determine which stages of the vertical structure of an industry are potentially competitive and which are structural monopolies. The regulation would then be directed to the natural monopoly stages that have been identified. How such issues might be resolved will be examined in the next section. While we will briefly review a number of alternatives, we argue that the regulatory governance is in need of significant change, including a re-evaluation of the objectives of regulation.

2. Changes in Regulatory Governance in Network Industries

Our approach takes into account that fact that, although there has been significant entry, entry has not been uniform. Entry has not occurred at all vertical stages of the industry. This is for good reason; some vertical stages may still have strong characteristics of natural monopoly because of the economies of scale, of scope, of contiguity, or for other industries depending on the industry. The residual natural monopoly parts of the business are, in our view, those with which regulation should be focused directly. Approaching this problem for each of the industries is complex. In this section, we will examine some of the details of the proposed approach for telecommunications, electricity, and gas. The application would have major differences in each of the industries. In addition, we will provide some evaluation of the efficiency consequences of the proposal in each industry.

2.1. Telecommunications

Continuing with the telecommunications industry example, there is a case for arguing that the monopoly is the wires, poles, trenches, conduits, and the like used to provide access from the subscriber to the network.[6] The next step calls for a decision as to the firm to divest itself of all its activities except its redefined core monopoly.[7] If divestiture is deemed appropriate, the firm would become a provider only of "access" or a "Loopco." As an access monopolist, it would only provide service to other firms. It would not provide retail service. Its customers would be other telephone companies. It would be regulated by a commission, which would adjudicate disputes between it and the other telephone companies.

While divestiture provides a very "clean" solution, it is not necessarily the only solution.[8] An alternative would require that the RBOC not offer any retail services in the area served by its Loopco. Thus, in the Loopco area in which the RBOC owned Loopco, the RBOC would have only wholesale customers, exactly as in the case of a divested Loopco. The RBOC would, however, be able to have retail customers anywhere outside its Loopco territory. So an RBOC would not be allowed to have any retail customers in its current territory but would be able to in the rest of the country. Its existing and new wireless customers would be unaffected. Thus, it would be itself a user of its Loopco for terminating its wireless calls and terminating the calls of its customers outside its territory.

A prohibition on retail customers within its Loopco area creates a problem for

---

6   This access system is used twice to make most telephone calls—at origination or at termination of a call. Where a wireless phone is used, the cellular company provides the origination portion of the call. A subscriber may also call a cellular customer or might use his telephone line to access the internet.

7   Alternatively, it could divest itself of its other businesses and retain just the monopoly core.

8   Recent proposals by LCI and C. Michael Armstrong, the Chairman of AT&T, argue for a clear "structural separation" between the RBOC's access facilities and the rest of the business if they are to be allowed into the business of long distance. See AT&T press release, May 5, 1998 and LCI Petition for Expedited Declaratory Rulings, Federal Communications Commission Docket No. 98-5.

the RBOC. It would presumably be seeking business from all types of customers except in its Loopco's territory. This would not present a problem for small residence and business customers as the RBOC would be banned from serving them within its Loopco region. Large business is sufficiently spread across the country that it might be significantly handicapped in competing for contracts to provide for a large company's business nationwide in that it could not offer service to a customer's plant located in its Loopco area. One approach would be to allow RBOCs to compete for large multi-location contracts over a certain size irrespective of whether the customer had a plant in its Loopco territory. Given the ubiquitous nature of the large corporation, most and probably all of the Loopcos would be involved. In many cases, they would only be involved in contracting with the company's telecommunications provider to supply special access, for example, a high capacity fiber link to the company and the telephone provider's switch. This might be a suitable boundary line. Provided certain conditions were met, including large-scale special access and multiple locations nationwide, the RBOC could seek a waiver to be allowed to provide retail service within its Loopco's territory. The process would involve a number of regulatory complications, with the regulator being required to adjudicate as to whether a particular customer qualified for this waiver. The other alternatives would be to have an absolute prohibition on retail business within its Loopco territory. If it found this unacceptable, it would still have the option of divesting its Loopco.

One model of the Loopco calls for divestiture and the other does not. To bring about the divestiture model might require new legislation or antitrust actions against the RBOCs. The other model might not require any changes. Any RBOC wishing to enter long distance would be allowed to do so provided it set up a Loopco and provided no retail service within the territory of the Loopco. In either case, the RBOCs and other local companies would be given their choice of whether to divest or not to divest under these conditions. The non-divestiture option might be attractive to them if they could sell their local customers to providers of what would now be end-to-end service. For example, each long-distance carrier could be offered the opportunity of buying the RBOC's local service customers who are currently receiving long-distance service. This would presumably raise a significant injection of funds that could be used to further its entry into long-distance outside the Loopco's territory.

Irrespective of whether divestiture occurred or not, the Loopco would be subject to regulation. Other telecommunications services normally would not be regulated.[9] The regulation of the Loopco would be by price not by profits. If the Loopco received an increase in its access demand, it would benefit in terms of increased profits. It would also have an incentive to build new capacity if demand was growing. Since it would be subject to price-cap regulation, the Loopco would be able to be flexible in its prices. If it found that it was losing access traffic to wireless

---

9   This would certainly be the intention at least. However, as the recent FCC ruling providing
    compensation for payphone owners for 800/888 calls made from payphones indicates,
    regulation can appear in all sorts of places.

companies, it would be able to adjust it rates accordingly.

The advantages of the Loopco approach are that it clarifies the regulatory and also severely restricts the scope of regulation. Most importantly, it offers the potential of opening up telecommunications to competition by making competition in the end-to-end market possible. The proposal has some disadvantages. Its adoption will not result only in efficiency gains. The main concern would be the loss of scope economies, which would occur primarily in two areas. Currently, RBOCs provide not only local access (the wires, etc.) but also local calling and intraLATA toll service, which requires that they own and operate switching and transmission plant in addition to loop plant. This plant is currently integrated into their loop plant. If the Loopco is required only to provide loop services, then any scope economies currently being achieved would be lost. A number of possible solutions exist to this problem in addition to divesting these facilities. One approach would be for the Loopco to retain these facilities and resell their services on a wholesale basis to competing carriers. The disadvantage of this approach is that it would expand the Loopco's activities beyond the loop and possibly make its regulation as a provider of monopoly services more complicated. The complications, however, may not be too severe. The RBOC would be able to decide whether to divest these non-loop facilities from the Loopco or to retain them. If they were retained, the solution might be for the Loopco to have two baskets. Basket 1 might be access and local usage and Basket 2 would be transmission services. The price cap on Basket 1 might offer the retail service provider a fixed fee per line for access and a per minute of use charge for charge for any calls made. It would then be for the retail service provider to decide whether he wished to offer flat rate or measured local service or other creative pricing option. Basket 2 would be the transportation services within the existing LATA. The retail services provider would buy such services depending on how many facilities he had colocated within the Loopco's central office.

If the Loopco provided not only loop services but also transportation and switching services within the LATA, it would be in many ways similar from a strictly network point of view to the existing RBOCs. However, the Loopcos would be in the wholesale business and not the retail business, as the RBOC is currently. For an RBOC, the choice would be between being in the retail business or in the wholesale business *in its existing territory*. Either it could divest its Loopco and provide end-to-end service nationwide or it could divest the retail business in its current territory and provide end-to-end service in the rest of the United States. Either option would focus on the monopoly and provide the regulator with the ability to offer some protection from monopoly exploitation.

There are undisputed scope economies of supplying local service and long-distance service. The Loopco proposal would forgo these. However, under the existing arrangement, these scope economies have been foregone entirely, and, if the lamentably slow progress of bringing about local competition as envisioned in the 1996 Act continues, this will never be fully achieved. So, at least compared with the status quo, the Loopco proposal involves an identical loss in efficiency from failure to achieve economies of scope from integrating end-to-end service. There may be some loss of scope economies from RBOCs ceasing to provide retail local service in their Loopco area. For example, to schedule a repair or an installation, the subscriber would contact his provider who would forward the customer's order to the Loopco for fulfillment. This is unlikely to be a huge loss as, given the call-forwarding ability of modern telecommunications, the provider would likely have all calls forwarded to the Loopco in any case. Absent a detailed study, it does not appear that there is likely to be a major loss of scope economies as a result of the Loopco proposal.

The Loopco proposal may be criticized on grounds that it may not promote innovation and other dynamic efficiencies. This could apply to a divested, fully independent Loopco whose only service was wholesale access. However, if RBOC predictions of increasing competition in the access market from CATV and wireless are true, then the Loopco may well have an incentive to innovate and, indeed, the Loopco's access monopoly will disappear. In this event, the LEC owning the Loopco would be able to show non-dominance and might then be in a position to petition for the lifting of any restrictions for it to provide full service, including long distance in its Loopco terrritory.

2.2. Electricity

Changes in the organization of the electric power industry continue to be the subject of much debate following the Energy Policy Act of 1992 and the start of a process of opening up of the industry to competition.[10] Here we will provide a brief statement of the problem and discuss, in somewhat simplistic and general terms, the implications for regulation. The approach we take is to focus on the core monopoly, in a similar fashion to our proposals for telecommunications. In a vertically integrated electric utility, it is the wires that are the monopoly and not the generating plants. Generating plants can compete with one another as long as they are connected to the wires of the transmission and distribution systems.[11] The wires from the plant to the distribution network take the power from the generator to the distribution system. The distribution system is like the local loop in that it provides for delivery to the final consumer. It is clearly a monopoly, at least until it is possible to install on site distributed generation, say in the form of fuel cells connected to the gas mains.

Given the nature of the industry, there seem to be three basic models for regulatory purposes. There are: the fully vertically integrated firm, regulated as presently (the Genco-Transco-Disco case); the firm which has divested generation but retains transmission and distribution (the Transco-Disco case); and the case of the distribution company only (Disco). Within each case there are a number of possibilities. Take the Disco case. Here the Disco might make the distribution wires available to an energy services provider (Esco). As in the telecommunications case, it would be the Esco who interacted with customer. The Disco would

---

10   See, for example, Kleindorfer (1998) for a discussion of such issues in the context of the
      transmission sector.
11   As Green and Newbery (1992) have shown, the location of the plant in relation to the
      transmission bottlenecks may give certain power plants monopoly power.

be supplying the Esco with wholesale use of the wires, which it would resell to its customers. The Disco would be subject to price-cap regulation and the Esco would not be subject to price regulation. The bundles of services supplied could be quite varied. For example, unbundling and rebundling could take place. Take metering as an example.[12] The Esco might be responsible for customer metering, or the Disco might perform this function or independent and competing contractors might perform it. There are other services that are needed for the supply of electricity. Some of these may involve significant market power. The provision of peak loads and backup power is an example. The supply of electricity requires back-up power otherwise significant damage or disruption costs might occur in the event of an outage. One source of back-up power would be an independent generator supplying power on site to a large industrial user. The independent generator will need back-up power to handle forced and scheduled outages. He could go to the Esco, the Disco, the Transco, or a Genco to provide this back-up.

Without going into details, the implications for an existing vertically integrated electric utility may involve a number of options. The utility could divest itself of all its generation and just operate as a Disco-Transco. It would then, like the Loopco, just provide services wholesale to Gencos, and Escos who would then deal directly with the final consumer. One model of the Disco-Transco would have it providing all the metering and other ancillary services, such as back up power and network support. An alternative model would allow provision of at least some of these services by others. For example, it might be possible to allow competition for all retail metering, but the Transco might be responsible for metering the power it receives at its bus from the Genco or Esco. Some back-up power and network support might be provided by individual Escos or Gencos or even by individual customers, for example, on-site back-up generation. The critical issue would be where the user provided his own back-up power that he could be made to bear the entire costs of his own failure to supply. If he could, then there is no reason why the Disco-Transco has to get involved. However, to insure the viability of the network, the Transco-Disco might provide the back-up in certain instances.

It is clear that a number of complex structures are possible. There may be distinct advantages in having vertically integrated utilities divest themselves of their generation and act only as a wholesale provider of energy and ancillary services to Escos and to the Independent System Operator responsible for transmission and load stabilization.[13] The regulator would then be concerned with regulating only the core monopoly, namely transmission and system operation, plus the wires portion of distribution. Like the Loopco case, this would be an extremely tidy solution from the regulatory point of view and would allow the regulator to focus on the core monopoly while allowing competition in all of the other services. A further advantage of this solution is that, in terms of resources employed, transmis-

---

12   See Croyle (1997) for a discussion of unbundling of the metering function.
13   Indeed, one major utility has made a move in that direction. GPU has, by it overseas acquisitions and its creation of a nuclear generating arm, begun to position itself to be a Disco-Transco. It has not announced any plans to exit the retail business.

sion and distribution accounts for about thirty percent of the investment and probably less than 10 percent of the total fuel, O&M, and other variable expenses. Thus, the vast bulk of the provision of the service would be subject to competitive supply, providing customers with the potential benefits of competition. A further benefit is that financial intermediation and brokering of contracts between generators and load managers (including Escos) could act as market makers and offer value added services including risk management.

2.3. Gas

Like other network industries, the gas industry consist of production, transmission, and distribution. Traditionally, gas distribution companies purchased gas from the pipelines or from the producer and paid pipelines for transportation. Now, however, gas distributors only provide this service for their smaller customers. Their larger customers either purchase gas directly themselves or through a broker, and the gas utility supplies transportation and other services, for example, storage for the servicing of peak demands. The structure is different from the current structure of telecommunications, as gas distribution companies are allowed to provide end-to-end service. Indeed, for small customers they do so. They buy the gas and arrange bulk transportation through the pipeline, which together with local storage enables them to provide end-to-end service.

While the structure of the industry continues to evolve, it is clear that the trend is clearly toward more unbundling.[14] Producers are largely unregulated.Transmission and distribution companies face regulation, currently in the form of the traditional cost-of-service variety but, increasingly, in the form of incentive regulation, which is also referred to as peformance-based regulation. The unbundling, which began in the late 1980s and has continued unabated, has promoted a transparent pricing of production, transportation, and distribution. This, with separation of ownership of the elements of the supply chain has also encouraged the entry of significant brokering and intermediation services into this market, including an active futures and options market and very significant competition arising from the activities of intermediaries. Local distribution companies can use the services of competing brokers to shop around for the best prices and delivery terms. They can contract for firm or interruptible supply, absorb uncertainties in various financial and technological ways, and generally profit from the tremendous increase in competition and variety available from it. While this unbundling process began with larger customers, just as in the case of electric power and telecommunications bypass, it is now moving into the arena of retail choice. For example, smaller customers, including residential customers, will increasingly be able to purchase gas through an energy-services company or broker. If this trend continues, gas companies may evolve into the equivalent of Loopcos, providing only wholesale delivery service. From a regulatory point of view, this would have all the advantages claimed for regulating only the core monopoly.

---

14   For a good introduction to the history of natural gas deregulation and the restructuring of the industry in the 1980s and 1990s, see Doane and Spulber (1994).

3. Changes in Postal Governance

While postal service has the basic characteristics of other fixed network industries, in that it displays economies of scale and scope in some parts, but not others, of the postal network, there are significant differences. The technologies differ in that utility networks are physically connected, while postal networks might be better described as virtual networks. Similarly, we might be more concerned with differences in the area of governance arising from the fact that postal service is still a public enterprise and therefore faces different incentives from the other (private) network industries. However, we are not going to address these issues specifically in this paper. While we would still argue that postal service should be privatized, we are not going to pursue this line of argument here.[15] Even ignoring these issues, our proposal for postal service differs somewhat from that for the other network industries. In the latter case, we argued that the monopoly should be confined to providing access to the distribution network with the monopolist generally taking on the role of a wholesale provider.

In what follows, we are going to assume that postal service will continue as a public enterprise. In the case of the U.S. Postal Service, this would mean that the current method of regulation would continue essentially unchanged, but that further legislative changes beyond those envisaged in the Postal Reform Act (H.R. 22) would need to be made. For other postal administrations, the government may have sufficient flexibility to make these kind of changes without requiring legislative action.

Postal service, like fixed network industries, has faced entry over the last ten years or so. Indeed, the U.S. Postal Service faced entry into its business at an early stage in the form of worksharing, namely discounts for presorting. Unlike privately owned companies, it did little to oppose entry in this form. Similarly, its parcels business was devoured by UPS, and FEDEX came to dominate courier service. Now postal administrations in Europe and the United States are beginning to face more serious threats to their traditional and basic letters business. Postal service is also facing competition from electronic communications in the form of fax, email, the internet, and electronic payment systems.[16] Thus, issues of regulatory governance when entry is allowed are now becoming as important in postal service as they are in the other network industries.

Currently, the postal monopoly is usually defined in terms of a weight or monetary limit. For example, the British Post Office has a monopoly of letters

---

15   We argued for privatization of the U.S. Postal Service in our testimony before the House
     sub-committee considering H.R. 22.

16   In view of the strong demand complementarities that exist between communications products
     and the increasing demand for communications, the soothsayers of doom have been
     confounded in the past. For example, the telephone did not displace the mail. Indeed, mail
     may have prospered in part because of its complementarity with telephone. However, based
     upon the work of Nikali (1997), Plum (1997), Ware (1997), and Wolak (1997), there may be
     reason to expect that the current electronic competition is having, and will continue to have, a
     significant negavitive impact on the demand for several postal products.

priced below one pound Sterling.   In the United States, this limit is under review in H.R. 22 but is currently three dollars or twice the postage whichever is greater. In addition, the Postal Service has a mail box monopoly. Applying our proposal to postal service would require that the monopoly be confined to the local delivery network only.   Local delivery would be the core or residual monopoly.   Postal services under such a proposal would take on the role of suppliers of services wholesale and not having any retail customers.   Postal administrations would provide only the local delivery networks and the sortation needed for local delivery.

The problem with this proposal is that it would potentially leave most residential postal customers high and dry for some services.   Unlike the other network industries, where the competitive market has the potential to rebundle the services required for residential and other small customers to obtain service, in postal service there may be major problems of bundling together the various parts of the postal value chain needed to provide end-to-end single piece service for residential or other small customers. This is likely to be an even more important problem in rural areas, which receive service only because of cross subsidization. These areas are not only highly vulnerable when it comes to delivery but also when it comes to collection. Similarly, very small residential customers, the Aunt Minnies, might be almost completely cut off from sending letters absent the "lifeline" offered by postal administrations. Given the low price of a stamp, it is rather unlikely that there is much profit opportunity for entrepreneurs in offering end-to-end service for single piece letters. We are saying, in effect, that almost nobody would want this kind of business. However, because of potential scale economies arising from their collection networks, most postal administration could handle this kind of business and receive a contribution over variable costs. We would therefore argue that the postal monopoly should consist of a statutory monopoly in local delivery of letters below a certain dollar limit and *a requirement* that it provide single-piece end-to-end service below a certain dollar limit.

This requirement to provide end-to-end single-piece service does not result in an increase in postal monopoly power but, rather, an increase in the universal service obligation (USO). While the national postal operator would be obliged to offer single-piece end-to-end service there is nothing to stop consolidators from collecting mail from small customers into large batches of mail for presorting or barcoding. For large users this is done now. Some small customers might have this option if the market offered sufficient profit to make it attractive to entrepreneurs. Indeed, customers who would be the targets for this option would likely be the postal administrations' profitable customers, i.e., the potential for cream skimming would exist. However, the gains from competition here are likely to be greater than the losses from cream skimming. Given that the postal administration has a monopoly in local delivery, through which it would fund its USO, we are not concerned that such losses, if any, would affect the financial viability of the postal administration or threaten its ability to meet its USO. Another reason for taking this route is that funding the USO in the postal context through uniform pricing and the local delivery monopoly would likely be preferable to setting up a universal service fund as is the case in telecommunications.[17]

We see considerable potential for increased efficiency arising out of our proposal. Despite the obligation to provide single-piece end-to-end service, our proposal would orient postal services very much toward local delivery networks. Even under public ownership, there would be an increased potential for much more contracting out. Independent contractors for the postal administrations might operate local delivery networks. Postal services might take on the role of franchisors for local delivery networks. Some of the networks would be operated by franchisees, while others would be owned and operated by the national postal administration. Hybrids might be possible in that franchisees might operate networks where the postal service owned the facilities. Under public enterprise, the absence of residual claimants would attenuate such incentives for efficiency. Even under public enterprise, some changes would occur, and the possible contracting arrangements are considerable. For these reasons, we regard further discussion as beyond the scope of this paper.

4. Summary, Conclusions, and Implications

We have examined the problem of regulatory governance when entry into a regulated monopoly is allowed. We have argued that, while such markets display competition, a residual or core monopoly remains, and it is this residual upon which regulation should be focused. Our proposals build on the apparent trends in most network industries toward unbundling of the various components of the value chain to assure greater transparency of the cost of each of these components (from generation to final customer distribution). Our proposal is to join this obvious trend and to reinforce it with appropriate changes in regulatory governance. We argue that the structure of present network monopolies, or their inherited partially deregulated descendants, should be restructured so that monopoly providers would, in most instances, provide only wholesale service. Furthermore, this monopoly would be confined to the core area (typically in local delivery), where overwhelming scale or scope economies continue to make monopoly provision desirable. Retail services would be subject to competition. Regulatory commissions, instead of acting directly on behalf of consumers, would now act directly on the part of the firms in competition for the consumer's dollars. Their key responsibility would be to assure fair and open access to competitors to the core monopoly-provided services and to regulate the price and quality of these latter services. Competition would be allowed to work within the industry where the industry was competitive. The monopoly segment of the industry would be regulated. The benefits of competition would be available, and monopoly regulation would rule in the residual monopoly segment. This approach would presumably offer greater efficiency gains compared to the older system, where the entire industry was treated as a monopoly and no entry took place. Shrinking the monopoly makes cross subsidies more difficult to hide, offering this benefit as well as the discipline provided by

---

17   We have examined the USO in the postal sector in a forthcoming paper (Crew and Kleindorfer 1998).

competitive entry.

The question must be asked as to whether this approach is worthwhile relative to the alternative governance structure of laissez-faire. Laissez-faire might be considered the only true form of deregulation or at least the ultimate outcome of a process of deregulation.[18] This is effectively the approach taken when the Civil Aeronautics Board was abolished in 1978 "letting the airlines be," with no regulator to set prices or otherwise act as referee. Laissez-faire is the ultimate in deregulation, and the question to be answered in this context is whether it should be considered as a governance structure to be implemented immediately or ultimately or whether it is even feasible in network industries. It would be relatively easy to craft an argument for laissez-faire on the grounds that the monopoly rents will be dissipated by rent seeking within the regulatory process along the lines of Posner (1969; 1975). A contrary argument is that by paring down the regulation to the residual monopoly that the rents are reduced. Another argument is that rents are no longer dissipated in thwarting entry to the competitive segment of the industry.

The arguments for laissez-faire in network industries are far from compelling. True laissez-faire would imply not just the abolition of regulation but also immunity from antitrust actions. Given that this is this is out of the question, effective laissez-faire would imply no regulation but the possibility of antitrust action. This much deregulation would, however, be considerable and would not likely to be politically feasible, in part because there would be a genuine concern about monopoly power in these situations.[19] Let us look at the consequences of laissez-faire in telecommunications and postal service.[20]

In telecommunications, prices of local service in rural locations could rise considerably. In some urban areas, prices for local service would fall or stay approximately the same. In others, they would fall. It might be even more difficult for long-distance carriers to get into the local market. Absent regulation, there might be no pressure for an RBOC to allow its long-distance rivals into the local market, since its own entry into the long-distance market was no longer barred. Competition from wireless and CATV has not developed as fast as once expected. So the RBOCs under laissez-faire would enjoy considerable monopoly power at the expense of long-distance carriers. In this case, the best option for a long-distance carrier would be to pursue a merger further consolidating the industry. Given the consolidation that has recently taken place and is continuing to take place,[21] it is not likely that this process would further enhance competition.

Laissez-faire for postal and delivery services would have a number of likely

---

18   Crandall (1997) provides an insightful analysis of the issues involved, including the major
      issues of political feasibility at this time.
19   Currently, the airlines are in this situation of being subject to the antitrust laws but not
      regulation. This has not necessarily made the industry competitive. There is a concern that
      the major airlines' control of gates and slots gives them considerable monopoly advantages.
20   Telecommunications, given the pace of technological change and the rapid growth in the
      market, seems likely to offer much better prospects than electricity and gas.
21   The latest proposed merger between Southwestern and Ameritech follows the acquisition of
      Pacific and Southern New England.

consequences. Universal service would disappear in its present form. Rural areas might get some kind of service but at a considerably increased price. In addition, quality of service would be likely to deteriorate.

Given the likely alternatives, namely the current situation and laissez-faire, the approach suggested here of identifying the residual monopoly and regulating the remaining core has much to recommend it.

References

Crandall, Robert W. 1997. "Is It Time to Eliminate Telephone Regulation?" In *Telecommunications Policy*, edited by Donald L. Alexander. Westport, CT: Praeger.

Crew, Michael A., and Paul R. Kleindorfer .1994. "Pricing, Entry, Service Quality, and Innovation under a Commercialized Postal Service." In *Governing the Postal Service*, edited by J.G. Sidak, pages 152-169. Washington, DC: The AEI Press.

Crew, Michael A., and Paul R. Kleindorfer. 1987. *The Economics of Public Utility Regulation*. Cambridge, MA: M.I.T Press.

Crew, Michael A., and Paul R. Kleindorfer. 1997. *Managing Change in the Postal and Delivery Industries*. Boston, MA: Kluwer Academic Publishers.

Crew, Michael A., and Paul R. Kleindorfer. 1998. "Efficient Entry, Monopoly, and the Universal Service Obligation in Postal Service." *Journal of Regulatory Economics* 14 (No. 2, September): 103-125.

Croyle, David R. 1997. "Unbundling Competitive Utility Services: What, Why, and How." Presented at the Tenth Annual Western Conference, July 9-11, 1997. Center for Research in Regulated Industries, Rutgers University, New Jersey.

"Developments in Incentive Regulation." 1996. Special Issue of the *Journal of Regulatory Economics* 9 (No. 3, May).

Doane, M.J., and D.F. Spulber. 1994. "Open Access and the Evolution of the U.S. Spot Market for Natural Gas." *Journal of Law and Economics* XXXVII (October): 477-517.

Kleindorfer, Paul R. 1998. "Ownership Structure, Contracting and Regulation of Transmission Services Providers." In *Designing Competitive Electricity Markets*, edited by Hung-po Chao and Hillard G. Huntington. Boston: Kluwer Academic Publishers.

Goldberg, Victor P. 1976. "Regulation and Administered Contracts." *Bell Journal of Economics* 7 (Autumn): 426-48.

Green, Richard, and David Newbery. 1992. "Competition in the British Electricity Spot Market." *Journal of Political Economy* 100 (No. 5, October): 929-53.

Nikali, Heikki. 1997. "Demand Models for Letter Mail and its Substitutes: Results from Finland." In Crew and Kleindorfer (eds.), pages 133-161.

Plum, Monica. 1997. "The Challenge of Electronic Competion: Empircial Analysis of Substitution Effects on the Demand for Letter Services." In Crew and Kleindorfer (eds.), pages 270-287.

Posner, Richard A. 1969. "Natural Monopoly and its Regulation." *Stanford Law Review* 21 (February): 548-643.

Posner, Richard A. 1975. "The Social Costs of Monopoly Regulation." *Journal of Political Economy* 83 (August): 807-27.

Ware, Harold. 1997. "Competition and Rate Restructuring for Postal Services." In Crew and Kleindorfer (eds.), pages 370-388.

Williamson, Oliver E. 1980. "The Organization of Work." *Journal of Economic Behavior and Organization* 1 (March): 5-38.

Wolak, Frank. 1997. "Changes in Household-Level Demand for Postal Delivery Services form 1986-1994." In Crew and Kleindorfer (eds.), pages 162-194.

2

MONOPOLY LEVERAGING, PATH DEPENDENCY, AND THE CASE FOR A LOCAL COMPETITION THRESHOLD FOR RBOC ENTRY INTO INTERLATA TOLL

T. Randolph Beard
David L. Kaserman
John W. Mayo

1. Introduction

One of the cornerstones of the Telecommunications Act of 1996 (without which the Act probably would not have been passed) is Section 271.[1] This Section establishes the criteria under which the Regional Bell Operating Companies (RBOCs) will be allowed to enter (or, more accurately, reenter) the interLATA long-distance market.[2] Specifically, under the 271 provisions, an RBOC's reintegration within its certificated geographic territory is made contingent upon the satisfaction of four necessary preconditions.[3]

First, the RBOC must be able to demonstrate that it is providing interconnection to competitive local exchange providers (at least one of which is predominantly a facilities-based carrier) or, at the very least, that interconnection is generally available to potential competitors. Moreover, the terms and conditions under which

---

1 Telecommunications Act of 1996, Pub. L. 104-104, 110 Stat. 56, to be codified at 47 §§ 151 et seq.

2 These firms had been excluded from that market under the terms of the settlement reached in the AT&T divestiture case. See Modification of Final Judgment, *United States of America v. Western Electric Company, Incorporated and American Telephone and Telegraph Company*, Civil Action No. 82-1092. Specifically, under Section VIII.C of the Modified Final Judgment issued in that case, the RBOCs were proscribed from reintegrating into interLATA long distance until they could demonstrate to the satisfaction of the Court that they would be unable to use their ownership of local exchange facilities for anticompetitive purposes in that market.

3 Reintegration into the provision of long-distance services outside the RBOC's certificated region is permitted immediately under the Act without any substantive preconditions.

the RBOC offers interconnection must conform to the standards established by a so-called "competitive checklist" contained in the Act.[4]

Second, the RBOC seeking approval to reintegrate must comply with the Act's nondiscrimination and structural separation requirements. Importantly, the Federal Communications Commission (FCC) has interpreted these provisions to mean that not only must the RBOC refrain from discriminating among third parties, but regulators must also be able to establish that the RBOC does not discriminate between itself (or its subsidiaries) and third party providers.[5]

Third, the Act requires the FCC to seek advice from the U.S. Department of Justice (DOJ) concerning each RBOC application. In conducting its evaluation of a 271 application, the latter agency may apply any standard that it deems appropriate. Although the resulting DOJ recommendation is not binding on the FCC's decision, the Act requires that "substantial weight" be given to it.

Finally, and perhaps most importantly, the Act instructs the FCC to deny the application unless it finds that the requested reentry is consistent with the "public interest." From an economic standpoint, such a determination would appear to require that the expected benefits accruing to telecommunications consumers exceed any likely harm inflicted on those consumers as a result of the reintegration.

The above criteria are clearly intended to establish some threshold level of competition in local exchange markets as a prerequisite to RBOC reentry into long distance. The question is what that level of competition will be. Today, more than two years after passage of the Act, that question remains very much an open issue. The Act's failure to resolve this issue, in turn, is attributable to the overall vagueness of its requirements. Despite the apparent specificity of certain portions of the criteria provided by the Act, the FCC and state commissions are, nonetheless, afforded considerable latitude under the provisions of Section 271. For example, depending upon the stringency with which the competitive checklist is enforced and the precise interpretation provided of the public interest criterion, these provisions could yield grossly different reentry standards. Virtually anything from a superficial appearance of "openness to competition" to a strict requirement of fully effective competition could be viewed as fulfilling the reintegration standard implied by the Act. As a result, there is considerable uncertainty at present concerning the required benchmark of the overall intensity of competition that will be required in local exchange markets before reintegration is allowed to occur. State and federal regulatory decisions ultimately must establish that benchmark.

Given this uncertainty, it is clearly in the RBOCs' interest to identify the lower bound. That is, these firms should be expected to seek out the minimum degree of

---

4   Economically, the checklist provides a set of conditions that, when present and fully operational, will help ensure (but cannot guarantee) parity in the quality of services provided by the RBOCs and entrants. Satisfaction of the checklist criterion will make it more difficult (though by no means impossible) for the RBOC to discriminate in the quality of the interconnection services provided to its competitors.

5   *First Report and Order*, CC Docket No. 96-98, Federal Communications Commission, August 8, 1997.

competition that will allow them to pass the 271 test and reenter the long-distance market, because any monopoly power they are able to retain in the local exchange market is a valuable asset. Moreover, as we explain below, the market value of the local exchange monopoly will be greatly enhanced by reentry into the interexchange market as monopoly provision of bundled service offerings and strategic options in the interexchange market will, thereby, be opened. At the same time, interexchange carriers (IXCs) who are concerned about the potential for anticompetitive behavior by RBOCs that retain control over monopoly bottleneck facilities will predictably seek to ensure that truly competitive access conditions are in place prior to RBOC re-integration. Thus, the opposing parties—principally, the RBOCs and the IXCs—have taken grossly divergent positions regarding the stringency with which the Section 271 provisions should be applied.[6]

In this paper, we explore the economic implications of allowing relatively early RBOC reentry that would follow from applying a comparatively less stringent interpretation of the 271 criteria. We find that due to both the incentive and ability of the RBOCs to engage in monopoly leveraging strategies, and the history of the use of such strategies by these firms or their integrated predecessor, a strict and uncompromising interpretation of the 271 criteria is called for. That is, any potential benefits resulting from early RBOC reintegration (where the term "early" is interpreted to mean reentry prior to the establishment of effective competition in local exchange markets) are likely to be overcome by the competitive harm inflicted on the long-distance market through monopoly leveraging.

Even more importantly, early reintegration will also retard the growth of competition in local exchange markets by eliminating any incentive the RBOCs may currently have to facilitate (or even tolerate) such growth. In fact, once the RBOCs have reentered the interLATA market, the asset value of any monopoly power they are able to retain or regain in local exchange markets will increase, because regulatory constraints on earnings may be partially or completely circumvented by a vertically integrated firm that participates in both regulated and unregulated markets.[7] As a result, regulatory approval of early reintegration is likely to slow or reverse progress toward competition in local exchange markets as well.

In addition, the problems encountered by regulatory efforts to prevent monopoly leveraging in long distance and promote competition in local exchange markets will intensify considerably. That is, with reintegration in the presence of local

---

6   The one conclusion on which both sides to this debate can, hopefully, agree is that society's interests will be best served by a policy that results in local exchange competition/deregulation sooner rather than later. Unfortunately, they do not agree on what that policy is. One side—the IXCs—advocate a relatively stringent interpretation of the 271 requirements that makes effective local exchange competition a prerequisite to RBOC reentry; while the other side—the RBOCs—advocate a more lax interpretation that allows such reentry upon a showing that local exchange markets are more or less "open to competition." We favor the former interpretation simply because we are convinced that it will lead to ubiquitous competition (and, therefore, deregulation) much sooner than the latter.

7   See Dayan (1975) and Brennan (1990).

exchange monopoly, regulators will be forced to do battle on two fronts—the local exchange and long-distance markets. And the opposition they will face on both fronts will be greatly fortified relative to the current, nonintegrated structure. Also, if the past is any indicator of the future, regulators are likely to experience little success in combating monopoly leveraging/monopoly preserving tactics by the vertically integrated Bells. But their efforts to do so will undoubtedly lead to increased regulatory controls in both markets. Therefore, premature reintegration is likely to undermine the Telecommunication Act's twin goals of increased competition and reduced regulation. It will result, instead, in less competition (in both long-distance and local exchange markets) and more regulation.

Our analysis is organized as follows. We begin, in Section 2, by describing the timing problem presented by Section 271 implementation. We explain that, as we look forward to the implementation of a pro-competitive telecommunications policy, a path dependency is likely to exist which makes the timing of RBOC reentry crucial in determining the future state of competition in both local exchange and long-distance markets. In Section 3, we describe the economic theory pertaining to the issue of monopoly leveraging by vertically integrated RBOCs that still hold substantial monopoly power in local exchange markets. Here, we argue that, as a theoretical proposition, early reintegration is likely to result in monopoly leveraging behavior. Section 4 then considers the evidence concerning monopoly leveraging in the telecommunications industry. Experience from both the pre- and post-divestiture periods supports the theoretical result that monopoly leveraging is likely to result. Finally, Section 5 concludes.

2. Path Dependency and the Timing of RBOC Reentry

It is important to note at the outset that, while Section 271 contemplates the eventual reintegration by the RBOCs into long-distance services, other sections of the Act contemplate immediate (or, at least, rapid) reintegration by interexchange carriers (and other firms) into local exchange services. Specifically, Sections 251 and 252 impose an extensive set of interconnection and provisioning obligations on incumbent local exchange carriers (ILECs)—both RBOCs and others—designed to facilitate entry into their markets on both a facilities-based and resale basis.[8] It is this latter reintegration, of course, that is intended to ignite the fires of competition in local exchange markets that ultimately will yield the competitive conditions required for RBOC reintegration to enhance rather than impede competition.

Thus, the Act can be seen as a comprehensive policy instrument that, if properly implemented, will produce symmetric (though not simultaneous) reintegration by local exchange and long-distance carriers. When the latter reintegration occurs, these firms, for the first time since divestiture, will be in a position to offer

---

8   Under the provisions of these sections of the Act, a firm may enter the local exchange market either as a pure reseller of ILEC-supplied wholesale services or as a provider of services created through lease of the ILEC's unbundled network elements. For a discussion of resale entry, see Beard, Kaserman, and Mayo (forthcoming).

consumers a complete menu of end-to-end telecommunications services—both local and long distance—from a single provider. The old Bell System will have been cloned successfully into multiple carriers, each of which is fully integrated. Consumers then will have the best of both worlds—the convenience of integration and the efficiency of competition.

The 1984 divestiture provided consumers a mixed blessing. While it facilitated the growth of competition in the long-distance market, it also denied customers the benefits (in terms of both cost and convenience) of vertical integration. Thus, the overarching and ambitious goals of the Telecommunications Act are to promote an industry restructuring that yields both vertical integration *and* competition. The latter of these two outcomes, of course, will also allow for extensive deregulation of this industry. If the Act's goals are realized, the resulting consumer benefits are likely to be quite substantial. Such benefits will derive from three primary sources: (1) increased competition; (2) reintegration; and (3) deregulation.

Importantly, these three market developments are inextricably related to one another. For example, as the reintegration process unfolds, it is widely anticipated that at least some consumers will place considerable value on the convenience of having a single firm provide the full range of their telecommunications needs. Some preliminary empirical evidence suggests, and many industry observers believe, that firms that are unable or unwilling to offer service bundles including, at a minimum, both local and long-distance calling will suffer a significant handicap in competing for customers' patronage in this new environment.[9] Consequently, both local exchange and interexchange companies are extremely anxious to enter each others' markets in a timely fashion. If either group succeeds in achieving the reintegration necessary to offer the bundled end-to-end service prior to the other group, considerable (and possibly irreversible) first-mover marketing advantages potentially could accrue.[10]

The competitive consequences of such non-simultaneous reintegration, however, are not likely to be symmetric. Specifically, if the IXCs achieve reintegration first by successfully entering local exchange markets (even if only on a resale or unbundled element basis) before local exchange carriers are able to enter the interexchange market, competition will survive intact, because the interexchange market is, in our opinion, already competitive.[11] Entry from a competitive market

---

9   Using survey data from Japan, Tardiff (1995) presents evidence of a price advantage of approximately 14 percent resulting from the ability to bundle local and long-distance calling. Other services that potentially may be bundled with local and long distance include cellular, Internet, and video services.

10   Without a credible threat of successful entry by interexchange carriers into local exchange markets (which will enable them to provide bundled end-to-end service offerings), the RBOCs have had little incentive to allow competition to develop in their markets. With such entry (hopefully enabled by implementation of the provisions of Sections 251 and 252 of the Act), however, they will feel considerable pressure to reenter long distance in order to be able to compete successfully on an integrated (bundled) basis.

11   That opinion is not ubiquitously shared by all economists who have examined this market. See, e.g., MacAvoy (1995; 1996), Taylor and Taylor (1993), and Sibley and Weisman (1998). We will return to this issue below.

into a monopoly market is unambiguously procompetitive. While local exchange *carriers* may suffer some competitive harm as a result of such entry, the *competitive process* (and, therefore, consumers) would not be injured. In fact, competition would be enhanced by such entry, and consumers would thereby benefit.

But if local exchange carriers are the first to reintegrate, and if such reintegration is allowed to occur prior to the advent of fully effective competition in local exchange markets, the competitive consequences could be both adverse and severe. Specifically, three undesirable consequences are likely to result from such premature reintegration. First, as noted above, reintegration by firms that continue to hold substantial monopoly power in the provision of local exchange services is likely to result in monopoly leveraging behavior that will cause a diminution in competition in the long-distance market. Second, such reintegration will immediately reverse whatever incentive the RBOCs might otherwise have to cooperate in the emergence of competition in local exchange markets, thereby reducing competition in those markets as well. And third, early reintegration will reduce substantially the benefits that consumers might receive from the provision of bundled service offerings.

This last outcome warrants a brief explanation. Suppose that consumers place a value (at the margin) on interexchange services of X, a value (at the margin) on local exchange services of Y and a corresponding value of the bundled offering of $(1 + \theta) [X + Y]$, $\theta > 0$, on the bundled offering. Under competitive provision of long distance and local services, prices will be driven to their respective marginal costs.[12] Moreover, with competitive supply of both services and freedom on the part of either to bundle, the premium value of the bundling $(1 + \theta)$ will accrue to consumers. That is, despite the fact that consumers place a premium on the value of the bundle, competition will ensure that the price of the bundle reflects the underlying costs of the bundled services.

Now suppose that an RBOC is able to integrate into the provision of interexchange services *before* IXCs (or other firms that seek to supply the full bundled offering of telecommunications services to consumers) are able to effectively compete in the provision of local exchange services. In this case, by virtue of being the monopoly supplier of local exchange service, the RBOC automatically becomes the monopoly provider of the bundle. The consequence is that the integrated monopolist of the bundled offering is in a position to extract the full premium value of the bundle from consumers. That is, by charging anything less than $(1 + \theta) [X + Y]$ for the bundle, the RBOC can entice consumers to purchase the bundled offering rather than the separate services.

In contrast, suppose that local exchange markets are opened to competition prior to the re-integration of the RBOCs. In this case, because there are numerous interexchange providers competing for the patronage of consumers, they will quite naturally be drawn to provide the bundled set of services to which consumers attach

---

12   For purposes of this example, we set aside the potential for vertical economies between local exchange and interexchange service. Changing this assumption does not alter the point of the example.

a premium value. Unlike the case of re-integration by a monopoly provider of the local exchange offering, however, in this case any rents that would accrue to a monopoly provider of the bundled offering are completely dissipated by competition among the many providers of the bundled offering. Suppose, for instance, that one of the providers of the bundled offering offered the bundle at a price equal to $(1 + \theta) [X + Y]$. Because the marginal cost of providing the bundled offering is only equal to $X + Y$, other competitors will bid down the price of the bundle. This competitive process will continue until the full value of the premium $(1 + \theta)$ is competed away. Thus, consumers' realization of potential bundling benefits depends crucially upon who enters which market first. Where regulators insist that the conditions for effective local exchange competition are fully implemented prior to permitting re-integration (i.e., where a relatively stringent interpretation of the Section 271 requirements is applied), consumers will be assured that they enjoy the benefits of any premium they attach to the bundled service offering.

Due to the above adverse consequences of early RBOC reintegration, the growth of competition in telecommunications markets (upon which all consumer benefits depend) is greatly affected by the timing of RBOC reintegration. In effect, a form of path dependency exists. That is, future opportunities for fully integrated effective competition depends upon the specific sequence of events contemplated by the 1996 Act—local exchange competition, RBOC reintegration, and deregulation. If RBOC reintegration is allowed to occur prior to the emergence of effective competition in local exchange markets and before interexchange carriers are able to offer bundled end-to-end service, market forces could reverse the trend toward greater competition in the provision of both local and interexchange services.

This path dependency problem is illustrated graphically in figure 1. Here, the vertical axis measures the intensity of competition in the two relevant markets, and the horizontal axis measures time. Prior to the AT&T divestiture in 1984, the interexchange market had begun to move in the direction of effective competition, while local exchange markets remained subject to considerable market power.[13] The divestiture itself greatly accelerated the former movement, resulting in a rapid realization of effective competition in the long-distance market.[14] This market evolution, greatly facilitated by the divestiture, led to the rapid divergence of the competitive time paths of these two markets. Long distance quickly became competitive while local exchange services remained monopolized.

Today, however, there are signs of emerging competition in local exchange

---

13   Some noted economists were proclaiming the long-distance market to be subject to effective competition as early as 1983. See Katz and Willig (1983).

14   The presence of effective competition in the long-distance market has been fully documented. See, e.g. Kahai, Kaserman and Mayo (1996) and Kaserman and Mayo (1996). The FCC has confirmed the presence of such competition. See *Order*, In re Motion of AT&T Corp. to be Reclassified as a Non-Dominant Carrier, CC Docket No. 79-252, FCC 95-427, October 23, 1995. Nonetheless, as noted above, some economists continue to argue that this market yields less-than-competitive results. See MacAvoy (1995; 1996), Taylor and Taylor (1993), and Sibley and Weisman (1998).

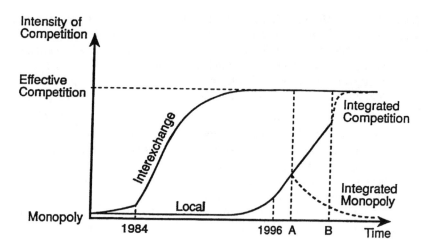

Figure 1. Path Dependency of Reintegration and Competition

markets as well, and the Telecommunications Act is specifically designed to facilitate and accelerate that trend. The question is whether this latter process will continue and the two time paths will converge to effective competition, or whether premature reintegration by the RBOCs will reverse these trends and pull both curves back down toward the monopoly asymptote. Which of these outcomes materializes will hinge critically upon the timing of RBOC reintegration relative to interexchange carriers' reintegration. If the former is allowed to proceed first (say, at time A), the competitive consequences could be extremely detrimental, as the reintegrated RBOCs pursue monopoly leveraging (in long distance) and monopoly preserving (in local) strategies. But if RBOC reintegration is postponed until local exchange markets have become sufficiently competitive (at time B), the reintegrated market structure is likely to converge to the upper, effective competition, asymptote.

The importance of the temporal order of vertical integration in telecommunications to the competitive outcome can be illustrated by the following simple model. Suppose that the provision of local exchange and long distance is comprised of only two players, an interexchange carrier (IXC) and an incumbent local exchange carrier (ILEC). The IXC initially participates in the long-distance market (LD) only, while the incumbent offers only local service (LOC). Both players earn profits from their respective markets, and consider entry into the other markets. While the ILEC initially enjoys a (presumably regulated) monopoly franchise in LOC, the IXC is constrained to price competitively, selling any products offered at economic costs. The simplifying assumption that the United States long-distance industry, composed of over 600 firms, can be represented as a single player, will strengthen our conclusions as explained below.

Additionally, suppose that there is a benefit from bundled service; that is, other things being equal, a bundled offering appeals to consumers more than a comparably priced dual provider's offering of the same quality. Finally, to make the model more realistic, we allow for the possibility that either IXC or ILEC may take actions that reduce the profits of their rivals, though these actions are privately costly to them. Such actions could include litigation, regulatory stonewalling, leveraging activities, and the like.[15]

We wish initially to consider a simple entry game in which first one player decides either to enter (E) their rival's market, or stay out (S). Observing this choice, the other player elects to either enter or stay out. Payoffs to both participants depend on the choices made by both participants. All of this is common knowledge.

The following market structures may occur. First, LOC may be a monopoly while LD exhibits competition. Second, both LOC and LD may both be competitive if either (1) IXC enters LOC and ILEC enters LD, or (2) IXC enters LOC and ILEC does not enter LD, a consequence of competitive behavior by IXC.

State-payoffs to ILEC, denoted $\pi_i^I \in \{1,2,3,4\}$, correspond to the incumbent's period profits in state i, where we have the following interpretations of the four possible market states.

π_i^I	State	Description
π_1^I	1	ILEC vertically integrated IXC not vertically integrated
π_2^I	2	ILEC not vertically integrated IXC not vertically integrated
π_3^I	3	ILEC vertically integrated IXC vertically integrated
π_4^I	4	ILEC not vertically integrated IXC vertically integrated

Conventionally, these payoffs satisfy the inequality chain $\pi_1^I > \pi_2^I > \pi_3^I > \pi_4^I$.

Next, consider the payoffs to the IXC. These payoffs should, in our context, be regarded as profits to the interexchange companies in *aggregate*: we assume the IXCs, while pricing competitively (and, in particular, dissipating any rents arising from bundling through price competition), still act to maximize their joint profits in their entry and obstruction decisions. (We will return to this issue below.) Profits to IXC are π_i^x, $i \in \{1,2,3,4\}$ for the states described above. We have the following inequalities: $\pi_4^x > \pi_3^x > \pi_1^x$ and $\pi_4^x > \pi_2^x > \pi_1^x$, although no comparison between π_2^x and π_3^x is generally possible, *a priori*.

Now consider the two simple entry games given in the figure 2. These games, denoted "Path 1" and "Path 2," differ in the move order. Payoffs are indicated at the terminal nodes, where δ, $0 < \delta < 1$, is the discount factor. We note that, consistent with reality, both IXC and the incumbent desire to move first, so IXC prefers Path 1, and ILEC prefers Path 2. This "competition for the first move" arises because of the transitory "monopoly" in bundled service obtainable by moving first is strictly valuable to ILEC, and may also be valuable to IXC.

---

15   The practical inability of IXC to undertake actions such as leveraging is ignored here, as this omission strengthens our conclusions.

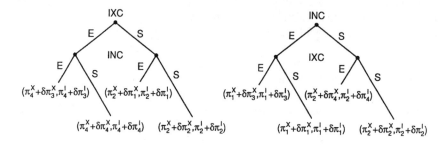

Path 1: IXC Enters First   Path 2: INC Enters First

Figure 2. Two Paths for Entry

Note: Payoffs to (IXC, INC), respectively

Subgame perfect equilibria for both games involve similar sequences of actions: the first mover, either ILEC or IXC, enters, and the second mover then responds to this entry by also entering. Entering (E) is a dominant strategy. Thus, in both cases here, full integration by both IXC and ILEC occurs, regardless of the move order.

We now modify the games depicted in figure 2 by allowing the first mover to elect, after either E or S, to engage in a costly obstructionist activity we term "harassment." Harassment consists of costly private activities that reduce rival's profits from entry. Such activities could consist of litigation, regulatory stonewalling, leveraging activity, failure to offer fully equal interconnection, or offering such interconnection but only at supracompetitive prices, and so on. While the structure of the United States telecommunications industry makes it difficult to see how the IXCs, lacking any bottleneck facilities, could engage in some kinds of harassment available to incumbent local service monopolies, our analysis treats ILEC and IXC symmetrically in this respect. The reason we take this conservative approach is that we wish in this example to illustrate the consequences of entry order for market structure when the only distinguishing difference between IXC and ILEC is the initial monopoly in LOC enjoyed by the latter, rather than to introduce additional differences in the strategic tools available to the players.

Specifically, we assume the following. After making a choice between E or S, the first mover (IXC on Path 1, ILEC on Path 2) can reduce the post entry profit of the second mover by an amount L, where $L = \alpha H$, and where H is the expenditure (reduction in profit) for the first mover, and α is a positive constant exogenous to this choice. We are interested in equilibria for both paths, the resulting market structures, and the optimal levels of harassment in both cases.

Several equilibria, with different consequences for market structure, are possible, depending on the values of the profit parameters and α. A consideration of the industry that suggested this analysis, however, allows us to select a quite plausible scenario from these possible equilibria with the following properties. On Path 1, IXC enters, $H = 0$, and then ILEC enters, resulting in a fully integrated market structure. On Path 2, ILEC enters, $H > 0$, the IXC chooses to stay out, and LOC remains a monopoly. The incentive compatibility constraints required for this scenario are:

$$(\pi_3^x - \pi_1^x) < \alpha \, (\pi_1^I - \pi_3^I), \text{ and} \qquad (A1)$$

$$\alpha \, (\pi_4^x - \pi_3^x) < \alpha \, (\pi_3^I - \pi_4^I). \qquad (A2)$$

If A1 and A2 are true, then the scenario outlined constitutes the unique equilibrium outcome for Paths 1 and 2. Condition (A1) makes it profitable for ILEC to engage in harassment of IXC (in Path 2) in an amount sufficient to deter entry by IXC. In effect, the maximum amount of profitable harassment cannot exceed the value to ILEC of keeping IXC out (of the local market) when ILEC is integrated, and this value is $(\pi_1^I - \pi_3^I)$. The level of harassment needed to keep IXC out is just $(\pi_3^x - \pi_1^x)$; hence condition (A1). Likewise, however, we required that the IXC not engage is harassment of ILEC sufficient to keep ILEC out on Path 1, and this requires condition (A2) to obtain.

Some insight into both the meaning and plausibility of these conditions is obtained by rewriting them in plain language, which produces:

(A1) "the value to IXC of integration against an integrated ILEC must be less than the efficiency of harassment spending multiplied by the value to an integrated ILEC of maintaining its local monopoly"

(A2) "the efficiency of harassment spending multiplied by the value to a vertically integrated IXC of keeping ILEC out of the competitive LD market must be less than the value to ILEC of integrating into a competitive LD market when IXC is vertically integrated"

Putting aside for a moment the size of α, it is clear that conditions (A1) and (A2) are quite plausible. Condition (A1), for example, requires that extra profits owing to monopoly provision of bundled services should be "large" compared to profits to "competitive firms" from introducing competition (by entry) into another market. If price competition by IXC drives bundle prices towards costs, entry by IXC into local services must be less profitable, on net, than monopoly provision of the bundle.

Condition (A2) is similar, and essentially requires that the extra profits earned by IXC, which prices everything competitively, from keeping ILEC out of LD, must be less than the value to the ILEC of vertically integrating into LD when faced with integrated competition from IXC. That there is likely to be little profit to be had for IXC from attempts to deter reintegration of ILEC stems from the competitive pricing of interexchange services even without ILEC re-integration. The value to the ILEC from re-integration when faced with a vertically integrated IXC, however, is likely to be large given that consumers value the provision of a bundled service offering more highly than comparable provision of the two services by separate firms.

The above discussion suggests the plausibility of (A1) and (A2) when, for example, $\alpha = 1$. Yet a much larger α may well be consistent with the equilibrium described above. In particular, $(\pi_4^x - \pi_3^x)$, the value to an integrated IXC of keeping ILEC out of toll markets, may well be small or zero. This can occur because, although a bundle might be relatively valuable, IXC prices it competitively (at costs) regardless of its value. Hence, the additional profit to IXC of keeping ILEC out of LD may be quite low.

The game-theoretic framework adopted here illustrates the following points. First, the monopoly enjoyed by incumbent local service providers introduces a fundamental asymmetry in the value attached by interexchange carriers and local monopolies to entry. Second, when the players can spend money reducing the post-entry profits of their rivals, their incentives to do so are fundamentally different. Third, due to the above, the *order of entry* may materially affect the final market structure obtained. If the monopoly enters first, competition in local markets may be delayed or derailed. If the competitor integrates first, such effects appear much less likely.[16]

The level of competition required to ensure a continuation of the upward time trend of local exchange competition is currently open to debate. The question is what level of competition is necessary to prevent a reversal of that trend once the RBOCs' incentive to cooperate in facilitating entry has been eliminated by their reintegration.[17] Specifically, will a *pro forma* satisfaction of competitive checklist items be sufficient to achieve this result, or will some threshold level of actual entry be required? Due to the public interest standard contained in the Act, this is, perhaps, *the* principal question raised by Section 271 implementation.[18] We shall return to this question below.

Moreover, as noted above, the pressure felt by the RBOCs to reintegrate (and to allow competition to develop within their markets in order to enable them legally to reintegrate) is directly affected by successful entry of interexchange carriers into local exchange markets. Even where such entry occurs at the retail stage only,

---

16   In reality, circumstances are worse than those assumed in our simple model. While we have treated IXC as a single "player," the interexchange industry is actually composed of many firms. All such firms have an incentive to "free ride" on the harassment activities of other IXCs resulting in more muted resistance by the IXCs. Antitrust considerations can outlaw some coordination among IXCs, reducing the effectiveness even further. Conspiracy law, ironically, cannot ordinarily be applied to coordinated activities within the monopoly firm. Finally, the harassment productivity constant may differ between the ILEC and the IXCs. Almost certainly, incumbent local service monopolies constitute the "home team" in many state regulatory venues. All of these effects serve to exacerbate the basic phenomenon described here.

17   In an affidavit filed on behalf of the Department of Justice in the Ameritech-Michigan 271 filing, Professor Marius Schwartz has advocated a reintegration standard that would require local exchange markets to be "irreversibly open to competition." To achieve irreversibility, Professor Schwartz argues that: (1) all checklist items be in place and proven to be operational by actual commercial usage; (2) entry by all three channels (pure resale, the purchase of unbundled network elements, and construction of competing facilities) be proven to be feasible; and (3) in the absence of such observed entry, a rebuttable presumption exist that irreversibility has not yet been achieved.

18   Several RBOC 271 filings have already been made as these firms probe this issue. The FCC has denied all such applications to date on the grounds that the checklist items have not been adequately satisfied. Consequently, the subsequent (and more difficult) question of the intensity of competition that will be required has not yet been clearly defined by the Commission. At some point, however, this question must be addressed.

through resale and the purchase of unbundled elements, it will nonetheless allow interexchange carriers to: (1) begin offering bundled end-to-end service offerings; and (2) establish customer bases from which facilities-based expansion can proceed. The competitive pressures created by these new market opportunities will make the RBOCs much more amenable to allowing whatever level of competition is required by regulators to permit them to reenter the interexchange market under Section 271.

Under the terms of the divestiture agreement, the RBOCs were faced with the following offer:

> If you will relinquish your monopoly over the local exchange market, you will be allowed to reenter the (now competitive) interexchange market.

It is little wonder that offer was not accepted. Abrogation of monopoly in return for permission to enter a competitive market is a distinctly bad deal. Under Section 271 of the Telecommunications Act, that same basic offer remains in place, albeit under a potentially different standard of what is meant by "relinquish your monopoly." The important difference, however, is that successful entry by interexchange carriers into local exchange markets along with a potentially strong preference by consumers for integrated service offerings is liable to rapidly erode the RBOCs' monopoly power over the retail portion of their business. Moreover, as entrants gain a foothold at the retail stage, the likelihood of facilities-based entry at the network level is enhanced as well.[19] This latter form of entry, of course, is ultimately required if the RBOCs' bottleneck monopoly power is to be eroded and deregulation is to be warranted.

Due to the expected advantage of bundled service offerings, however, even retail-stage entry by IXCs will create market pressures (and not just the unattractive opportunity presented by prior judicial decree) on the RBOCs to offer the bundled end-to-end service in order to remain viable competitors at the downstream stage. This aspect of the new environment (the presentation of a credible threat of bundled retail competition) substantially alters the RBOCs' incentive to allow competition to emerge. Thus, successful entry by interexchange carriers (or others) into local exchange markets, along with strict enforcement of an effective competition standard under Section 271, holds the key to promoting competition in local exchange markets while sustaining competition in long-distance markets.

Finally, the issue of whether the interexchange market presently is subject to effective competition has been raised by parties advocating early RBOC reentry. The essence of the argument here is that tacit collusion among the industry leaders has resulted in noncompetitive prices.[20] It is then claimed that the benefits of enhanced competition that would allegedly result from RBOC entry will exceed any potential (and speculative) harms that might be felt in local exchange markets. As a consequence, these parties argue for immediate approval of RBOCs' 271 applications.

---

19 For a more complete development of this argument, see Beard, Kaserman, and Mayo (1998).
20 See MacAvoy (1995; 1996), Taylor and Taylor (1993), and Sibley and Weisman (1998).

In our view, this argument is flawed on at least two grounds. First, on any objective basis, there are good reasons to believe that the long-distance market today is effectively competitive. There is simply too much evidence pertaining to industry structure, conduct, and performance to believe otherwise. Moreover, the conclusion that effective competition is present in this industry, while not shared by all parties, has been supported by several prior analyses and endorsed by numerous regulatory decisions.[21] Moreover, in this regard, the obvious question emerges: If the interexchange market currently exhibits collusively-determined, supracompetitive prices, then why have the RBOCs refrained from entering that market out-of-region thereby sharing in the alleged monopoly profits? As noted earlier, under the terms of the Telecommunications Act, these firms were authorized to enter the interexchange market outside their certified regions the day after the Act was signed into law. Their refusal to do so provides strong testimony to: (1) the competitiveness of that market; and (2) the RBOC's interest in confining their reentry to those regional markets in which they continue to hold substantial monopoly power in the provision of local exchange services, where monopoly leveraging is feasible.

The second reason the early reentry argument fails is that, if such reentry results in monopoly leveraging behavior in the long-distance market, RBOC reintegration will *lessen* competition in that market, not increase it. Consequently, even if one believes that the long-distance market is not performing competitively, it does not follow that RBOC reentry will improve matters. Once one acknowledges the competition-reducing effects in long distance and the monopoly-preserving effects in local, the case for early RBOC reentry clearly fails.

3. Monopoly Leveraging: Strategies and Theory

The above discussion suggests the likelihood of substantial harm to competition in both long-distance and local exchange markets resulting from early RBOC reintegration under a relatively lax implementation of the Section 271 standards (i.e., an implementation that allows reintegration to occur prior to the advent of a sufficient level of competition in local exchange markets). The potential for such harm results, in part, from the incentive and opportunity for these firms to pursue monopoly leveraging strategies in an environment where they: (1) still have monopoly power to leverage; and (2) are allowed to participate in an adjacent market that is susceptible to such leveraging. Conversely, if monopoly leveraging is unlikely to occur with early RBOC reintegration, at least a portion of the path dependency problem described above (that portion pertaining to the long-distance market) will not exist. Thus, in this section, we examine some specific strategies that may be used for monopoly leveraging and explore the economic theory

---

21   See, e.g., Bernheim and Willig (1996), Katz and Willig (1983), and Kaserman and Mayo
      (1996). Also, see the FCCs October 23, 1995, Order reclassifying AT&T as a nondominat
      carrier, in CC Docket No. 79-252. In addition, numerous state regulatory orders dating back to
      1984 have reached similar findings.

pertaining to these strategies in order to determine whether leveraging would be likely to arise in a prematurely reintegrated environment.

Strategies. Monopoly leveraging is said to occur when a firm with monopoly power in one market is able to exploit or extend that power to another market through various strategies.[22] A variety of leveraging strategies have been identified in the literature, but the most familiar fall into four categories: tying arrangements or bundling, vertical price squeezes, price discrimination, and service or quality discrimination. At the risk of oversimplification, but to form the foundation for discussion of the monopoly leveraging literature, we first provide a brief characterization of each of these strategies.[23]

Tying or bundling works as follows. Consider two products, A and B. Suppose a firm has a (legal) monopoly over product A, and, accordingly, is regulated in Market A.[24] Suppose also that the firm is allowed to participate in an unregulated market, B. The monopolist over A can evade the profit-restraining influences of price regulation on A by requiring that purchases of A be accompanied by purchases of B as well. By increasing the price of B above the competitive level, it is possible for the partially regulated firm to capture significant monopoly profits from the sale of the competitive product despite regulation of its monopoly service. The potential for anticompetitive tying or bundling of a monopoly and an (otherwise) competitively supplied service has been noted by the Director of the Bureau of Competition at the Federal Trade Commission, who noted that "Tie-ins can be used to evade price regulations, to discriminate in price against customers who place the highest value on the tying product, and, less commonly, to increase barriers to entry or leverage a monopoly in one market into another."[25]

Interestingly, it would appear that a widespread consumer preference for bundled service offerings could exacerbate monopoly leveraging through tying. Specifically, where such preferences exist, it is not necessary to *force* customers to purchase A and B together. All that is required is that the A, B bundle be offered at a mark-up above cost that does not exceed the premium consumers are willing to pay for the packaged service offering. No explicit tie-in or restriction of choice is necessary to pursue this leveraging strategy in the presence of such preferences.

Vertical price squeezes may be an important leveraging strategy when the monopolized product or service is employed as a necessary input in the production process of the firm's competitors. This occurs when, for instance, an upstream monopolist is vertically integrated and controls an important input but faces competition at the downstream (final output) stage. By controlling the price of the

---

22   This definition is consistent with the economic and antitrust literature. For example, see Sullivan and Jones (1992), Kaplow (1985), and Bowman (1957).

23   For a complementary discussion of the related problems of cross-subsidization and cost misallocation by regulated monopolists, see Brennan (1990).

24   Monopoly leveraging theory does not require regulation of either market. Regulation, however, can enhance the incentive for such leveraging to occur. See Ordover, Sykes, and Willig (1985, 123-127). Also, see Dayan (1975), Beard, Kaserman, and Mayo (1997), and Blair and Kaserman (1983, 110-114).

25   See Arquitt (1992, 932-933).

input (i.e., the cost to its downstream rivals), the vertically integrated monopolist may exclude competitors at the downstream stage by simultaneously raising their costs (by pricing the monopolized input high) and lowering their revenues (by pricing the output low). The resulting profit squeeze drives these firms from the downstream market.

Price discrimination can also be employed as a monopoly leveraging device. For instance, a firm providing a monopoly (regulated) input to both its own downstream service and to its competitors' services may charge different rates to itself and to its competitors.[26] Alternatively, if overt price discrimination is not possible, it may be possible to accomplish this same effect by shifting "costs" between the regulated and unregulated services.[27]

Finally, because firms compete on more than one dimension (price), equivalent results may be obtained if the monopoly provider of an essential service is able to discriminate on non-price terms (availability, quality, timeliness, etc.). For instance, Ordover and Willig (1979) describe what they call predatory product innovation, which involves introduction of a new product that has the effect of driving existing rivals from the market. For such exit-inducing innovation to be considered predatory, its profitability must hinge on an increase in monopoly power that results from the decreased number of competitors. More recently, we have shown that a dominant regulated input supplier that competes with unintegrated firms at a downstream stage will have an incentive to engage in sabotage against its rivals, where "sabotage" refers to input quality degradations that raise these firms' costs.[28] Thus, non-price (or service) discrimination and product innovation can have precisely the same exclusionary effects on competition as more overt anticompetitive pricing policies.

In order to employ these strategies in an anticompetitive way, it is necessary only that the firm in question have monopoly power in the provision of the leveraging good or service A. The leveraged service B to which the monopoly power is being extended may or may not bear some economic relationship (either horizontal or vertical) to the monopolized good.[29] Such a relationship exists where the monopolized product or service is either employed as a necessary input in the production of the other good or service or where the two products are either direct substitutes or complements (e.g., components of a system). As we shall see below, the existence of some economic relationship between the two goods, while not necessary for leveraging to occur, can facilitate the exercise of a leveraging strategy.

The Early Theory. In one of the first theoretical examinations of monopoly leveraging (via tying arrangements), Bowman (1957) distinguished between leveraging as a revenue maximizing device (which exploits existing market power)

---

26   The price the firm "charges to itself," of course, is simply the marginal cost of producing the intermediate product.
27   See Brennan (1990) for a formal discussion.
28   See Beard, Kaserman, and Mayo (1997). Also, see Economides (forthcoming).
29   See Whinston (1990) for a demonstration of monopoly leveraging in the case of independent goods. Also, see Burstein (1960).

and as a monopoly power-creating device (which involves the creation of new monopoly power). Bowman's analysis focuses on the former—leveraging as a revenue-maximizing device. In that context, Bowman found that monopoly leveraging was not always a profitable strategy.

Suppose that there is an unregulated firm with monopoly power in one market (the tying good) that is considering requiring its customers to also buy an otherwise competitively purchased product (the tied good) at greater than the competitive price. In this situation, it is not obvious that the monopolist will benefit. The reason is straightforward: if the monopolist were already charging the profit-maximizing monopoly price for the tying good, then requiring those customers to additionally purchase another good is economically equivalent to a price increase on the monopoly good. Because the price of the monopoly good was already at the profit-maximizing level before the tie-in arrangement, the addition of the tie-in will necessarily reduce the profits associated with the sale of the monopoly good. At the same time, however, sales of the tied good will add profit for the firm. Thus, the profitability of the leveraging strategy, and, therefore, the economic rationality of employing it, will depend upon whether the increased profits from sales of the tied good more than offset the decreased profits of the tying (monopoly) good.

Bowman then notes a specific example of when monopoly leveraging does not make economic sense—when the products involved are used in fixed proportion. Suppose, for instance, that a firm has monopoly power over bolts, but nuts are supplied competitively. Clearly, the only price that matters to the customers is the price of the combination of bolts *and* nuts. Thus, the monopolist could usurp all of the monopoly profit from this market by setting the price of bolts at the monopoly level and selling nuts at the competitively determined price (or, for that matter, allowing other firms to sell nuts). Any attempt by the monopolist to raise the price of nuts in this situation without simultaneously lowering the price of bolts simply raises the level of the *combination* price above the profit-maximizing level and, therefore, results in reduced profits for the firm.

Having identified this basic case where monopoly leveraging fails to enhance the firm's profits (and, therefore, is unlikely to occur), Bowman then describes a series of situations where monopoly leveraging can represent a profitable strategy (and, therefore, is likely to occur). These include: (1) situations where the monopoly good is price regulated, (2) situations where tying the monopoly good facilitates price discrimination, (3) situations where the goods involved are complements and are used in variable proportions, and (4) situations where the goods involved are technologically interdependent.

While Bowman found that monopoly leveraging, through tying, was not a universally profitable strategy, several subsequent authors have been much more critical of the concept of monopoly leveraging. The most noted examples of such criticism are Posner (1976) and Bork (1978). According to these analyses, monopoly leveraging will not be a profitable strategy under any conceivable circumstances; and, therefore, questionable practices (such as tie-in sales) must be driven by procompetitive motivations. The lack of profitability of monopoly leveraging stems from what Kaplow (1985) refers to as the "fixed-sum" perspective. That is, there is only one monopoly profit to be earned, and the firm may earn that profit without any strategic pricing or practices in other markets simply by establishing the correct (monopoly) price in the monopoly market. Indeed, Bork (1978, 372) went so far as to say "[t]he law's theory of tying arrangements is merely another example of the discredited transfer-of-power theory, and perhaps no other variety of that theory has been so thoroughly and repeatedly demolished in the legal and economic literature." Thus, while some of the early literature acknowledges the possibility of anticompetitive consequences of monopoly leveraging, much of that work denies the general profitability and, therefore, likelihood of such behavior.

Recent Developments. The essence of the early economic analysis was that a monopolist over product A can earn all the possible monopoly profits from appropriately pricing product A. Consequently, there is no (anticompetitive) reason to attempt leveraging.[30] There is only one monopoly profit to be earned and it can be fully captured without leveraging, so the only reason that one would observe, for example, bundling or tying arrangements is for pro-competitive reasons.

The validity of this analysis, however, relies on a special set of circumstances. In particular, the legitimacy of the early work rests on at least three fundamental assumptions: (1) no regulation of prices occurs for either product A (the monopolized product) or B (the erstwhile competitive product), (2) A and B are consumed (or employed) in fixed proportions, and (3) the monopolist over A takes the output price of product B as given (i.e., the market for B is fully competitive both before and after the leveraging has taken place). Under these stylized conditions, monopoly leveraging is, indeed, not profitable and has appropriately been discredited by the economics profession.

Over the past two decades, however, considerable economic research has been conducted to evaluate the robustness of the early conclusions on monopoly leveraging. The development of the more modern literature has roughly been along the lines of each of the above assumptions, and in each case the early conclusions on the irrationality of monopoly leveraging have been shown to be erroneous. Monopoly leveraging has now been demonstrated to be a profitable strategy in a variety of settings that are more realistic than those embodied in the strict assumptions of the early analyses. That is, modern economic research has resulted in a substantial rehabilitation of monopoly leveraging theory. We now turn to that literature.

In situations where monopoly leveraging occurs by extending an input monopoly to a downstream stage, the process involves vertical integration by the upstream firm. The theoretical literature pertaining to this process is fairly extensive.[31] The early work in this area assumes that the downstream industry employs the monopolized input in fixed proportions with other inputs in the production of some final output. Given this assumption of a fixed proportion production technology at the downstream stage, it is shown that the input monopolist has no profit incentive to extend its monopoly to the final product.[32] This result is, in effect, the vertical

---

30   Much of the early work on leveraging came from scholars at the University of Chicago, which
         has led Kaplow (1985) to label the early work the "Chicago School" approach to leveraging.
31   For surveys of this literature, see Kaserman (1978) and Perry (1989).

equivalent of the early literature's conclusion concerning the absence of an incentive for leveraging under similar (fixed proportions) circumstances.

In an important series of papers that appeared fully two decades later, however, the assumption of fixed proportions was shown to be crucial to the conclusion of no incentive for the monopolist to vertically integrate forward. First, Vernon and Graham (1971) show that, where the more general case of variable proportions production prevails, an upstream monopolist will, in fact, have a profit incentive to vertically integrate into production of the final product. And second, Schmalensee (1973) showed that the incentive for this firm to vertically integrate forward will persist until the final output stage is also monopolized.[33] Thus, relaxation of the assumption of fixed proportions results in an incentive for (vertical) monopoly leveraging to occur.

In an important break with the earlier literature, Ordover, Sykes, and Willig (1985) demonstrate that, in several other plausible cases, the early conclusions on the unprofitability of monopoly leveraging are similarly erroneous. These cases include price caps on the dominant firm, rate-of-return regulation, implicit price discrimination, and alternative (but inferior) sources of supply. For instance, suppose that a regulated multiproduct firm with monopoly power in one market produces complementary or vertically-related products also. In this case, Ordover, Sykes, and Willig demonstrate that the monopoly firm will have an incentive to engage in anticompetitive behavior toward other (perhaps more efficient) producers of the complementary or vertically-related products. As Ordover, Sykes, and Willig note,

> [T]he firm may use vertical mergers, tie-ins, predatory systems rivalry, and other tactics to monopolize production of complementary products, notwithstanding that other firms may have a comparative advantage in production of these products.

Moreover, the anticompetitive strategies employed by the monopolist may not be detected by standard regulatory tests of predatory behavior.[34]

Indeed, Ordover, Sykes, and Willig (1985, 125-126) note that

> To avoid regulatory or antitrust sanctions ... firm A may employ one of several more subtle tactics to induce the exit of firm B and its rivals, tying the sale of service 1 to the sale of service 2, redesigning service 1 to make it incompatible with variants of service 2 produced by rivals, or combining services 1 and 2 in a physical package while refusing to sell service 1 to its rivals at a price that allows them to remain viable competitors. *All such tactics facilitate extension of the market power of firm A to service 2, as well as lower economic welfare by excluding the most efficient suppliers of service 2* (emphasis added).

---

32   See Spengler (1950) and Machlup and Taber (1960).

33   Schmalensee (1973) also finds that monopolization of the final stage of production may be pursued through use of a vertical price-cost squeeze.

34   Such tests include the Faulhaber (1975) cross-subsidization criteria, the Baumol (1986) net burden test, and the Areeda-Turner (1975) standards for predatory pricing.

Ordover, Sykes, and Willig's results regarding the feasibility of monopoly leveraging directly contradict the principal conclusions of the earlier literature on this subject. The difference in results is easily seen to stem from the unrealistic assumptions (*viz*, no regulation, fixed proportions, etc.) embodied in the earlier analysis. Indeed, Judge Robert Bork, who generally has been thought of as the intellectual leader of the anti-leveraging school, has now acknowledged the viability of leveraging in the context of regulated industries. Specifically, with respect to the telecommunications industry, Judge Bork has argued that, were the Bell operating companies unregulated and vertically integrated, then monopoly leveraging strategies would not make sense. But, according to Bork:

> The situation and conclusion change, however, when the monopoly level of the firm is regulated and the other level is, or could be, competitive. This situation so alters the firm's opportunities that antitrust can no longer view vertical integration as necessarily benign. That was the situation that led to the AT&T divestiture, and it is the situation that would be recreated if Ameritech's regulated monopoly were permitted to enter the long-distance market. As a vertically integrated firm, Ameritech would be able to increase its revenues by damaging consumers in the monopolistic as well as competitive markets.[35]

Similarly Ordover, Sykes, and Willig (1985, 127) state:

> In sum, when a regulated firm is subject to a binding rate-of-return ceiling that exceeds its true marginal cost of capital, it has a profit incentive to expand into the production of vertically related services ... If, however, the regulated firm is comparatively inefficient in producing vertically related services, it may still endeavor to extend its monopoly by means of such tactics as below-cost pricing, tie-ins, and predatory systems rivalry—all to the detriment of economic welfare.

Other recent research has also emphasized the plausibility of anticompetitive monopoly leveraging strategies employed by a multiproduct firm that holds monopoly power in one or more of its markets. In separate papers. Carbajo, De Meza, and Seidmann (1990) and Whinston (1990) have used modern game theoretic models of oligopoly behavior to rigorously demonstrate the potential for monopoly leveraging. A key feature of both of these papers is that they relax the assumption, implicit in earlier analyses, that strategic behavior on the part of the monopolist cannot affect pricing, output, or market structure in related markets.[36] Once this assumption is relaxed (even in unregulated markets), monopoly leveraging strate-

---

35   See Affidavit of Robert H. Bork on behalf of AT&T Corp., In the matter of Application of Ameritech Michigan For Authorization under Section 271 Of the Communications Act to Provide In-Region, InterLATA Service In the State of Michigan, CC Docket No. 97-137, June 5th, 1997.

36   Whinston (1990), in particular, is critical of the earlier literature, stating that "[I]n an important sense, however, the existing literature does not really address the central concern inherent in the leverage theory, namely, that tying may be an effective (and profitable) means for a monopolist to affect the market structure of the tied good market (i.e., "monopolize" it) by making continued operation unprofitable for the tied good rivals" (p. 838).

gies become both feasible and profitable. As Carbajo, De Meza, and Seidmann (1990, 286) conclude, "[T]here is a sense in which our model identifies 'an extension of monopoly power ...' In this sense our results, like those of Whinston, vindicate the jurists' criterion of extending monopoly power ..."

Thus, the more recent research has demonstrated the economic plausibility of monopoly leveraging in a more general context. Its relevance to any specific industry or market, however, depends upon the particular industry characteristics that may enhance or deter the likelihood of anticompetitive monopoly leveraging. From the generic literature, several industry characteristics can be seen to enhance the likelihood of such leveraging. These characteristics are listed in table 1.

Table 1. Factors that Facilitate Monopoly Leveraging
1. Significant monopoly power in one or more markets.
2. A complementary or vertical relationship between the products involved.
3. Presence of price or profit regulation.
4. The monopoly firm's influence on entry/exit, pricing, or investment decisions by rival firms.

First, the primary condition necessary for monopoly leveraging is that the firm in question has significant monopoly power in one or more of the markets in which it operates. Second, the likelihood of monopoly leveraging is enhanced by a complementary or vertical relationship between the products involved (although this is not a necessary condition for leveraging to occur). For instance, should an input monopolist also operate in a downstream (and otherwise competitive) market, the prospects for monopoly leveraging are enhanced. Third, the presence of price or profit regulation of the monopolist increases the prospects for anticompetitive monopolistic leveraging into other markets. And fourth, the prospects for monopoly leveraging are enhanced where the monopoly provider can influence entry, exit, pricing, or investment in the "related" market. That is, where the monopolist has the potential for inducing either the exit of rivals in the related market or affecting price in that market, the possibility of successful leveraging is also enhanced.

Arguably, all of the above conditions will be present in the event of premature reintegration by the RBOCs. Thus, theoretical considerations suggest that monopoly leveraging is likely to occur if such reintegration is permitted. We now turn to consider the historical evidence pertaining to the occurrence of monopoly leveraging in this industry.

4. The Legacy of Monopoly Leveraging in the Telecommunications Industry

Not only do the economic conditions in the telecommunications industry appear ripe for monopoly leveraging in the event of premature RBOC reintegration, but there is also a demonstrable propensity of telecommunications firms with monopoly control over vital industry assets to engage in monopoly leveraging. That is, monopoly leveraging is not just a theory in this industry. It is a long-standing and widely observed practice. Thus, while a host of economic factors point toward the likely emergence of monopoly leveraging should the RBOCs prematurely be permitted to reintegrate into the interLATA market, the reality of this threat is underscored by a review of the history of the telecommunications industry. Indeed, such a review indicates that monopoly leveraging behavior has been a recurring source of competitive problems throughout the history of this industry. Thus, while telecommunications markets have undergone considerable technological, structural, and regulatory changes, it is the repeated reemergence of monopoly leveraging that perhaps serves as the enduring legacy of the industry.

While more recent antitrust cases stemming from the abuse of the ownership and control of monopoly bottleneck facilities are better known, recent research has demonstrated that monopoly leveraging practices emerged in this industry as early as the beginning of the century. When the Bell company patents expired in 1894, competition began to arise from a host of independent companies. In a detailed study of this period, Professors David Weiman and Richard Levin have identified a three-fold response by Southern Bell Telephone Company (SBT) to the emergence of this competition (Weiman and Levin 1994). Specifically, these authors argue that SBT engaged in a purposeful strategy of: (1) pricing below cost in response to entry; (2) making preemptive investments in order to deter new entrants; and (3) influencing local regulatory policy to weaken rivals and ultimately institutionalize the Bell monopoly. From their research, Professors Weiman and Levin conclude that "[I]ts combination of aggressive pricing, preemptive investment, and strategic use of regulation had the undeniable effect of eliminating competition." (p.106)

Beyond the strategies chronicled by Professors Weiman and Levin, SBT also employed the monopoly preserving/enhancing technique of denying competitors access to its network. Indeed, it was only under the imminent threat of a Department of Justice and Interstate Commerce Commission investigation that Bell acquiesced to grant access to its network to independent companies. Thus, as a vertically integrated, regulated utility with complete control over local exchange facilities, the Bell System was able to implement a variety of monopoly leveraging techniques that closely correspond to the strategies described above to exploit and extend its monopoly control over customers.

Subsequent to this early history, two prominent antitrust cases sprang up in the 1970s, both stemming from the abuse by the Bell System of its monopoly position over local exchange and access facilities.[37] Both cases centered around the behavior of an incumbent regulated vertically integrated monopolist when faced with the prospect of competition from nonintegrated rivals at a downstream stage of production. Indeed, the events surrounding MCI's persistent attempts to enter the long-distance telecommunications market provide powerful testimony to the ability of an incumbent vertically integrated firm to thwart the emergence of

---

37   See *MCI Communications v. American Telephone and Telegraph Company*, 708F. 2d 1081
      (1983); and *United States of America v. American Telephone and Telegraph Company; and
      Western Electric Company Inc., and Bell Telephone Laboratories, Inc.*, United States District
      Court for the District of Columbia, Civil Action 74-1698.

competition, even in the presence of legal and regulatory attempts to prevent such behavior.

While MCI's attempts to enter began in 1963, it was not until 1969 that it overcame the Bell System's regulatory and legal roadblocks to entry. Even the most preliminary provisioning of services by MCI that followed in the early 1970s was met with a variety of monopoly preserving tactics on the part of the Bell System. Recall that in the early 1970s, the Bell operating companies, as part of a vertically integrated AT&T, held (as they still do today) nearly complete control over local exchange and access facilities. Thus, in response to entry by MCI, the Bell system engaged in a host of practices that were designed to entrench the firm's grip on consumers and to squelch the emergence of competition.

In a recent monograph, Professors Douglas Berheim and Robert Willig have recounted the Government's charges brought against the integrated Bell system:

> [T]he Bell companies repeatedly chose not to comply with pro-competitive rulings, and instead continued to obstruct competitive entry through tactics as blatant as outright refusal of services, and as subtle as foot-dragging, time-consuming regulatory appeals, complex price discrimination, and a general reluctance to cooperate with competitors." (Bernheim and Willig 1996, 7).

Moreover, not only were these charges brought against the Bell System, but, at the trial, substantial evidence was presented to support the Government's position. Indeed, after hearing the Government's case, Judge Harold Greene formed the opinion that: "the testimony and documentary evidence adduced by the government demonstrate that the Bell system has violated the antitrust laws in a number of ways over a lengthy period of time."[38]

In the parallel private litigation brought by MCI, evidence pertaining to a host of monopoly leveraging tactics was introduced into the record.[39] For instance, it was pointed out that the Bell system had alternatively refused to provide interconnection services or had provided interconnection at discriminatory rates. MCI also charged that the integrated incumbent monopoly had taken actions before state public utility commissions that were anticompetitive because they constituted attempts to delay competitive entry and to impose heightened costs on *entrants*. After weighing the evidence, the court ruled, inter alia, that the Bell system's state level regulatory activities were indeed part of an anticompetitive strategy to inhibit the ability of MCI to compete on its merits, and awarded MCI trebled damages totaling $1.8 billion.

Thus, when conditions have been ripe for monopoly leveraging, such leveraging has, indeed, arisen in this industry. Premature RBOC reintegration will create

---

38   See Judge Greene's *Opinion*, September 11, 1981, U.S. v. AT&T, Ca No. 74-1698
      (D.D.C.), 524 F. Supp. 1336 at 1381. It is now widely accepted that it was the strength of the
      Department of Justice's case against the Bell system that drove AT&T to the negotiating table
      and, ultimately, to the divestiture agreement. See, e.g., Temin (1987, 217).

39   *MCI Communications v. American Telephone and Telegraph Company*, 708 F. 2d 1081
      (1983).

precisely those market conditions that have repeatedly given rise to anticompetitive behavior in the past. Therefore, these conditions will arise again unless reintegration is delayed until *after* the emergence of effective or irreversible competition in the provision of local exchange services. Failure to require this specific sequence of events—competition first and reintegration second—will condemn this industry to repeat its past.

Finally, while both the prevailing and prospective economic conditions and the history of the industry point unambiguously toward the likelihood of monopoly leveraging in the event of premature reintegration, any remaining skepticism on this issue is quickly put to rest by a close examination of recent marketplace actions of the RBOCs. Consistent with the economic incentives for monopoly leveraging and the legacy of such behavior in this industry, these firms have apparently been engaged in a host of practices that clearly indicate a positioning and predisposition to pursue monopoly leveraging once again in the face of threatened competition.[40] Such proclivities will only intensify if these companies are permitted to reintegrate prematurely. Indeed, recent actions provide a strong sense of *deja vu* to anyone who has objectively observed the performance of this industry over any substantial period of time.

5. The Effective Competition/Irreversibility Standard: Some Practical Indicia

Given the path dependency of the growth of competition in local exchange markets and the continuation of competition in long-distance markets on the timing of regulatory approval of RBOC 271 applications to reenter the interLATA market, the question that naturally arises is: What sort of practical indicia can be used to verify that local exchange competition is sufficiently established to satisfy the public interest standard of Section 271? That is, what set of objective criteria can be applied to signal the presence of effective, or irreversible, competition?[41] In our view, four such indicia may be applied. First, the operational support systems (used for pre-ordering, ordering, billing, and maintenance) required to achieve full parity between the incumbent's and entrants' retail-stage services should be in place, tested, and successfully employed. Moreover, we agree with Professor Schwartz that such systems be "demonstrated to work on a commercially significant scale, under real-world strains."[42] Such a demonstration is necessary to aid in the

---

40   A number of recent actions by the RBOCs are clearly intended to slow, halt, or reverse the emergence of competition in local exchange markets. The discussion in Bernheim and Willig (1996) documents many of these actions. See also, Testimony of Robert V. Falcone, Docket No. P-00971307, Before the Pennsylvania Public Utility Commission, 1998.

41   As over 100 years of antitrust enforcement has taught us, there is no set of objective, readily observable criteria that can unambiguously confirm either the presence or absence of effective competition. Some judgement will always be required. Nonetheless, certain criteria may be identified that can minimize the amount of judgment that must be applied. It is such a set of criteria that we seek to establish here.

42   Schwartz affidavit, p. 26. Bernheim and Willig (1996) also emphasize the need for operational

prevention of at least some forms of non-price discrimination by the RBOC that can be used to severely hamper competitive market forces and delay the development of effective competition in local exchange markets. Promises to implement such systems or installation of untested or unproven systems are not sufficient to meet the irreversibility or effective competition standards. One should not rely upon good intentions when those intentions are likely to change with the 271 approval. Moreover, by observing ongoing, satisfactory commercial provision of the operational support systems required for new entrants, policy makers can establish a set of performance benchmarks against which to judge the continuation of satisfactory provision of these systems in the wake of RBOC reintegration.

Second, before the RBOCs are allowed to reenter the interLATA market, it is absolutely essential that the prices their competitors will pay for the inputs required to compete in local exchange markets be set at economically efficient levels. That is, both wholesale discounts and the prices of unbundled network elements (including non-recurring charges) must be set on the basis of the relevant economic costs. Any deviation of such prices from these costs creates opportunities for cross-subsidization (or price discrimination) that can be used to stifle emerging competition. Non-competitive (i.e., non-cost-based) prices invariably yield non-competitive results. Quite simply, firms paying input prices that exceed competitive levels are vulnerable to predatory attacks such as price-cost squeezes; and such vulnerability is inconsistent with irreversible competition. Consequently, establishing competitive wholesale discounts and prices for unbundled network element prices are important prerequisites to the irreversibility of competition in the RBOCs' local exchange markets.

Third, as objective evidence that existing operational support systems and input prices are, in fact, not obstructive to local exchange entry, a non-trivial amount of non-facilities-based entry should be observed prior to approval of the RBOC's 271 application. The most probative evidence of an absence of entry barriers is actual observed entry. And RBOC entry into long distance should not be allowed until entry barriers (both regulatory and economic) to the local exchange market have been sufficiently lowered to allow the forces of potential competition to begin to be felt.[43] Therefore, new entrants actually purchasing the incumbent's wholesale services and unbundled network elements in competitively significant amounts should be a prerequisite to RBOC reentry.[44] In the absence of such competitive

---

support systems that have been demonstrated to function effectively on a commercially significant scale.

43 In this vein, it is interesting to note that AT&T recently announced that it is putting on hold its plans to enter local exchange markets through resale and the use of unbundled network elements. The reasons given for this decision were the unattractive (i.e., unprofitable) prices for RBOC wholesale services and network elements. Due to the terms offered to companies seeking to resell RBOC wholesale services, AT&T's chairman characterized resale entry as a "fool's errand."

44 We agree with Professor Schwartz that the absence of such entry should create a rebuttable presumption that non-regulatory entry barriers have not yet been lowered sufficiently. Moreover, the burden of proof to rebut that presumption should fall on the RBOCs.

activity, one can have little confidence in the irreversibility of local exchange competition.

Finally, the fourth indicator of the existence of effective, or irreversible, competition is the presence of one or more significant facilities-based competitors in the RBOC's local exchange markets. This last indicator is a particularly crucial signal of irreversibility of the path to effective competition for two reasons. First, until alternative facilities are put in place, new entrants will be forced to rely upon the RBOC for the essential inputs required to provide local exchange services to their customers. Such reliance obviously creates a vulnerability that is fundamentally inconsistent with irreversible competition. And second, due to the large sunk costs associated with facilities-based entry, a demonstrated willingness of investors to commit substantial resources of this nature to the local exchange market provides *prima facie* evidence of an expectation of irreversibility. In this sense, a significant amount of facilities-based entry provides a sort of market signal that competition is irreversible. That is, an irreversible commitment of resources suggests an expectation of irreversible competition. In fact, once a significant amount of costs have been sunk, predation and exit become considerably less likely. As a result, where significant facilities-based entry has occurred, regulators can be much more confident that the competition that is in place will be irreversible.

Where all four of the above indicia are present, effective and irreversible competition can be presumed to be in place. Then, and only then, can the future path toward vertically integrated competition be ensured and the public interest standard for approval of an RBOC's 271 application satisfied.

6. Conclusion

Given the dependency that exists between the time path of competition in telecommunications markets and the timing of RBOC reentry into long distance, and the likelihood of monopoly leveraging in a reintegrated environment in which the RBOCs still retain significant monopoly power in local exchange markets, the case for adopting a relatively stringent local exchange competition threshold for RBOC reentry into the long-distance market is compelling. Reentry in the presence of substantial local exchange monopoly would be likely to have two serious adverse consequences. First, it would eliminate whatever incentive the RBOCs might otherwise have to facilitate the emergence of competition within their own local exchange markets. Quite simply, in the absence of an effective competition standard under Section 271, effective competition is substantially less likely to materialize. As a result, the RBOCs' extant monopoly power over local exchange markets will be prolonged with early reintegration.

Second, RBOC reentry with the local exchange monopoly still intact is also likely to diminish (rather than enhance) competition in the long-distance market as a consequence of monopoly leveraging practices. The competitive strides made in that market over the past decade-and-a-half could be placed in jeopardy. At the extreme, the end result of this combination of reintegration and monopoly leveraging would be the emergence of seven (or, depending upon merger activity among the RBOCs, three or four) regional reincarnations of the old Bell system. That is, what started as a procompetitive vertical restructuring of the industry at divestiture could evolve into a simple geographic segmentation with a fully integrated monopoly within each region. Such a turning back of the clock would cause substantial harm to consumers by denying them the benefits of competition in both local exchange and long-distance markets.

This extreme scenario is, in our opinion, unlikely to materialize fully. Once the fires of competition have been lit, it is difficult to extinguish them altogether. Firms like AT&T, MCI, Sprint, and others are unlikely to be completely run out of the market. The real concern is that competition, particularly vertically integrated competition, will be delayed rather than that fully integrated monopoly will be restored. Nonetheless, any tendency in that direction would be harmful to competition and, therefore, to consumers. As a result, effective or irreversible competition in local exchange markets should provide the operable standard for RBOC reintegration under the provisions of Section 271.

References

Areeda, Philip, and Donald Turner. 1975. "Predatory Pricing and Related Practices Under Section 2 of the Sherman Act." *Harvard Law Review* 88:637-733.

Arquitt, Kevin J. 1992. "Market Power in Vertical Cases." *Antitrust Law Journal* 60, 3:921-934.

Baumol, William J. 1986. *Superfairness: Applications and Theory.* Cambridge, MA: The MIT Press.

Beard, T. Randolph, David L. Kaserman, and John W. Mayo. 1998. "The Role of Resale Entry in Promoting Local Exchange Competition." *Telecommunications Policy* (forthcoming).

Beard, T. Randolph, David L. Kaserman, and John W. Mayo. 1997. "Vertical Integration, Regulation, and Sabotage." mimeograph.

Bernheim, S. Douglas, and Robert D. Willig. 1996. "The Scope of Competition In Telecommunications." Working Paper.

Blair, Roger D., and David L. Kaserman. 1983. *Law and Economics of Vertical Integration and Control*, pages 110-114. New York: Academic Press.

Bork, Robert. 1978. *The Antitrust Paradox.* New York: Basic Books.

Bowman, Ward, S. 1957. "Tying Arrangements and the Leverage Problem." *Yale Law Review* 67:19-36.

Brennan, Timothy J. 1990. "Cross-Subsidization and Cost Misallocation by Regulated Monopolists." *Journal of Regulatory Economics* 2:37-51.

Burstein, M.L. 1960. "The Economics of Tie-In Sales." *Review of Economics and Statistics* 42:68-73.

Carbajo, Jose, David De Meza, and Daniel J. Seidmann. 1990. "A Strategic Motivation for Commodity Bundling." *Journal of Industrial Economics* 38:283-298.

Dayan, David. 1975. "Behavior of the Firm under Regulatory Constraint: A Reexamination." *Industrial Organization Review* 3:61-76.

Economides, Nicholas "The Incentive for Non-Price Discrimination by an Input Monopolist." *International Journal of Industrial Organization* (forthcoming).

Faulhaber, Gerald. 1975. "Cross Subsidization: Pricing in Public Enterprise." *American Economic Review* 65:966-977.

Kahai, Simran K., David L. Kaserman, and John W. Mayo. 1996. "Is the 'Dominant Firm' Dominant? An Empirical Analysis of AT&T's Market Power." *Journal of Law and Economics* 39:499-517.

Kaplow, Louis. 1985. "Extension of Monopoly Power Through Leveraging." *Columbia Law Review* 85(3): 515-555.

Kaserman, David L. 1978. "Theories of Vertical Integration: Implications for Antitrust Policy." *Antitrust Bulletin* 23:453-510.

Kaserman, David L. and John W. Mayo. 1996. "Competition and Regulation in Long Distance Telecommunications: An Assessment of the Evidence." *CommLaw Conspectus* 4:1-26.

Katz, Michael and Robert D. Willig. 1983. "The Case for Freeing AT&T." *Regulation* (July/August): 43-49.

MacAvoy, Paul W. 1995. "Tacit Collusion Under Regulation in the Pricing of Interstate Long-Distance Telephone Services." *Journal of Economics and Management Strategy* 7:147-185.

MacAvoy, Paul W. 1996. *The Failure of Antitrust and Regulation to Establish Competition in Long-Distance Telephone Services.* Cambridge, MA: The MIT Press; and Washington, DC: American Enterprise Institute.

Machlup, Fritz, and Martha Taber. 1960. "Bilateral Monopoly, Successive Monopoly, and Vertical Integration." *Economica* 27:101-119.

Ordover, J.A., A.O. Sykes, and R.D. Willig. 1985. "Nonprice Anticompetitive Behavior by Dominant Firms towards the Producers of Complementary Products." In *Antitrust and Regulation: Essays in Memory of John J. McGowan,* edited by F.M. Fisher, pages 123-127. Cambridge MA: The MIT Press.

Perry, Martin K. 1989. "Vertical Integration: Determinants and Effects." In *Handbook of Industrial Organization* Volume 1, edited by Richard Schmalensee and Robert D Willig. New York: North-Holland.

Posner, Richard A. 1976. *Antitrust Law: An Economic Perspective.* Chicago, IL: The University of Chicago Press.

Schmalensee, Richard. 1973. "A Note of the Theory of Vertical Integration." *Journal of Political Economy* 81:442-449.

Sibley, David S., and Dennis L. Weisman. 1998. "The Competitive Incentives of Vertically Integrated Local Exchange Carriers: An Economic and Policy Analysis." *Journal of Policy Analysis and Management* 17:74-93.

Spengler, Joseph J. 1950. "Vertical Integration and Antitrust Policy." *Journal of Political Economy* 53:347-352.

Sullivan, Lawrence A., and Ann I. Jones. 1992. "Monopoly Conduct, Especially Leveraging Power from One Product Market to Another." In *Antitrust, Innovation and Competitiveness,* edited by T.M. Jorde and D.J. Teece. Cambridge, MA: Cambridge University Press.

Tardiff, Timothy J. 1995. "Effects of Presubscription and Other Attributes on Long-Distance Carrier Choice." *Information Economics and Policy* 7.

Taylor, William E., and Lester D. Taylor. 1993. "Post-Divestiture Long-Distance Competition in the United States." *American Economic Review, Papers and Proceedings* 83:85-90.

Temin, Peter. 1987. *The Fall of the Bell System.* Cambridge, MA: Cambridge University Press.

Vernon, John, and Daniel Graham. 1971. "Profitability of Monopolization by Vertical Integration." *Journal of Political Economy* 79: 924-925.

Weiman, David F., and Richard C. Levin,. 1994. "Preying for Monopoly: The Case of Southern Bell Telephone Company, 1894-1912." *Journal of Political Economy* 102:103-126.

Whinston, Michael D. 1990. "Tying, Foreclosure, and Exclusion." *American Economic Review* 80(4): 837-859.

3

LOWERING PRICES WITH TOUGHER REGULATION:
Forward-Looking Costs, Depreciation, and the Telecommunications Act of 1996[1]

Michael A. Salinger

1. Introduction

The preamble to the Telecommunications Act of 1996[2] (henceforth, "the Act") states that Congress' objective in passing it was "[t]o promote competition and reduce regulation in order to secure lower prices ... for American telecommunications consumers." Several features of this objective should be noted. First, the ultimate objective is to lower prices.[3] Second, the mechanism that is supposed to lower prices is competition, not regulation. Indeed, easing regulation is an explicitly-stated objective. Of course, a major issue in the implementation of the Act is the sequencing of the development of competition and the easing of regulation; and it is reasonable to suppose that Congress intended most of the easing of regulation to come at some point in the future. Still, nowhere does the Act say that the intent is to lower prices by tightening regulation.

The implementation of the sorts of broad principles in the Act to systems as complicated as the telecommunications sector necessarily entails myriad detailed choices and judgments. These details are breeding grounds for unintended consequences. One such detail is the treatment of depreciation in the calculation of costs. Depreciation seems like one of those details that can safely be delegated to some mid-level accountant or engineer. It cannot.

This paper has both a narrow and a broad theme. The narrow theme is the difficulty of measuring costs and, in particular, the depreciation component of cost. The broader theme is that the details of implementing the Act might cause it to have quite different effects from those Congress intended.

---

1   I have benefited from comments by Ingo Vogelsang, William Moore, and Christopher Babb.
2   Public Law No. 104-104, 110 Stat. 56 (1996).
3   The preamble also states the objective of accelerating the adoption of new technology.

There are several steps in making this argument. Section 2 provides a perspective on the nature of the regulatory changes the Act makes. Section 3 discusses how depreciation is treated in the cost models that are being put forth to implement the Act and makes the case that this treatment is a reason to be concerned that cost models are understating costs. If price regulations are based on these models, the result will be price reductions through regulation. Section 4 then discusses what it means for price regulation to be eased or tightened. With just one layer of regulation, easing regulation means increasing the allowed price and tightening regulation means lowering it. Determining whether the Act eases or tightens regulation is more complicated, however, because there are two layers (wholesale and retail) of regulation. Section 5 concludes with a policy recommendation. It proposes that wholesale prices be high enough so that a competitor cannot offer lower prices than the incumbent simply by renting the incumbent's facilities.

2. The Nature of Regulatory Changes made by the Act

2.1. Simultaneous Wholesale and Retail Regulation

Prior to the Act, incumbent local telephone companies (ILECs) primarily faced what might be termed retail level regulation. State regulatory commissions regulated the price that they could charge to residences and businesses for local telephone service and intra-LATA toll, and the FCC regulated what they could charge to interexchange carriers (IXCs) for exchange access. A fundamental change brought about by the Act is that incumbents now face regulation of both wholesale and retail prices.

The Act allows for three types of interconnection/competition with the incumbent local telephone network. Competitors can purchase the services of the ILEC at wholesale and resell it; they can install an entire network and interconnect; or they can assemble their own network making at least partial use of unbundled network elements (UNEs) provided by the ILEC. It is this last form of competition that creates the primary reason to question whether the Act makes regulation stricter than it had been.

The statutory standard for the pricing of UNEs (as well as interconnection) is particularly problematic. According to the Act, "[t]he price (A) shall be—'(i) based on the cost (determined without reference to a rate-of-return or other rate-based proceeding) ... and (B) may include a reasonable profit."[4] In contrast, the standard for the price of wholesale services is retail prices "excluding the portion ... attributable to any marketing, billing, collection, and other costs that will be avoided by the local exchange carrier."[5] Since this latter standard seems intended to embody the efficient components pricing rule (ECPR),[6] the different wording for

---

4   Telecommunications Act of 1996, §252 (d)(1).
5   Telecommunications Act of 1996, §252 (d)(3).
6   Consider a service that consists of separable components. An incumbent company can sell the
        service (as a bundle) as well as at least some of the individual components. The ECPR states
        that the price of a component should be the price of the entire service minus the supplier's

the standard for the pricing of interconnection and UNEs was probably chosen to preclude the ECPR. What the standard does not mean is, however, clearer than what it does mean. The wording begs several obvious questions. First, if the prices are to be based on costs, why preclude reference to rate-of-return proceedings? After all, the objective of rate-of-return proceedings is to measure costs. Second, what is the meaning of the qualification that the cost might include a "reasonable profit?" It makes no sense that Congress would have (or Constitutionally could have) required incumbent companies to charge a price that did not reflect a required return on invested capital. As any Freshman student of economics knows (or is supposed to know), the required return on capital is just as much a component of cost as any out-of-pocket expense. The wording seems to suggest the possibility of allowing prices to exceed costs provided that the excess is "reasonable."[7] The FCC has not, however, accepted this interpretation. The FCC has proposed that the pricing of UNEs and access be based on forward-looking economic costs.[8]

The objective in requiring ILECs to sell UNEs is to facilitate competition by making it possible for firms to enter without installing an entire network. Indeed, the provision might have been designed with the expectation that some firms will choose to compete without ever installing network elements with natural monopoly characteristics. Still, despite the stated intent of fostering competition, this provision imposes an additional layer of regulation.

Two layers of regulation are not necessarily more stringent than one. Whether they are depends on the details of the regulated prices. Nevertheless, adding a new level of regulation without easing the existing level either makes the regulation more stringent or has no effect; the additional layer cannot by itself ease regulatory constraints.

2.2. Leveraging

The possibility that the additional layer would in fact result in a tightening of regulation is heightened by concerns that ILECs will resist entry by leveraging their market power in some network elements. The requirement that ILECs sell UNEs

---

avoided cost of not having to provide the remaining components. For example, if telephone service consists of loops and switches, then the ECPR for the price of a loop is the price of telephone service minus the firm's avoided cost of not having to provide switching. See, for example, Baumol and Sidak (1994, chapter 7).

7   The standard that prices be "based on costs" does not necessarily mean that they must equal costs. Ingo Vogelsang has suggested to me that the phrase about rate of return proceedings was intended to allow for the use of benchmark models. In other words, the UNE prices for a firm could be set without reference to its own actual costs. He also suggested that the wording about a reasonable profit is standard statutory language that indeed means that the prices should allow the investing company a normal rate of return.

8   *First Report and Order*, Implementation of the Local Competition Provisions in the Telecommunications Act of 1996, CC Docket No. 96-98 (Aug. 8, 1996), ¶¶630-703. As of this writing, the FCC's order has been vacated by the U.S. Court of Appeals for the 8th Circuit. See *Iowa Utilities Board v. FCC*, 120 F.3d 753 (8th Cir. 1997), which vacated the FCC order, and *Iowa Utilities Board v. FCC*, 135 F.3d 535 (8th Cir. 1998), in which the 8th Circuit ruled that the FCC had tried to circumvent its (i.e., the Court of Appeals) ruling.

in essence creates a market for individual components of local telephone service rather than just for telephone service as a whole.[9] While there are, of course, many potentially separable components of telephone service, it will suit our purposes to suppose that telephone service consists of just two elements, loops and switches. Absent the requirement that an ILEC sell UNEs, a competitor would have to install both loops and switches. With the requirement, it can install just one and rent the other or, for that matter, rent both.

The leveraging concern is that if an ILEC prices non-competitive elements above costs, it will have an advantage that allows it to preserve market power in elements that are potentially more competitive. There is, of course, an economics literature on leveraging that grew out of legal doctrines against leveraging. The so-called Chicago critique of leveraging doctrine stems from what might be termed the "single-lump" model. According to this model, a monopolist at one stage of a multi-stage industry can get all of the monopoly profits that a vertically integrated firm could earn. As the result of the model is usually explained, there is a "single lump" of monopoly profits available and the incumbent cannot get more than that lump by leveraging market power from one stage to another.[10] The assumptions needed to obtain this result are, however, quite strong. In particular, one must assume that the adjacent stages are perfectly competitive with constant returns to scale and that the underlying production technology entails "fixed coefficients."

While the single-lump model was originally formulated in light of an unregulated industry, there is a natural extension to a multi-stage regulated industry. If the regulated final price exceeds costs, then the level of profit allowed constitutes the single lump. A monopolist at just one stage can get the entire lump if the other stage becomes perfectly competitive and there are no opportunities for substitution between the two stages. Under these assumptions, basing the price of unbundled elements on the ECPR leaves no incentive for leveraging. While the FCC's motive in establishing the forward-looking cost standard may have been to prevent leveraging, the standard actually creates an incentive to leverage. The price regulations may prevent using prices as a leveraging tool, but a cost-based standard provides more of an incentive to the incumbent to use non-price means to exclude rivals in the provision of some elements.

A simple example illustrates the point. Suppose that the retail price of telephone service is regulated to be $3, that service consists of two components (loops and switching) and that the cost of each component is $1. According to the ECPR, each element should be priced at $2. The incumbent makes the same profit by selling an element to a competitor for $2 as it does by selling telephone service to

---

9   In contrast to proposals for deregulating retail electricity markets, customers do not necessarily
     see that different companies are providing different parts of the service. Each customer simply
     chooses a telephone company that is selling some combination of service that it provides itself
     and service that it first buys and then resells. Nonetheless, the underlying economics are
     similar to the case in which each customer can choose different providers for different
     components of telephone service just as electricity customers will be able to choose a
     generator that is different from the distributor.
10   For an articulation of the "single-lump" theory, see Bork (1978, 373).

an end user for $3. Moreover, potential entrants with lower costs than the incumbent for just one element would find entry profitable and potential entrants with higher costs would find entry unprofitable. To the extent that more efficient rivals exist, prices to consumers would drop below $3.

If, instead, the price of each element is held below $2, then the incumbent strictly prefers to be the retail provider rather than selling just one element to the ultimate provider. In turn, this difference provides an incentive to use non-price mechanisms to exclude rivals.

It has long been known that the single lump theory does not apply when the underlying production technology makes it possible to substitute away from a monopolized input.[11] There is a more recent literature that explores market outcomes when successive stages of an industry are imperfectly competitive.[12] When they are, the single lump theory no longer applies and concerns about leveraging have some merit. If, for example, switching is inherently oligopolistic, than a price for unbundled network elements above marginal cost gives the ILEC an advantage in the provision of telephone service. If retail price competition were eliminated altogether, then the market price would be determined by some oligopolistic equilibrium. Unless other firms were more efficient than the incumbent in the provision of some elements, the incumbent would have a cost advantage which would tend to translate into a larger market share.

If a bottleneck element exists, the likely explanation is that there are scale economies in providing it. If so, marginal cost is less than average cost; and it is mathematically impossible to set (linear) prices of unbundled elements at compensatory levels (i.e., at average cost) and not give the incumbent a marginal cost advantage. Still, a UNE price equal to average cost would provide less of a marginal cost advantage than one that allows some economic profit.

3. The Forward-Looking Cost Standard and Depreciation

The determination of the prices of UNEs can be divided into two stages: conceptualization and implementation. These stages may be logically distinct, but the interaction between them can have important effects in practice. The FCC's proposal of forward-looking cost as a conceptual standard is at the bottom of the plausible range of pricing standards. As this section will discuss, forward-looking costs are hard to measure. If the concern with leveraging that makes regulators choose a forward-looking cost standard also causes them to be more willing to understate costs than to overstate them, then the regulated prices of UNEs will fail to be compensatory.

---

11   See Vernon and Graham (1971). There is, in fact, substitutability between loops and switches in the design of a telephone network.
12   For informal discussions, see Klass and Salinger (1995), Riordan and Salop (1995), Reiffen and Vita (1995), and Krattenmaker and Salop (1986). For formal analyses, see Salinger (1988, 1991), Hart and Tirole (1990), Ordover, Saloner, and Salop (1990), and Riordan (forthcoming).

3.1. The Nature of Forward-Looking Costs[13]

The forward-looking cost standard is much more complicated than is generally acknowledged. This observation is not about the likely difficulty of measurement, although measurement is indeed likely to be difficult. Rather, the statement concerns the very concept of forward-looking costs. The conceptual complications generally arise because some of the inputs are durable. The economist's mantra that cost means opportunity cost is of little help in clarifying these conceptual issues.

The prices of UNEs are rental prices, and the conceptual difficulty stems from what it means for a rental price to be cost-based. A rental car company provides a useful analogy for illustrating the issue. What would it mean for the price that Hertz charges for car rentals to be cost-based? Vertical integration with Ford and unobservable contracts might make it difficult for us to know precisely the price that Hertz pays for a car, but the cost of purchasing a car is at least conceptually clear. Simply observing the cost of purchasing a car is not, however, sufficient to determine the cost-based rental price.[14]

Some fundamental distinctions lie at the heart of the complication. A price is associated with a unit sold, so a cost-based rental price is a cost per unit sold (CPUS). In order to sell units, however, firms must invest in capacity; and there are many reasons to suppose that firms will not use all of their capacity. Most notably, to the extent that demand is uncertain and capacity takes time to install, any company must make a trade-off between the risk of unused capacity and the risk of not being able to satisfy all demand. Also, if capacity is lumpy and demand is growing, firms will necessarily have excess capacity at some time.

A firm's capital costs are a total cost. While they can be put on a per-unit basis, the units directly driving capital costs are capacity, not sales. Thus, a cost of capital on a per unit basis is a cost per unit of capacity (CPUC), not a CPUS. To get a CPUS that includes capital costs, it is necessary to divide the CPUC by a utilization rate. In traditional regulatory parlance, capital costs determine a revenue requirement. Prices are then determined by dividing the revenue requirement by the quantity sold.

The other crucial distinction that complicates the meaning of cost-based prices is between the purchase cost of capital and the CPUC. The purchase price, i.e, the price of a switch or the cost of installing a loop, is relatively easy to observe but is associated with many periods. The CPUC is the cost over a period that is presumably shorter than the life of the asset. To go from the purchase price of capital to the CPUC requires an allocation of the cost over time.

While the standard that prices be cost-based seems to suggest that it is necessary to try to observe costs, there is an alternative approach to the problem. Cost-based

---

13   The material in this section is the subject of Salinger (1998), which treats the topic in more detail. While I have tried to minimize repeating the arguments in that article, some repetition is necessary to make this paper understandable as a self-contained unit.

14   The existence of a market for used cars of virtually any vintage makes it easier to determine the cost-based rental price for a car than the cost-based rental price of telecommunications equipment.

prices have the following feature:

> The cost-based rental price is the *minimum* rental price needed for
> the *direct* revenues from the asset to compensate the firm for the
> cost of investment.

The above statement contains two important qualifications. First, the cost-based
price is the *minimum* price that makes investment profitable, so an ILEC would
earn no *economic* profits from investing in an asset and renting it at cost-based
prices. The other is that it is the direct revenues from the investment that compensate the firm. The term "direct revenues" includes revenues jointly provided by the
asset but excludes the effects of renting the asset on revenues received for other
investments the firm makes. As the term is used here, the forward-looking cost
standard does not mean the ECPR. Also, irreversible investment entails the
exercise of a real option; [15] it imposes an opportunity cost to a firm by precluding
subsequent investments that have positive net present value. The forward-looking
cost standard does not compensate the firm for exercising this option. [16]

The "zero economic profit" feature of forward-looking prices is not sufficient
to define them uniquely. The current price needed to make investment just
profitable depends on expectations about future prices and utilization. One might,
for example, make the static assumption that the price and utilization will remain
constant throughout the life of the asset. Given market and regulatory conditions
in the telecommunications industry, however, such an assumption flies in the face
of economic reality. The prices of some types of telecommunications equipment,
such as switches, have declined over time and can be expected to continue to
decline. As a result, the rental price of switches can also be expected to decline.
One of the uncertainties about the future of telecommunications is the role of
wireless technologies. It is possible, although by no means certain, that fixed point
wireless technology will develop to the point that wireless drops will be used to
provide residential telephone service. If, as is likely, wireless drops turn out to be
much less expensive than wire-line drops, then the price of loops will decline as
well.

One way to pin down the forward-looking cost standard is to impose the
expectation that future prices be set to equal forward-looking costs. It is this
assumption that underlies the definition of forward-looking costs in Salinger
(1998). There, the forward-looking cost of an asset is defined as the rental price
that makes the net present value of investing in the asset equal to 0 assuming that
all future rental prices will be set so that the net present value of new investment
equals 0. [17]

---

15   McDonald and Siegel (1986) were the first to point out the option value of waiting to invest.
      See, also, Dixit and Pindyck (1994).
16   Hausman (1997) argues that this value is potentially large. Salinger (1998) argues that this
      option value is theoretically 0 under a true forward-looking cost standard. However,
      implementation of such a standard requires that prices be continuously adjusted, which would
      not happen in practice.
17   To be more precise, future prices are expected to be set so that the net present value of

The solution for forward-looking costs is well known for two special cases. One is the static expectation case described above. The other is when both the physical product of the asset and the price of new equipment are expected to decay or grow at an exponential rate. Under this assumption, the sum of the rates of physical and price decay can be taken as a depreciation rate, which can then be used as a cost component for the purposes of defining forward-looking costs.

Salinger (1998) shows how to solve for forward-looking costs for any path of expected utilization provided that the path is expected to be stable over time and that the price of new equipment is expected to change at an exponential rate.[18] Specifically, the forward-looking cost is

$$P(0) = \frac{I(0)}{\int_{t=0}^{T} X(t)e^{(\delta-r)t}dt}, \tag{1}$$

where $P(0)$ is the forward-looking rental cost at time 0, $I(0)$ is the cost of new investment at time 0, $X(t)$ is the expected quantity sold from the asset at time t in the asset's life, T is the maximum possible life of the asset, δ is the expected percentage change in the price of new assets, and r is the discount rate.[19]

3.2. Approach of Forward-looking Cost Models

While one can think of annual revenue requirements as the sum of an allowed return and depreciation, the models that are being used to measure forward-looking costs in the provision of local telephone service do not calculate costs in this way.[20] Rather, they take an assumed life and discount rate and calculate an annual revenue requirement (CPUC) with an annuity formula. The models then calculate a price by dividing the CPUC by an average utilization rate.

On one level, this approach is conceptually correct. The price is not calculated as the sum of input costs. Rather, it is calculated as the price that, under certain assumptions, yields cash flows that make the net present value of investment equal to 0. This present value calculation is, however, based on assumptions about the time pattern of cash flows; and the details of these assumptions are crucial. The assumptions under which the annuity formulas are appropriate are quite strong.

---

investment equals 0 only in those periods when investment is expected to occur. In periods with 0 investment, the price is set either at the market-clearing price or 0, whichever is greater.

18 It is important to be clear on what is being held constant. It is not necessary to assume that expected utilization of an asset is constant over its life. Rather, the assumption is that whatever is assumed about the time path of utilization over the life of a new asset today can also be assumed for the expected utilization for new assets in the future. If it is assumed that expected utilization in 2002 of an asset purchased in 1998 is 40%, then it is also assumed that expected utilization in 2003 of an asset purchased in 1999 is 40%.

19 Some additional assumptions are needed for this solution to be unique, but it is always a solution.

20 The two most prominent models are the HAI model, which was previously known as the Hatfield model, and the Benchmark Cost Proxy Model (BCPM).

One rationale for the annuity approach might seem to be that telecommunications equipment is what economists call "one-hoss shay" capital. This term refers to capital that does not decay physically (in the form of diminished capacity) during its life. At some point, it ceases to function altogether, but it remains fully functional up to the point of death.

This argument is not, however, persuasive. The annuity formula requires not only that capital have constant usage over its expected life, but also that the life be known with certainty at the time the asset is purchased. The forward-looking cost must be based on the time shape of the expected units sold, where the term "expected" is used in its mathematical sense. As of the date that an asset is purchased, the expected usage at some point in the future is the product of its usage conditional on survival multiplied by the probability of survival. Since the probability of survival necessarily decreases as the time horizon lengthens, constant usage during an asset's expected life implies declining expected usage over time.

An example serves to illustrate this point. Consider an asset that costs $100 to purchase and that yields a single unit of output during its actual life. Suppose that the discount rate is 10% and that the expected life is 10 years. If, at the time the asset is acquired, it is known that the asset will last exactly 10 years and if it is expected that the forward-looking price will remain constant, then it is straightforward to use an annuity formula to calculate a forward-looking cost of $16.27. Note that the present value of 10 successive annual receipts of $16.27 starting one year after the purchase price and discounted at a 10% rate is $100.

Now, suppose that the 10-year life is not a known life but, rather, an expected life. To keep matters simple, assume that the asset has a 50% chance of lasting only 5 years and a 50% chance of living 15 years. If the asset lasts only five years, then the present value (as of the time the asset is purchased) of the actual payments, assuming a price of $16.27, is $62. If the asset lasts 15 years, then the present value of the cash flows is $124. As of the time the asset is purchased, the expected present value of the cash flows is $93, which is the average of the two. The important feature of this estimate is that it is less than $100. Thus, the $16.27 provides an adequate return when the ten-year life is known with certainty. In the example with uncertainty about the asset life, the $16.27 does not provide an adequate return.

Although illustrated with a single example, this point is completely general. Holding constant the expected life at 10 years, increased uncertainty about the actual life increases the forward looking cost. This point is a natural consequence of present discounted value. Increasing uncertainty about the life of an asset while holding the expected life constant necessarily entails increasing the probability of cash flows late in the potential life of the asset and a reduction in the probability of cash flows early in the asset's potential life. Because of discounting, such trade-offs on a one-for-one basis lower the expected present value of cash flows.

The use of an annuity formula might also seem to be dictated by the following dilemma. At any point in time, a telephone company is using assets that were purchased at different times. The price of telephone services does not (and should not) depend on the vintage of the precise equipment used to deliver the service. Thus, one might expect that to use the output of a forward-looking cost model to apply to all vintages, the model must assume a constant price throughout the life of the asset.

This justification for the use of a level revenue requirement is simply wrong for two reasons. First, the assumption of a level revenue requirement is not simply a matter of the price being constant. It also requires that expected utilization (and maintenance costs) be constant over the asset's life. As explained above, uncertainty about the time of death makes it unlikely that expected utilization is constant. The second reason arises from a fundamental confusion about the interpretation of prices for equipment after the first period in models of forward-looking costs. These prices are not the forward-looking prices of current old equipment. Rather, they are expectations about what forward-looking costs will be when equipment that is currently new becomes old. That is, the price of equipment in the asset's second year is what the forward-looking price is expected to be one year in the future. The price of equipment in the asset's tenth year is the expected forward-looking price nine years in the future. Ultimately, the forward-looking price standard dictates that those prices will be calculated at the time the prices are used. Thus, the prices in the model are expected prices. Nothing in the forward-looking cost standard requires that future prices must be expected to be the same as current prices. Indeed, it is inherent in the forward-looking cost standard that prices change as technology and the cost of new equipment changes.

3.3. Factors to Consider

The most difficult aspect of implementing the forward-looking cost standard is likely to be to determination the $X(t)$ series—i.e., the expected utilization rate over the life of the asset. To do so, one must consider the following factors.

3.3.1. Risk of Physical Death

Assets cease to work. Sometimes it is the asset itself that simply ceases to function. At other times, the asset is destroyed by natural or man-made events.

3.3.2. Technology Risk

Many and perhaps all types of telecommunications equipment run the risk of becoming technologically obsolete. The probability that an asset will be taken out of service before the end of its physical life because it is replaced by an asset embodying new technology must be captured in the $X(t)$ series.

One relatively recent develop in the treatment of capital in cost estimation is the substitution of "economic" lives rather than physical lives. In some cases, the estimates of economic lives are based on a projection of technological substitution. While the details of how these estimates are obtained are inherently controversial, it is necessary to take account of this effect in some way. At the same time, however, the prospect of technological substitution is not the only reason for divergence between physical and "economic" lives.

Technological change can affect the estimate of forward-looking costs both through the expected utilization series $[X(t)]$ and through the rate of price decay (δ). The example of personal computers serves to illustrate the different effects. Consider a personal computer with an Intel 486 chip purchased in 1994. How would one determine the forward-looking rental price for the machine in 1994? It is likely (but not certain) that the machine would still be in use in 1995. By that time, however, the cost of the same machine would have dropped, and the price of that model could be expected to decline each subsequent year. This price reductions are captured in δ. Also, as time goes on, the likelihood that the machine would simply be discarded for a machine with a Pentium processor would increase. The probability of completely retiring the machine would be captured in the $X(t)$ series.[21]

3.3.3. Competition Risk

As noted in the introduction, the stated objective of the Act is "[t]o promote competition ... in order to secure lower prices for American telecommunications consumers." The implication is that competition will bring prices down. While competition might ultimately have that effect, there is at least one important sense in which competition raises costs, at least in the short run.

Recall that the forward-looking cost is the price for output that makes investment just profitable. In a competitive market, it is not possible to insure that an investment will turn out to be profitable. The forward-looking cost standard means, however, that investment is just profitable on an expected value basis. These expectations must take into account all risks that any rational business would take into account when making an investment.

Given passage of the Act, no rational ILEC would make irreversible investments without taking account of the possibility that competition might reduce use of the asset some time during the asset's life. This risk necessarily lowers expected use and raises forward-looking costs. Measuring competition risk is likely to be difficult. This difficulty is, however, no excuse for not trying to do so. The failure to account for competition risk makes the implicit assumption that it does not exist. It does, however, and ignoring it necessarily results in an understatement of costs.

3.3.4. Planned Excess Capacity

For some telecommunications assets, installing capacity has a large fixed cost but the marginal cost of installing more capacity is relatively low. A good example is loops, since the labor needed to install the loops is a substantial fraction of the cost and does not depend much on the amount of capacity installed. Under such circumstances, it is generally efficient to install excess capacity whenever capacity is being installed and demand is either growing or uncertain.

It is certainly not surprising that planned excess capacity lowers average utilization rates. All else equal, this reduction raises forward-looking costs. Planned excess capacity has an additional, more subtle effect that can be illustrated with a simple example. Consider an asset that has a capacity of 4 units of output, an initial cost of $100, and a known life of two years. Suppose that in the first year, only 2 units will be sold. In the second year, demand growth will result in all 4 units being

---

21 Note that what matters for the $X(t)$ series is the possibility that the machine is literally discarded. If the original owner sells (or in some other way reallocates) the machine to another user, it remains in use for the purposes of calculating forward-looking costs.

sold. Finally, let the discount rate be 10% and assume that the cost of new equipment is expected to be constant. Using a discrete time analog of equation (1), $X(1) = 2$ and $X(2) = 4$. The forward looking price is then calculated as:[22]

$$P(1) = \frac{100}{\dfrac{2}{1.1} + \dfrac{4}{1.1^2}} = 19.52. \tag{2}$$

Over the life of the asset, the average quantity sold is 3. If one made the simplifying assumption that actual quantity sold was 3 in both periods, the forward-looking price would be:

$$P(1) = \frac{100}{\dfrac{3}{1.1} + \dfrac{3}{1.1^2}} = 19.21. \tag{3}$$

Comparing the two cases, the estimate of forward-looking cost is lower in equation (3) than in equation (2). To the extent that equation (2) reflects the economic reality, equation (3) underestimates the forward-looking cost.

3.3.5. Other Uses

The four factors listed so far all have the effect of increasing the estimate of forward-looking costs. One factor that, all else equal, reduces forward-looking costs is the possibility of technical advance that makes sunk assets more valuable. Telephone lines are, of course, already used to transmit data and can be used to transmit television signals. If, for example, improvements in signal-compression technology make it possible to transmit data over existing wires at higher speeds and allow for the carriage of more video signals, then existing assets will have greater future value than they otherwise would. All else equal, increases in the expected future value of existing assets lowers the current forward-looking cost.

3.4. Likely Magnitudes of Alternative Treatments

In the preceding examples, the difference between the alternative treatments is small, but these examples are highly stylized. There are two primary reasons why it is difficult to assess the precise amount by which the annuity approach in forward-looking cost models understates forward-looking rental prices. First, the amount of understatement depends on how lives are estimated. Indeed, there would be some estimate of a life that would generate the correct forward-looking cost in the annuity model. The estimate would not bear any necessary relationship to the actual or expected life, but a sufficiently short "effective life" would generate the right answer. Second, while the constant expected utilization (and price) assumption underlying the annuity approach is generally implausible, the correct time path

---

22   In equation (1), the forward looking price is denoted as $P(0)$. In going from a continuous to discrete time formulation, a timing convention must be adopted. Here, I assume that the initial cash in-flow is one period after the investment is made. Under this convention, the forward-looking cost is $P(1)$.

of expected use is much harder to know.

Still, to see that these effects are potentially large, it is useful to compare the annuity approach to another simple alternative. In particular, suppose that the process generating expected lives is a "constant probability of death" model. That is, each year, an asset has a constant probability of dying conditional on surviving to that point. The attractive feature of this model is that if π is the constant probability of death, then $1/\pi$ is the expected life. Thus, to the extent that the actual estimates of lives are expected lives, one can use these estimates to calibrate the expected probability of death model. That is, one can estimate π as $1/L$, where L is the estimate of the useful life. Given a constant probability of death (and no other sources of depreciation), then the probability of death can be considered an expected depreciation rate. Henceforth, I refer to this approach as "1/L depreciation."

Table 1 shows the differences in estimates of forward-looking costs based on the annuity approach and on "1/L depreciation."[23] To provide some intuition for the source of the differences, it also reports the differences in the rate of depreciation implied by the two approaches. Depreciation for the annuity approach is calculated as the total revenue requirement (stated as a percentage of the cost of purchasing capital) minus the required rate of return.

As column (3) indicates, the annuity values allow for virtually no depreciation for assets with lives greater than 15 years. The values in column (3) are absolute values. It is arguably more relevant to place these in perspective by comparing the annuity value to 1/L depreciation, which is given in column (4). Column (5) shows the ratio of the two. As it indicates, the depreciation implicit in the annuity approach for a 50-year asset is just 1% of 1/L depreciation. While not much telecommuni-

Table 1. Annuity versus "1/L Depreciation"					
(1) Life	(2) Annuity Value	(3) Depreciation Implicit in Annuity	(4) 1/L Depreciation	(5) Annuity/ 1/L Depreciation	(6) Annuity/ 1/L Cost of Capital
5	0.26	0.16	0.20	0.82	0.88
10	0.16	0.06	0.10	0.63	0.81
15	0.13	0.03	0.07	0.47	0.79
20	0.12	0.02	0.05	0.35	0.78
30	0.11	0.01	0.03	0.18	0.80
50	0.10	0.00	0.02	0.04	0.84
Note: Calculations assume 10% required rate of return and that investment occurs 1 year prior to first year of returns.					

---

23   Straight-line depreciation is an example of 1/L depreciation. The straight-line method refers, however, to an entire path of depreciation. In a forward-looking cost model, however, cost is directly linked only to depreciation in the first year. Another process that gives rise to 1/L depreciation is when an asset has a constant probability of death each period. The expected life is 1 divided by that probability, and the probability is also an expected depreciation rate.

cations equipment is assumed to have 50-year lives any more, the difference in depreciation between the two methods is substantial (23%) even for 5-year capital; and the annuity depreciation is less than 40% of 1/L depreciation for 15-year capital.

The result that the annuity approach provides for virtually no depreciation for long-lived assets should be of no surprise to anyone who has calculated the tax-deductible portion of a home mortgage. A conventional mortgage is an annuity payment. Each payment consists of two components, a tax-deductible (in the United States) interest payment and a non-tax-deductible repayment of principle. The interest component corresponds to the allowed return and the repayment of principle corresponds to the implicit depreciation. In the first year of a home mortgage, virtually all of the payment is tax-deductible.

While the ratio of annuity to 1/L depreciation is a decreasing function of asset life, so is depreciation as a fraction of the total cost of capital. The effect of assuming annuity values rather than 1/L depreciation is more accurately gauged by its effect on the total cost of capital. The last column of table 1 reports this ratio. It shows that the difference is roughly flat at approximately 80% for assets with lives between 10 years and 30 years. It is less for both very short-lived and very long-lived assets. [24]

One way to place these results in further perspective is to compare the choice between the annuity approach and 1/L depreciation to choices about the allowed rate of return. For a 15-year asset and an allowed return of 10%, the annual revenue requirement for a unit of capital is 16 2/3% with 1/L depreciation and only 13% with the annuity method. Thus, the choice between the two methods is comparable to a difference of nearly 4% in the allowed rate of return.

4. Intended versus Actual Effects

We now return to Congress' intention to increase competition and ease regulation. To do so, it is instructive to consider the stylized example in which the retail price is $3 and the apparent cost of each of the two elements is $1. The ECPR would mandate a price of $2 for each element and a cost-based standard mandates a price of $1.

Suppose that the cost-based standard is adopted. The retail price would then necessarily drop to $2 because it would be possible to put together a virtual network entirely from rented elements and charge a price of $2. Telephone calls would still be going through the same wires and switches. Customers would, however, perceive a difference because some or all of them would write checks to companies other than the ILEC.

Superficially, it would appear that the intent of the Act would have been achieved. The presence of alternative (retail) suppliers would create the appearance of competition, and the increase in competition would be associated with a decline

---

24   The results in table 1 depend on but are not very sensitive to the assumed allowed rate of return.

in prices. Moreover, having regulated the price of each element to be $1, the regulation on the retail price could be eliminated altogether, thus creating the appearance of deregulation.

The reality would, of course, be quite the opposite. Under this scenario, regulation is not eased and it is not competition that brings down the price. Rather, the reduction in price would be due to the tightening of regulation.

As was argued in section 2, the nature of the Act was to add a layer of wholesale regulation to an existing layer of retail regulation. Even if the retail regulation was eventually phased out, the nature of the Act would be to substitute wholesale regulation for retail regulation, not to lessen regulation or to substitute competition for regulation.

Wholesale regulation is neither inherently tighter nor inherently looser than retail regulation. The tightness of regulation depends on the level of prices that are set. If the wholesale prices were set sufficiently high and the ceilings on retail prices were raised sufficiently at the same time, then the addition of a layer of regulation would be associated with an effective easing of regulation. If, however, the wholesale prices are such that a competitor can undercut prevailing retail prices simply by renting all network elements from the incumbent at regulated wholesale prices, then regulation is tightened even if retail price regulation is relaxed or eliminated.

The use of the ECPR for wholesale price regulation while maintaining retail price regulation provides an interesting benchmark. In this case, the combination of regulatory and competitive constraints on the incumbent are the same as they would be if the ILEC did not need to sell unbundled elements at all. The incumbent's profits would be preserved as long as all competitors rented at least one UNE from the ILEC. Any reduction in cost under this scenario could be attributed to competition, since a competitor could only cause a price reduction by being more efficient than the incumbent for the provision of one of the elements.

Given this standard for when the strength of pricing regulations is constant, we can establish certain conditions under which the strength of the regulations either increases or decreases. First, the ECPR as a standard for wholesale prices in combination with an easing of retail price regulation would be an easing of regulation. By the same token, maintaining retail prices while setting prices less than the ECPR would be a tightening of regulation.

Another interesting benchmark would be a set of wholesale prices that add to existing retail prices in conjunction with an elimination of retail price regulation. Such a policy could not be considered an easing of regulation, since the wholesale price regulation would prevent any increase in retail prices above previous levels. Whether or not it would constitute a tightening of regulation would depend on the individual wholesale prices. For example, if one of the wholesale prices was below the cost of providing the element while another was above cost, then an entrant could rent the underpriced element and supply the over-priced element itself, thus causing a reduction in the retail price.[25]

5. Conclusions

This paper has had both a broad and a narrow theme. The narrow theme is that in determining forward-looking prices, measuring the capital component of costs is quite difficult. The broader theme is that despite its stated intent of easing regulations, the Telecommunications Act added a layer of wholesale regulation without easing retail regulation. To the extent that the wholesale price regulations are binding, regulation has become tighter, not looser.

To understand the link between the two, return to the stylized example of a regulated retail price of $3 and estimated forward looking costs of $1 for each of two UNEs. The estimated forward-looking cost of the two UNEs are inherently suspect because forward-looking cost is hard to measure. Given the difficulty of measuring forward-looking cost, one might argue for the constraint that the forward-looking costs of the UNEs be high enough that it is not possible to compete at retail simply by renting UNEs. In part, the constraint serves as a reality check on the estimates. It is easy for Congress, the FCC, state regulators, academics, and others to speculate that current prices for telecommunications services are above what it would cost an efficient provider to offer them. If regulators could really ascertain, however, that prices are above costs, they could lower them through regulation. The level of current price regulations presumably means, however, that regulators cannot be confident that an efficient competitor could do better. Thus, any cost model that says that the price of service should be much lower than it is should be met with suspicion. Even if one knew, however, that prices equal to the forward-looking cost of UNEs would allow competitors to compete just by buying wholesale UNEs from the ILECs, one could reject using them on the grounds that their effect would be inconsistent with the Act's stated objective of bringing prices down through competition.

References

Baumol, William J., and J. Gregory Sidak. 1994. *Toward Competition in Local Telephony.* Cambridge: MIT Press.

Bork, Robert H. 1976. *The Antitrust Paradox: A Policy at War with Itself.* New York: Basic Books, Inc.

Dixit, Avinash K., and Robert S. Pindyck. 1994. *Investment Under Uncertainty.* Princeton: Princeton University Press.

Hart, Oliver, and Jean Tirole. 1990. "Vertical Integration and Market Foreclosure." *Brookings Papers on Economic Activity – Microeconomics*, pp. 205-76.

---

25   These general points about elements apply equally well to the provision of services in different areas. To market efficiently, for example, there might be advantages to offering service throughout a metropolitan area. One can think of capacity in different parts of a metropolitan area as being unbundled elements for providing service throughout the area. To the extent that the cost varies throughout the area (because of density, say) and both the retail and wholesale rates are geographically averaged, then an entrant can rent facilities in high cost areas and install facilities in low-cost areas.

Hausman, Jerry. 1997. "Valuation and the Effect of Regulation on New Services in Telecommunications." Presented at American Enterprise Institute conference entitled, "Pricing and Costing a Competitive Local Telecommunications Network," November 4, 1997.

Krattenmaker, Thomas G., and Steven Salop 1986. "Anticompetitive Exclusion: Raising Rivals' Costs to Achieve Power over Price." *Yale Law Journal* 96:209-93.

McDonald, Robert, and Daniel Siegel. 1986. "The Value of Waiting to Invest." *Quarterly Journal of Economics* 101:707-728.

Ordover, Janusz A., Garth Saloner, and Steven C. Salop. 1990. "Equilbrium Vertical Foreclosure." *American Economic Review* 80:127-142.

Reiffen, David, and Michael Vita. 1995. "Is there New Thinking on Vertical Mergers? A Comment." *Antitrust Law Journal* 63:917-941.

Riordan, Michael H. forthcoming. "Anticompetitive Vertical Integration by a Dominant Firm." *American Economic Review*.

Riordan, Michael H., and Steven C. Salop. 1995. "Evaluating Vertical Mergers: A Post-Chicago Approach." *Antitrust Law Journal* 63:513-568.

Salinger, Michael A. 1988. "Vertical Mergers and Market Foreclosure." *Quarterly Journal of Economics* 103:345-56.

Salinger, Michael A. 1991. "Vertical Mergers in Multi-Product Industries and Edgeworth's Paradox of Taxation." *Journal of Industrial Economics* 39:545-556.

Salinger, Michael A. 1998. "Regulating Prices to Equal Forward Looking Costs: Cost-Based Prices or Price-Based Costs?" *Journal of Regulatory Economics* (forthcoming).

Salinger, Michael A., and Michael Klass. 1995. "Do New Theories of Vertical Foreclosure Provide Sound Guidance for Consent Agreements in Vertical Merger Cases." *The Antitrust Bulletin* 40:667-698.

Vernon, John M. and Daniel A. Graham. 1971. "Profitability of Monopolization by Vertical Integration." *Journal of Political Economy* 79:924-925.

4

STRANDED ASSETS IN NETWORK INDUSTRIES IN TRANSITION[1]

Michael A. Crew
Paul R. Kleindorfer

Stranded assets are assets that have lost a large amount of their value and may even be worthless. However, "worthless" and "stranded" are not synonymous. To be considered stranded, assets generally must be assets of a regulated industry and must have lost their value as a result of legislative or regulatory changes. Stranded assets have recently taken on considerable significance in network industries, especially electric utilities. The resulting demands for compensation or recovery of stranded assets have made it one of the major public policy problems that must be addressed by regulators and legislators today. The purpose of this paper is to examine the problem of stranded assets and consider some possible directions that might be taken in addressing the problem. In section 1, we begin by reviewing and defining the problem of stranded assets. In section 2, we comment on a number of approaches to the problem. Some of these might be characterized as variations of network access pricing schemes. In section 3, we develop a simple model to illustrate the problem of stranded asset recovery by various means, including access pricing. Section 4 is by way of summary and implications.

1. Stranded Assets

Before providing our definition of stranded assets, we first review some of the issues. For an asset to be considered stranded, it must incur a significant loss in value. However, losing its value alone does not necessarily make an asset stranded. Some assets become worthless in the normal course of the operation of the market. Their loss in value is attributed to the normal operation of the competitive market. In the competitive market, the entrepreneur faces the consequences of his own actions and, if he cannot meet the standards of the market, pays the price. Take the

---

1   The authors would like to thank Shimon Awerbuch, Mark Beyer, Robert Graniere, Sally Johnston, Richard Schuler, Richard Simnett, and Larry Spancake for helpful comments.

example of an entrepreneur who buys a country house and converts it into a charming hotel and restaurant. Unfortunately, he misjudges the conversion costs and ends up having to sell the property at a loss. The loss should not be considered a stranded asset but rather the necessary consequence of failing to meet the standards of the competitive market. Indeed, losses and the threat of bankruptcy are the principal disciplines imposed in a competitive market to encourage prudent investment on the part of entrepreneurs and investors.

Critical to the determination of whether assets are stranded is whether they have lost a significant portion of their value as a result of legislative, government, or regulatory changes. However, not all losses in asset value resulting from action by government are expected to be compensated. For example, the gas, electric, telephone, and water companies that supplied an automobile assembly plant should not expect to be compensated if the plant is forced to close because it is too expensive to modify it to produce zero-emission vehicles which were mandated by government decree. This kind of loss would be considered part of the normal risks of doing business and is not significantly different from the risks faced by unregulated businesses. Thus, stranded assets arise primarily in regulated industries, but the mere act of losing value as a result of a regulatory change is not sufficient for assets to be considered stranded. For assets to be considered stranded, the loss must be directly related to the actions of the industry regulator or legislation specific to the industry.

Based on the above discussion, we propose the following definition of stranded assets:[2]

> Assets are considered stranded when they were prudently acquired but have lost economic value as a direct result of an unforeseeable regulatory or legislative change specific to the industry in question.

We note the following characteristics of a stranded asset:

1. The investment decision to acquire the asset or contract for its use would have to be considered "prudent" in the light of the information available at the time it was made.
2. The loss in value must be the direct result of regulatory or legislative change and not the result, foreseeable or not, of changes in factor or product markets.
3. The change must have been unanticipated when the original investment was made.
4. The change in the economic value of the asset must be evaluated against the prospects for cash flows from use of the asset in the future.

Before proceeding to examine the problem of stranded investments as manifested in regulated industries today, we develop a simple statement of the problem. We summarize the principal aspects of stranded investment symbolically with the

---

2   Stranded assets can be in the form of financial assets, such as contracts, as well as physical assets, such as plants or equipment.

following expression:

$$S(y, y', \theta) = PV\{\Pi[x(y), y, \theta] - \Pi[x(y), y', \theta]\},$$

where

$S(y, y', \theta)$ = Loss in value of the regulated firm's assets at (y, y', θ);

θ is the state of the world, observed after both x and y are chosen;

y is the initial regulatory regime, which is expected by the firm to continue;

$x(y)$ is the firm's optimal choice of long-run assets, technologies, etc., given y;

y' is the changed regulatory regime, possibly unanticipated by the firm;

$PV\{\}$ is net present value; and

$\Pi[x, y, \theta]$ is a vector of profits per period over the life of the assets in regulatory regime y, when the firm chooses long-run factors x and state of the world θ obtains.

Assuming that x is chosen to maximize expected discounted profits $E\{PV\{\Pi[x, y, \theta]\}\}$, given y and some distribution over θ, it is clear that the change in regulatory regime to y', if unanticipated, will lead to a decline in expected profits. Of course, it may or may not lead to a decline in actual profits, depending on the state of the world θ which obtains. And this is the nub of the problem of determining stranded assets. The loss in value of assets is state dependent, and the distribution of θ used to determine $x(y)$ (and therefore expected profit) is known or verifiable only to the firm's owners/managers.[3] How then is a regulator to determine ex post the magnitude of stranded investment?

One approach is to attempt to assess ex post the difference between what the firm would have earned under y and under y' given its actual investments and the state of the world θ which obtained, with assets being called stranded only if this difference is positive. This amounts to defining stranded investments as $Max[S(y, y', \theta),0]$. A little reflection will lead the reader to see that this is a very generous definition of "stranded assets." It essentially guarantees in all states of the world complete immunity from downside risk and attributes all negative outcomes to regulatory choice, when in fact some, if not most, downside risk is the result of normal business uncertainty as captured in the uncertain state of the world θ. Thus, under such a regime, favorable changes in the state of the world imply that a regulator can change the regulatory regime without being presented with a claim for compensation. However, there may be an asymmetry for unfavorable changes in the state of the world. If $S(y, y', \theta) > 0$, that is, the regulated firm shows a loss of value in his assets ex post, the firm may seek to have the regulator compensate it for the entire loss in value, despite the fact that some of the loss arose from the changed state of the world θ or from the regulated firm's choices x. Indeed,

---

3   This is very much in the spirit of Buchanan's (1968) work on the subjectivity of costs. Thus, costs and profits are only known at the time when economic resources are irrevocably committed to a course of action by a decision maker.

it should be clear that full indemnification of the firm against downside risk, if anticipated ex ante, will lead the firm to make exceedingly risky choices, since it will in effect be playing with "house money."

It is because of this difficulty in the real world of identifying how much of the stranded investment arises from the firm's own actions and from changes in the state of the world θ and how much is the result of actions y by the regulator that the issue of stranded assets will be highly contentious and difficult to resolve. As economists, we can provide some analysis of the issues, but the ultimate resolution will be highly judgmental. Before proceeding to a discussion in section 2 of ways of addressing the stranded asset problem, we will provide some background on the stranded-asset problem in electric utilities and telecommunications.

Some firms in the electric utility industry, at least *prima facie*, have a strong case for claiming that they face a problem of stranded assets. For many years, the electric utility industry has been highly regulated not just in terms of traditional rate-of-return regulation but also in terms of environmental regulation and acting as an agent for the state in promoting energy conservation through demand-side management (DSM) and other policies. Government policy has lead the industry to make decisions that have turned out to be very poor and have resulted in assets which now have a very low market value relative to their book value. The prime example is nuclear power. The public has come to think of nuclear power plants as costly white elephants. Under rate-of-return regulation, the public would bear the cost of such mistakes over a long period of time. As the utilities were monopolies with entry blocked by the regulator, the original investment would be recovered slowly over time through long depreciation lives. All this changed beginning in 1978 with the Public Utility Regulatory Policies Act, which made access to the utility network much easier for independent power producers. The process quickened in 1992 with the Energy Policy Act, which further opened up their networks, signaling an end to the traditional guarantee by the regulator to protect the utilities from entry. This presented some utilities with the immediate prospect that they would be unable to recover a large portion of their investment in their nuclear plants and other assets. The rate of capital recovery through depreciation was too slow to allow them to recover the original cost of these assets, as competition could be expected to drive down the prices they could charge for the electricity they generated.[4]

In telecommunications, the effects of competition and technological change started to become apparent in the late 1970s with the entry of resellers and facilities-based competition into the long-distance business. With the divestiture by AT&T of its local exchange business, the process gathered momentum. AT&T and the local exchange carriers (LECs) showed an awareness of the problem and sought relief from regulators who allowed faster capital recovery. However, despite the progress made in bringing about faster capital recovery, there is still a concern on the part of LECs that they may be faced with stranded assets. The

---

4   We first analyzed this problem in relation to local exchange carriers. See Crew and
     Kleindorfer (1992a).

Telecommunications Act of 1996 and the resulting arbitrations to determine the terms under which long-distance companies can enter their markets as resellers and as facilities-based providers has resulted in claims that the LECs face severe problems of stranded assets and under-recovery of capital. There have also been claims that the regulators were in breach of what is called "the regulatory contract" or "an implicit regulatory compact."[5] The regulatory compact or contract refers to the notion that firms would be guaranteed a reasonable rate of return on their assets in return for controlled prices; and prices and price variability would be kept low by regulation and by long depreciation lives and extended capital recovery. With technological change and the entry of competitors with newer technology, however, LECs with a capital recovery deficiency would be unable to recover their capital, since now the market and not the regulator was determining the rate of capital recovery. Unless the regulator permitted them an immediate increase in capital recovery while they still had some residual monopoly power, perhaps by delaying entry, the regulator would be in breach of the regulatory contract because they would not be able to recover their capital. Arguments for such increased capital recovery have had all the elements of the above dilemma in them, including judgments as to whether the investment had been prudently undertaken, whether changes in industry regulation were unanticipated, and whether states of the world which obtained were more or less favorable to the stranded investment argument put forth by the regulated firms.

At first sight, both industries have what looks like a compelling case that the regulator is in breach of the existing regulatory contract. However, these claims need closer examination. In both of these industries, not all of the assets are stranded. In the case of telecommunications, the value of the LECs' networks have already increased in value since divestiture because of the booming demand for telecommunications brought about by rapid technological change in the industry. The fax machine, the internet, competition in long distance, and the growth of 800 service have benefited the LECs in the form of increased demand for their local exchange networks. New technologies, for example asymmetrical digital sub-scriber line (ADSL), have made it possible to increase bandwidth of copper wire potentially increasing the value of the LECs networks. In addition, the LECs themselves will be entering the long-distance markets, further increasing the value of parts of their networks. Rapidly growing markets and advancing technology imply that the argument for significant stranded assets in telecommunications is, at least at the present time, a difficult one to make. In terms of our definition, many of the assets in telecommunications would not qualify as stranded because their economic value is growing not declining.

The situation facing the electric utility industry is quite different. The industry

---

5   A stalwart proponent of this argument on behalf of the LECs has been Robert Harris in testimony in numerous jurisdictions. Crew and Kleindorfer (1992b) describe the regulatory contract and indicate ways in which LECs and regulators can work to maintain its viability. We offered a form of *quid pro quo* price-cap regulation which, at least in theory, offered the opportunity to make the companies and customers better off.

faces stringent environmental regulation and demand is sluggish. The technological change that is taking place, notably the combustion turbine, seems to work mostly to reduce the value of the assets of existing utilities. However, although the picture in electric utilities is much weaker than in telecommunications, there are instances where some companies—those with low-cost fossil fuel plants or hydro plants—do not have any stranded assets. Indeed, the value of their assets has increased as the markets for their low cost power are opened up. As the example of the United Kingdom shows,[6] moreover, even slow growth markets offer significant potential for earnings through internal and institutional restructuring and the resulting increased flexibility for companies to reduce X-inefficiencies and respond to market opportunities without regulatory intervention. Similarly, companies relying on purchased power may find that the value of their assets has increased if they get increased access to lower cost power as a result of competition. Even companies with heavy investments in nuclear may find that the value of their transmission and distribution systems has increased. They have a natural monopoly in distribution and increased competition will mean increased demand and, therefore, increase the value of their distribution system. Similarly, their transmission network may have bottlenecks from which they can extract high congestion prices. Thus, it is vital to consider not just the loss in value of a utility's generating assets but also the increase in value of its transmission and distribution networks. If the loss in value exceeds the gains, then the net loss in value (if attributable to unforeseeable regulatory action) would be considered stranded investment. It is this net figure that has to be addressed. If the net is positive, we would argue for doing nothing, even though this means that the shareholders have received a windfall. If the net is negative, then the question of what to do becomes an issue to which we will devote the remaining sections of this paper.

These examples from the electricity and telecommunications point to a further difficult problem of determining whether an asset is indeed stranded and the extent of the loss. The problem is that, particularly in network industries, assets do not have value in isolation, but rather their economic value is determined jointly through their use with other assets. The system-wide basis for defining economic value of a group of assets makes the problem of judging changes in value for subsets of these assets particularly thorny. A variety of methods have emerged for dealing with this valuation problem in networks, but none are completely satisfactory, as we will see.

2. Some Approaches to the Problem of Stranded Asset Recovery

In this section, we examine a number of solutions to the problem of stranded asset recovery. We do not claim to be comprehensive in our treatment, but we have attempted to identify the major approaches to stranded asset recovery. They fall

---

6   See, e.g., Newbury (1995) for a discussion of the United Kingdom restructuring and its impact on firm profitability.

into three categories. The first is to open up markets as soon as possible and let competition rip. The implication of such a policy is that the losses, if any, should lie where they fall. In this context, stranded asset recovery is perceived as a misguided or irrelevant concept. Thus, the free market solution implies no provision for stranded asset recovery. The second approach attempts to define estimation methods, including a variety of scenario-based and auction approaches, for identifying, valuing, and recovering stranded assets. The third approach involves a *quid pro quo* approach derived from a forward-looking market-based approach, which attempts to provide the regulated firm with additional flexibility to generate earnings to recover stranded asset costs while providing assurances that customers will not be disadvantaged. We examine each approach in turn.

Open Markets to Competition and No Provision for Stranded Asset Recovery
Opening up markets immediately to competition is one approach which is proposed and employed on occasions, notably, De Vany (1997) and Michaels (1997). De Vany argues for opening up the market to competition, and Michaels argues that attempts to provide recovery of stranded investment are mistaken. He specifically addresses the situation in the electric power markets in California, which he criticizes as anticompetitive. De Vany argues, *inter alia*, competition will mean that "[t]here are no stranded assets or customers in an open market because electricity generation assets are no longer specialized to a particular service or set of customers" (1997, 49). Michaels argues that the anti-competitive nature of the California plan will result in not only static but also dynamic inefficiency. Consumers will not see significant price reductions, which will be further delayed by the ability of incumbent utilities to bar entry to competitors with more efficient plants. In addition, he argues that the plan may not benefit investors, the group that are at risk from failure to recover stranded assets. He argues that, although the plan provides over-recovery of stranded assets, it also provides no guarantee that investors will benefit from the full amount of the recovery. He argues that management may appropriate some of the revenues allowed by entering all sorts of unregulated ventures rather than returning the funds to the investors.

The DeVany-Michaels approach does not specifically disallow recovery of stranded investment. It sees it as something that a market opened up to competition will resolve. There are instances, however, where stranded investment is explicitly disallowed. This would be the case where a regulatory body judges that the claims by a company to have stranded assets are groundless and disallows them. For example, a company might claim breach of the regulatory contract, and its commission might counter by ruling that there was no breach.[7]

---

7   In a recent case before the Washington Utilities and Transportation Commission, docket no. UT-951425, Robert Harris claimed a breach of the regulatory contract. However, the matter was effectively deferred, as the Commission was never required to make an explicit ruling on the matter with USWEST Communications, Inc. reaching a settlement with the parties. The settlement, presumably, does not affect the company's right to raise the argument again in the future. Such claims are currently being made in several cases the outcomes of which will be known shortly.

The no-recovery solution is one that has a strong following and one that cannot readily be dismissed. It is attractive in that it avoids inefficiencies of the type Michaels discusses. However, it does raise certain legitimate concerns of a more general nature going beyond just the narrow interests of the companies concerned. If claims for stranded asset recovery are understood to be summarily dismissed in one industry, this may have an adverse impact on investment in other regulated industries. If investment in a regulated industry is seen as something that the regulator can effectively confiscate through haphazard changes in regulations, then this is an added risk making investment less attractive and requiring significantly higher returns than associated with traditionally regulated industries. The concern is not just with the industry suffering the losses. If the precedent created by this treatment in the eyes of investors is that the regulator and the government are prepared to make changes in policy without any intention of compensating investors for losses, then investment in all regulated industries will be adversely affected.

"Reasonable" Recovery of Stranded Assets

We use the term "reasonable" in this context because we are considering methods of recovery that would rely on the tradition legal and administrative institutions that operate in regulation. These have traditionally been based on a "just" price and "reasonable" return on assets. Claims for stranded assets imply that investors have not achieved the presumed reasonable return on assets. Hence our use of the shorthand and familiar term "reasonable."

The disadvantages of this approach have been stated, for example, by Michaels and are clear from the model in section 1; it is extremely difficult ex post to sort out what the actual loss in value in an asset is and how much of this is due to unanticipated regulatory actions. However, the benefits of this approach are several. It would use an approach that was familiar to most of the parties. While this may not be the case for prospective entrants to the industry, even here, most potential competitors would understand the importance of the regulatory process before considering entry. The approach would emphasize considerations of fairness and openness and might therefore be more acceptable than some other approaches. It may have low transactions costs, at least relative to the alternative of litigation. The latter, given the legal resources available to the industry, would result in significant delays and very high transactions costs. In addition, it is unlikely that courts, lacking knowledge of the industry, will be any better able to resolve specialized technical matters concerning the industry than experienced regulatory commissions. The litigation route then promises to be protracted and likely to come up with a result that is less satisfactory than that which could be reached by means of the administrative and regulatory process.

If the route of "reasonable" recovery is chosen, two main problems have to be resolved. One is the valuation of the stranded assets. The other is the actual compensation mechanism. A number of methods might be feasible for valuing the stranded assets along the lines of the discussion in section 1. One approach may be to auction off the stranded assets, for example, along the lines of Ainspan and Lesser (1996). This would have the advantage of putting a market valuation on the stranded assets which may be preferable to alternative approaches. Having determined the value of the stranded assets, the design of the mechanism to compensate the firm for the loss in value of its assets would have to be resolved. This is the subject of section 3, where we examine some of the problems of various compensation mechanisms by means of a simple model. However, before turning to this issue, we will briefly examine one more alternative.

Price-Cap Regulation: Using a *Quid Pro Quo* **Approach to Stranded Asset Recovery**

We first proposed this approach in the context of increasing the rate of capital recovery in the context of the situation facing LECs (Crew and Kleindorfer 1992b). Throughout the 1980s, the LECs had protested that their rates of depreciation were too slow given the rapid technological change that was taking place in telecommunications and given the increasing competition they were expecting to face. We, therefore, proposed an approach to address this issue which had the potential to make both ratepayers and the LECs better off. Our approach involved adjusting the initial price level and the X factor to enable faster capital recovery to take place.[8] There are several variations on the theme. One possibility is a higher price now and a higher X factor. The other is that the company would get higher prices in the initial periods but would face a higher X factor later. The idea was to enable the LECs to gain faster capital recovery immediately in return for guaranteed greater price reductions in the form of a higher X factor. The idea was intended to be attractive to them not only in that they would recover their capital more quickly but also in that the pattern of recovery was reflective of the increasingly competitive situation they were facing. It is fairly straightforward to demonstrate that companies would find such a proposal attractive if demand is growing.

Despite the apparent attractions of our proposal, at least to our knowledge, there were no takers. There may have been a number of reasons for this. The LECs continued to prosper and continued to be successful at increasing their rate of capital recovery without "renegotiating" the terms of their regulatory contract. The continued stability and health of their earnings also made it difficult to sell the argument for increased flexibility to their regulators. In addition, perhaps the *quid pro quo* aspect may have been problematical for the LECs if they were not completely convinced about the increasing intensity of the competition and the robustness of demand growth.[9] For electric utilities today, some variation on this theme might address the problems they face of increasing competition and stranded assets. It seems likely that the attractiveness of such an approach in electric power would be based on opportunities for pricing flexibility and improved productivity under deregulation. This could come about either through a formal *quid pro quo*

8   Price-cap regulation allows the firm to change prices annually without permission of the regulator. The increase allowed employs an economy-wide price index, for example, the consumer price index (CPI) less the X factor. The X factor acts as a guaranteed percentage reduction in real prices.

9   In recent arbitrations, the LECs have not generally offered any *quid pro quo* when requesting faster capital recovery. This may in part have been because the nature of the forum, dominated as it was by cost models, meant that this was not feasible.

approach embedded in the price cap or through less explicit approaches which provide the regulated firm cash flows through more flexible competitive pricing allowances or other regulatory relief.

One common variant of the negotiated *quid pro quo* regulatory settlement of stranded asset claims which does appear to be used in practice is the delay of regulatory changes to allow for a suitably long period of protected transition, during which the regulated firm clears up its capital recovery deficiency.[10] This and other informal or less explicit approaches are probably the most common approaches to settling the stranded asset problem. Given their relative efficiency in transactions cost terms, they may represent an appropriate balance between the dangers which explicit recognition of stranded assets presents, as argued by Michaels, and the legitimate claims of some regulated firms for stranded asset recovery. However, this under-the-table or more informal approach is not likely to work where the magnitude of stranded assets is very large. In these cases, some explicit identification and valuation must be undertaken. Once stranded assets are explicitly recognized, there must also be explicit mechanisms for recovering the losses associated with these assets. We now consider various approaches for implementing "reasonable" recovery of stranded assets.

3. Compensation Mechanisms for Stranded Asset Recovery

In this section, we consider a simple model which allows us to compare various mechanisms for stranded asset recovery. Since the transition in network industries is primarily concerned with promoting competition, we will be especially concerned with the impact of stranded asset recovery on competitive entry.

We assume two classes of economic agents, an incumbent and entrant(s). The incumbent I operates with a technology with (long-run) unit cost of C_X. Entrants E operate as a perfectly competitive fringe with a technology with (long-run) unit cost of C_Y. The incumbent offers a product X which is an imperfect substitute for the entrants' product Y. In addition to the cost C_X associated with producing output X, the incumbent has additional costs S which may be only imperfectly observed by a regulator and which represent the costs of stranded assets in the sense defined earlier. Whether and how I is compensated for S will have a significant impact on the efficiency of the resulting outcome. We consider three approaches to compensation:

1. Covering I's stranded assets from general tax revenues, e.g., through tax

---

10   For example, when many national post offices are seeing liberalization of market entry restrictions to promote competition, the German Post Office (Deutsche Post AG) was recently granted a continuation of its letter monopoly through 2002. This legislative action was recognized by many as a *quid pro quo* for the significant stranded assets of the German Post Office arising from its merger with the former East German Postal Service as well as its existing labor contracts and pension obligations. While the costs of these stranded assets could have been assessed and assumed by the taxpayers, the solution adopted was to have the German Post Office assume these costs in return for a period of continuing entry protection.

credits to I.

2. Taxing E per unit of output to pay for I's stranded assets.

3. Providing no compensation; letting I pay for its own stranded assets.

We follow the standard model for public utility pricing (e.g., Crew and Klein-dorfer (1986)). Define willingness to pay WTP for a consumer of type t as $v(x, y, t)$, where x is the amount of service provided by the incumbent and y the amount provided by the competitive fringe (as noted, we assume product differentiation between x and y). We represent consumer preferences in the usual quasi-linear form:

$$u(x, y, m, t) = v(x, y, t) + m,$$

where m is the numeraire good and $t \in T$ is the consumer type. Consumer demand in response to prices P_X and P_Y for services $x(t)$ and $y(t)$ will then be the solution to $Max[v(x, y, t) - P_X x - P_Y y]$. Given these constraints and assumptions, we can use the following notation to represent demand for the various services of interest and the resulting welfare and profit functions:

Demand for Incumbent's Services

$$X(P) = \int_{t \in T} x(P, t) \, dF(t) . \tag{1}$$

Demand for Competitive Services

$$Y(P) = \int_{t \in T} y(P, t) \, dF(t), \tag{2}$$

where P is the price vector (P_X, P_Y) and $dF(t)$ is the number of consumers of type t, T being the set of types.

We assume that entrants pay the incumbent a tax per unit of output (or capacity installed, which in the deterministic model here equals output). We denote this tax by $\rho \geq 0$. Since the Y market is competitive, entry will occur until $P_Y = C_Y + \rho$. Incumbent's profits can, therefore, be represented as

Incumbent's Profit

$$\Pi_I(P) = (P_X - C_X) X(P) + \rho Y(P) \tag{3}$$

or alternatively, since $P_Y = C_Y + \rho$, as

$$\Pi_I(P) = (P_X - C_X) X(P) + (P_Y - C_Y) Y(P). \tag{4}$$

We assume that prices are regulated. We will treat the price vector $P = (P_X, P_Y)$ as the decision variable, although the real decision variables are P_X and ρ. Consumer surplus $U(P)$ is given by

$$U(P) = \int_{t \in T} [v(x(P, t), y(P, t), t) - P_X x(P, t) - P_Y y(P, t)] \, dF(t)$$

$$= V(P) - P_X X(P) - P_Y Y(P) \tag{5}$$

with $V(P)$ equal to aggregate WTP.

Welfare

The traditional welfare function, the sum of consumer and producer surpluses, can be expressed as

$$W(P) = U(P) + \Pi_I(P) = V(P) - C_X X(P) - C_Y Y(P). \tag{6}$$

We have in mind solving a Ramsey-like problem of determining the optimal compensation arrangement subject to a breakeven constraint for I, using revenues from sale of X as well as any external compensation, through the "competition transition charge" ρ, I may receive to pay for S. We can now consider the three options of interest for compensating the incumbent for the costs S of stranded assets.

3.1. Guaranteed Stranded Assets Recovery from General Tax Revenues

Consider first the case where S is paid for from general tax revenues and assume efficient regulation, i.e., P_X set so that I just breaks even. If such payments are not anticipated by I (i.e., they are non-distorting) and if they do not impose a deadweight loss themselves through the general inefficiency of taxation, then the welfare optimal solution results. That is $P_X = C_X$ and $P_Y = C_Y$ would result and entry would occur at the efficient level. However, given the likely infeasibility of funding stranded assets by general taxation, we do not consider this option further.

3.2. Guaranteed Stranded Assets Recovery by Taxing Entrants

The welfare optimal solution for the option of paying for stranded assets by taxing entrants is the solution to the following problem (note that this is posed in terms of the price vector P rather than in terms of P_X and ρ):

$$\underset{P \geq 0}{Maximize} \left\{ W(P) \,\middle|\, \Pi_I(P) \geq S \right\}. \tag{7}$$

Let $P^*(S)$ be optimal solution to this problem and denote the optimal solution value by $W^*(S) = W(P^*(S))$.

3.3. Stranded Assets Recovery Placed on the Incumbent

This option is along the same lines as the Devany-Michaels proposal discussed earlier, where the incumbent pays for S out of revenues. The welfare optimal solution is the solution to the following problem:

$$\underset{P \geq 0}{Maximize} \left\{ W(P) \,\middle|\, \Pi_I(P) \geq S, \rho = P_Y - C_Y = 0 \right\}. \tag{8}$$

Let $P_0(S)$ be the optimal solution to this problem and denote the optimal solution value by $W_0(S) = W(P_0(S))$. The reader will note immediately that if the same S is present in both (7) and (8), then $W^*(S) \geq W_0(S)$, since (8) entails additional constraints (namely the constraint that only price vectors with $P_Y = C_Y$ are feasible). This result is just a restatement of the well-known Ramsey result that if a given burden (in this case S) must be borne by an economy, then welfare is enhanced if additional products are brought in "under the Ramsey umbrella" to pay for the burden.

3.4. Taxing Entrants versus Burden Placed on Incumbent

The key point we wish to make is that raised in the discussion in section 2, namely the incentive effects of guaranteeing I repayment of stranded costs. To make the point in the context of the above two options (taxing entrants or having I pay for S from I's revenues), we wish to analyze the case in which, because of asymmetric information, the regulator cannot determine precisely what the value of stranded assets are with the result that I is able to negotiate a higher stranded cost settlement $S' > S$ when entrants are taxed than when I goes it alone. This assumption seems reasonable in view of the fact that I will face stronger incentives to economize when paying for S from revenues.

We first note that both $W^*(S)$ and $W_0(S)$ are decreasing in S. This follows since increasing S while requiring breakeven operations imposes a more stringent breakeven constraint on the associated Ramsey problem (so that if $P(S')$ is feasible in this problem at S', then $P(S')$ will certainly be feasible in the problem at $S < S'$). Thus, assuming the profit constraint is binding at optimum, it follows for $S' > S$ that

$$W^*(S) = U(P^*(S)) + \Pi(P^*(S)) = U(P^*(S)) + S > U(P^*(S')) + S' = W^*(S') . \quad (9)$$

In particular, note that if I can misrepresent stranded cost to be $S' > S$, where S is the actual value, then total welfare will decline (since $W^*(S') < W^*(S)$) relative to the pricing regime that would obtain if stranded costs were not overestimated. Of course, the incumbent will be better off by misrepresenting S to be S', but collecting the additional profits to fund the misrepresentation will cause a deadweight loss in welfare.

We, thus, have two regimes possible. In one, taxing entrants, the Ramsey advantage of pricing both X and Y under the Ramsey rule leads to welfare gains relative to I going it alone. However, if the incentive effects of taxing entrants leads to a negotiated outcome (i.e., a mispresentation) of stranded cost, and if this misrepresentation is less when I goes it alone, then going it alone is the appropriate rule. To make this plain, we note what happens as the misrepresentation $(S' - S)$ grows, where S' is the effective stranded cost when entrants are taxed and S is the stranded cost when I goes it alone. When $S' = S$, we have from the above $W_0(S) < W^*(S)$, so if no misrepresentation occurs when taxing entrants, then doing so is efficient. However, as $S' - S$ grows (keeping S fixed), the welfare associated with the entry taxation regime declines, i.e., $W^*(S') = U(P^*(S')) + S'$ is decreasing in S'. The result is that for sufficiently large $S' - S$, having I go it alone is a preferable regime. We illustrate this result in figure 1.

As the reader will discern, the region where taxation is preferable to the

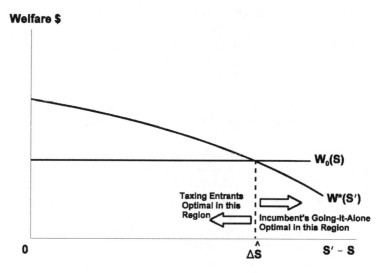

Figure 1. Comparing Two Compensation Regimes

incumbent's covering S will depend on all of the parameters of this problem. Clearly, if S is small, if misrepresentation can be prevented, and if entrants have no product or cost advantages (so entry taxation will not have adverse dynamic efficiency effects), then taxation of entrants to pay for stranded assets is likely to be superior, although under the noted circumstances the welfare differences will not be great relative to having I go it alone. The most advantageous case for entry taxation (e.g., using a rule like Efficient Component Pricing) would appear to be when S is large, when there are no product or cost advantages for entrants, and when misrepresentation can be prevented.

These simple results illustrate the interdependence of designing appropriate compensation mechanisms for stranded cost and procedures for determining the magnitude of these costs.

4. Summary and Implications

We have shown that the problem of stranded asset recovery confronts regulators and policy makers with quite serious problems. We have examined a number of proposed and actual solutions to the problem—none of them entirely satisfactory. The biggest dangers in the current situation are that inefficiencies will be perpetuated or increased. Regulators are in a bind. Not to compensate may create inefficiencies in the form of less investment in the future not just in the industry concerned but more generally. However, the decision to compensate is an extremely difficult one. If the regulator decides to compensate, there is the danger of the creation of an entitlement mentality. This could lead to a situation where the regulated firm does not care very much whether it makes bad or very risky decisions, because it expects the regulator to cover its losses. If this continues, it may be very difficult to break out of the entitlement environment and move to a competitive industry.

The policy that is most likely to be followed when sizable stranded assets are involved is the "reasonable" compensation approach. Our analysis in section 3 showed some of the difficulties in implementing this policy. The difficulties arise from a number of sources, including information asymmetries and the effects of asset-value guarantees on incentives. Because of its impact on incentives, this approach is particularly vulnerable to the entitlement mentality. Also, if access pricing or taxes on entrants are used to compensate incumbents for their stranded assets, then further losses in efficiency result, especially in the presence of information asymmetries which allow the incumbent to negotiate compensation requirements in excess of real economic loss in value of the assets in question. Even if the worst excesses can be avoided with this approach, it will still have the immediate effect of impeding entry and causing static and dynamic inefficiencies along the lines argued by Michaels (1997).

It is for such reasons that a negotiated *quid pro quo* arrangement, for example, in the form of a price-cap regime that allows the recovery of claimed losses in value over time through improved productivity and service innovations by the regulated firm may be attractive. Such a *quid pro quo* arrangement reduces the transactions costs resulting from the necessity of determining the loss of value which is apparent in the other approaches. It does this by striking a negotiated agreement between the regulator and the regulated firm (which is transparent to other parties as well), rather than attempting to determine a net amount of allowed stranded asset recovery. It has the disadvantage that, because of asymmetric information, it may result in excessive compensation to the industry. A common variant of the negotiated approach which is being implemented is the delay of regulatory changes to allow a continuing period of protected transition for the regulated company to recover its capital. A further variant would be the transition to a price-cap regime in which the parameters of the price-cap regime were negotiated to reflect the needed flexibility for the regulated firm to "earn" its stranded asset recovery. This approach would again have the benefit of reducing transactions cost, promoting a smooth transition to competition, and protecting consumers through the normal operation of price-cap regulation. The increasing popularity of price caps in network industries in transition is no doubt a result of the recognition of these benefits by regulators and regulated firms alike. However, the details of appropriate price-cap regimes in different industries are themselves complex and require considerable judgment in practice.[11]

References

Baumol, William J., and Gregory J. Sidak. 1994. "Pricing of Input Sold to Competitors." *Yale Journal on Regulation* (Winter): 171-202.
Buchanan, James M. 1968. *Cost and Choice.* Chicago: Markham.

---

11   For a review of recent experience with price caps in different industries and national contexts, see Crew and Kleindorfer (1996).

Crew, Michael A., and Paul R. Kleindorfer. 1986. *The Economics of Public Utility Regulation*. London: Macmillan.

Crew, Michael A., and Paul R. Kleindorfer. 1992a. "Economic Depreciation and the Regulated Firm under Competition and Technological Change." *Journal of Regulatory Economics* 4 (No. 1, March): 51-62.

Crew, Michael A., and Paul R. Kleindorfer. 1992b. "Incentive Regulation, Capital Recovery and Technological Change in Public Utilities." In *Economic Innovations in Public Utility Regulation*, edited by M.A. Crew, pages 57-79. Boston: Kluwer.

Crew, Michael A., and Paul R. Kleindorfer. 1996. "Incentive Regulation in the United Kingdom and the United States." *Journal of Regulatory Economics* 9 (No. 3, May): 211-225.

De Vany, Arthur S. 1997. "Electricity Contenders." *Regulation* 20 (No. 2, Spring).

Economides, Nicholas, and Lawrence J. White. 1995. "Access and Inteconnection Pricing: How Efficient is the 'Efficient Component Pricing Rule'?" *Antitrust Bullentin* (Fall): 557-579.

Lesser, Jonathan, and Malcolm Ainspan. 1996. "Using Markets to Value Stranded Costs." *Electricity Journal* 9 (No. 8, October): 66-74.

Michaels, Robert J. 1997. "Stranded in Sacramento." *Regulation* 20 (No. 2, Spring).

Newbery, David M. 1995. "Power Markets and Market Power." *The Energy Journal* 16 (3): 39-68.

5

COMPARING "STRANDED COST" ARGUMENTS IN TELECOMMUNICATIONS AND ELECTRICITY[1]

Timothy J. Brennan

1. Introduction

As the prospect of competition has gained salience with regard to the electricity industry in the United States, a number of transitional issues have garnered substantial attention. Certainly among the leaders, if not the leader, is the extent to which policy makers should impose *ex post* fees in the competitive environment to provide utility stockholders with revenues to cover the otherwise not recovered *ex ante* costs of generator investments and power purchasing contracts made during the regulatory era.

Less noticed, until recently, is the expansion of the stranded cost[2] issue into the other industry undergoing a major transition from competition to regulation, telecommunications. To facilitate independent entry into local telecommunications markets, the 1996 Telecommunications Act imposed duties on incumbent carriers to provide unbundled "network elements" to entrants at just and reasonable rates based on their cost of provision (U.S. Congress 1996, Sec. 251- 252). The Federal Communications Commission (FCC) interpreted these provisions as warranting rates based on forward-looking incremental costs (FCC 1996).

The courts have so far prevented the FCC from setting these prices directly, and later in requiring that they must be included in the terms of interconnection agreements offered by Regional Bell Operating Companies (RBOCs) to entrants before the RBOCs can get the FCC's approval to offer long-distance service. The

---

1   Discussions with Paul Kleindorfer, Dale Lehman, Colin Loxley, Molly Macauley, Glenn Meyers, Karen Palmer, Richard Simnett, and Tom Spavins were quite helpful. Errors of commission and omission remain the author's sole responsibility.
2   Others often use and advocate the term "stranded assets," but "stranded costs" is more accurate. The policy problem is financial, not physical: Should investors recover the unrecovered costs of the investments they have made?

courts' proscriptions were based on beliefs that the FCC had overstepped its jurisdiction. However, they also noted that allowing these forward-looking cost-based rates to go into effect might do irreparable harm to incumbent telephone companies because they would not generate sufficient revenues to recover "historical" or "embedded" costs (*Iowa Utilities Board v. FCC* 1996).

Consequently, the "stranded cost" issue is arising in the telecommunications context (Council of Economic Advisers 1997, 204-05; Linhart and Weber 1997; Moore 1998). Using the economics of implicit contract interpretation, we can compare the arguments for and against stranded cost recovery in the now-traditional setting of electricity and in the newly pertinent telecommunications arena. Among the factors to examine are the initial responsibility for making the investments that might not be recovered, the nature of the policy changes that create the possibility of stranded costs, and the availability of efficient means for generating revenues to recover these costs. Such an examination should improve the positive economics of the interpretation of implied regulatory "compacts" between regulators and regulated industries, and perhaps more importantly, inform our normative judgments whether the case for stranded cost recovery is stronger or weaker in telecommunications than it is in electricity.

The paper begins with overviews of the stranded cost debate as it has evolved in electricity restructuring and, more recently, surfaced in the development of competition in markets for local telephone service. Because it has been more prominent in the electricity era for a longer time, and because the responsibility for it lies with state regulators, there has been a wide range of proposals for whether and how much recovery there should be. On the telephony side, the salience of stranded costs is a more recent phenomenon, arising most notably from the processes by which the FCC and the states have implemented pricing provisions in the 1996 Telecommunications Act. Following these descriptions will be a review of how the economics of contract interpretation can inform judgments regarding the conditions under which regulators should be obligated to compensate regulated firms for losses the latter incur as a result of changes in the economic and political environment.

Applying the economic principles in the latter section to the events described in the former leads to a series of questions one would need to address to determine whether electric utilities have a stronger or weaker case for recovering stranded costs. While I can and will speculate on the answers to these questions, the purpose here is primarily to get the questions on the table. My hope is that those knowledgeable about electricity, on either side of the issue, will implicitly or explicitly compare their cases against a potentially similar situation in telecommunications, and *vice versa*.

To see how we might be able to use a comparison to lead to more informed policy, imagine a simple partition of stranded cost policy contestants into four (simplified) positions, indicated in table 1.

It is not hard to imagine that quite a few groups would fit into boxes 1 and 4 and would tend to employ policy rhetoric that would emphasize similarities regarding the virtues or vices associated with stranded cost recovery in both industries. However, in either case, if the trend is going against a position in one context, the

Table 1. Stranded Cost Positions			
		Telecommunications	
		Pro-recovery	Anti-recovery
Electricity	Pro-recovery	1	2
	Anti-recovery	3	4

policy debate in the other context may bring out informative differences, pro or con cost recovery, between electricity generation and local telephone service.

Perhaps more interesting is that there may be parties in the "off-diagonal" boxes. Electric utilities attempting to enter telecommunications markets by interconnecting their internal monitoring system to elements of an incumbent local telephone carrier's switched network could fit in box 2. They would ideally want to preserve stranded cost recovery in the electricity context while hoping to ensure that telephone interconnection fees they might pay to their incumbent competitor do not include embedded cost recovery components. Thus, we might see these parties developing distinctions between the telecommunications and electricity settings, showing the merits of stranded cost recovery in the latter. I am less sure that I can identify participants in the debate who would opt for box 3 from a position of self-interest. But as we will see, my current speculation is that box 3 may have the strongest theoretical support, given the differences in policies that have led to "stranded cost" allegations in the two great remaining regulated monopolies.

2. The Problem Defined

Stranded costs can best be thought of as losses in undepreciated capital resulting from reductions in output prices. The recent performance of the stock market notwithstanding, stranded costs defined as such are ubiquitous in a market economy with durable assets and uncertainty. Investors and entrepreneurs have to gamble their savings on research and development, plants, equipment, and long-term contracts for factors used to supply products, where the future prices of those products are not guaranteed. Sometimes they will lose, "stranding" those portions of the investments and obligations that had not been depreciated or amortized.

At least in theory, to a first approximation, the possibility of stranded costs is not a policy concern. Capital markets will provide investors with a rate-of-return commensurate with the (undiversifiable) risk associated with such investments. Practice, of course, need not match this theoretical ideal. Stranded costs may matter, e.g., when industries invoke the prospect of bankruptcy to demand special tax breaks or trade protections.

Stranded costs, however, may become a more legitimate object of public policy when they arise as a result of policy decisions. The United States's constitutional obligation to provide "just compensation to citizens for private property taken for public use" could be interpreted along these lines.[3] While this may be a necessary

---

3   U.S. Constitution, Amendment V. Some go farther and presume that "stranded costs" are an

condition for conveying such legitimacy, it is not a necessary condition. For example, the government's decision to construct the Interstate Highway System surely reduced the value of investments in hotels and restaurants situated along the roads that formerly handled such traffic, but in general those roadside businesses were not compensated for undepreciated investments that were never recovered as a consequence.

The factor that brings stranded costs into policy prominence is that policy not only had something to do with the capital losses, but it played a role in the decisions to make the capital investments in the first place. For this reason, the "stranded cost" phenomenon is one centered around regulated industries, where investment decisions were intimately tied up with public policies regarding franchises, construction permits, output prices, depreciation rates, service obligations, policy mandates, and cross-subsidies. The policy controversy, arising first in electricity and now in telecommunications, is the extent to which these factors impose an obligation on the government to ensure that equity holders in these regulated firms can fully depreciate their investments, despite losses that may accrue from policy changes.

To compare these obligations in the electricity and telecommunications contexts, we briefly describe at the scenarios in each of these sectors that have led to stranded cost concerns, and then set out a framework for understanding how these scenarios may or may not lead to stranded cost recovery obligations.

3. Scenarios

3.1. Electricity

"Stranded cost" entered the policy lexicon as a result of a series of legislative and regulatory actions at the state and federal level to open up markets for generated electric power. The Public Utility Regulatory Policy Act of 1978 (PURPA) provided the first significant evidence of the feasibility of an independent generation market functioning with monopolized wire distribution systems. The primary purpose of PURPA was to promote fossil fuel conservation by requiring that utilities purchase power from "qualifying facilities" that generated electricity using renewable, non-fossil fuels, or as a byproduct of energy-intensive industrial processes.

The merits of that particular objective may well be less than obvious, particularly as the threat of Middle East oil boycotts becomes a more distant memory. PURPA's specific requirements that utilities purchase such power when it is available at less than the "avoided cost" of marginal generation exacerbated the stranded cost problem, as we will see shortly. However, PURPA did show that utilities could purchase, transmit, and distribute independently purchased power, hence that vertical integration with "natural monopolies" in the "wires" sectors of the industry—long-distance transmission and local distribution—was not necessary to main-

---

unconstitutional public taking (Sidak and Spulber 1997).

tain the integrity of the electricity network.[4]

The feasibility of independent electricity markets became important when natural gas prices and innovations in power production reduced the minimum efficient scale of generation. Not only were independent power markets feasible, but independent power now became an economical alternative to the existing large-scale generation plant. Industrial users of large amounts of electricity began to lobby for more competitive markets. States with high electric power costs, particularly New England, New York, and California, began to see the merits of being able to ship in electricity produced at lower costs in other parts of the country.

As a response to these pressures, Congress passed in 1992 the Energy Policy Act (EPAct), which ordered the Federal Energy Regulatory Commission (FERC) to formulate rules that would give all power producers "open access" to transmission lines owned by the incumbent utilities. In 1996, FERC issued Orders 888 and 889, which set out those rules and established information systems to facilitate the distribution of information regarding tariffs and availability of transmission capacity.

FERC's jurisdiction is limited to "wholesale" electricity markets, which may be roughly understood as covering sales to distribution companies that then sell power to consumers. Consequently, FERC's order, while enabling local distribution companies to seek out lower cost power, did not empower end users, particularly households and businesses, to seek out low cost power directly. A utility, under rate-of-return regulation, might have no compelling incentive to reduce its power costs by going to outside suppliers; requirements that plant must actually be used in order to receive depreciation allowances would actively discourage switching to more efficient suppliers. However, some industrial users, perhaps because of the ability to threaten to leave a state, could lead the utility (and its state government regulator) to give them substantial volume discounts for power purchases.

Differences between industrial and residential prices illustrated potential price benefits that could be reaped if all end users had similar opportunities to bargain

---

4   Our purpose here is not to argue that transmission and distribution are natural monopoly. But, for completeness, the argument for monopoly in local distribution is that it is wastefully redundant to overbuild local electricity networks, since one wire or bundle of wires can carry local loads at less cost than two separate lines. In addition, a single network manager can provide the control necessary to ensure that power supplied equals power demanded on a minute-by-minute basis.

The argument for monopoly in long-distance transmission is trickier. Essentially, it arises first because uncertainty in where power is demanded and where it can be made available on short notice makes it economical to interconnect separately-owned transmission networks, so power can be go from any generating location to any using location on relatively short notice. Once interconnected, however, electricity essentially uses all paths between two points to get to those two points. This lack of excludability effectively makes the grid a single "commons" for the transmission of power. Unlike the long-distance telephone business, where switching ensures that calls stay on a single carrier's facilities, separately interconnected electricity transmission lines are not independent and potentially competing suppliers. Consequently, transmission has a natural monopoly character, at least over regions covered bysingle or interconnected grids.

among competing power suppliers. This led high-cost states initially, followed by others, to facilitate competition in the "retail" markets that fall under their jurisdiction. Again, California and New England were among the leaders, but numerous other states have joined in. The federal government has not ignored these developments. Some proposed bills would force states to adopt retail competition by specified dates. The Clinton Administration's recently announced "Competitive Energy Competition Plan" would mandate retail competition by 2003, but would allow a state to opt out if it finds in a "public proceeding" that an alternative, including the current monopoly regime, "better serves" customers (Department of Energy 1998).

Competitive pressure resulting from opening retail powers markets should reduce prices. These reduced prices could make it more difficult or impossible for utility stockholders to recover the capital invested in generation. Estimates of the costs that would be stranded in a move to retail competition run in excess of $100 billion or more (Council of Economic Advisers 1996, 186; Moore 1998, 4). The sources of these stranded costs include plant built in anticipation of high demand for electricity that failed to materialize, nuclear plants that proved to be more expensive than some anticipated, and high-cost contracts for renewable power mandated by PURPA. Ironically, the statute that led to the development of independent, competitive power markets exacerbated the stranded cost problem that such competition could bring.

3.2. Telecommunications

Stranded costs have recently arisen in telecommunications also through government actions to open markets, but in a significantly different manner. A primary goal of the Telecommunications Act of 1996 was to promote competition in local telephone service against the incumbent local carriers. However, two factors have inhibited the development of such competition.

First, local telephone service possesses network externalities, in that the value of one's telephone service depends upon how many other parties one can reach. In that sense, there is and should be only one "network." However, the Telecommunications Act presupposes that the one "network" can be provided by a number of potential suppliers of network services, *if* they all can interconnect with one another so that subscribers to any one service can reach subscribers of other services.[5] Because incumbent local carriers could maintain their monopoly by simply refusing to interconnect, the Act begins by establishing general duties of those carriers to negotiate interconnection arrangements with actual or potential entrants.

However, interconnection alone would not suffice to produce local telephone competition. An incumbent may act perfectly willing to interconnect with a competitor that can itself provide local telephone service. But willingness to interconnect will not lead to competition unless entrants that can provide telephone

---

5   The Internet is perhaps the paradigmatic arrangement, where agreements to share
     communications and routing protocols permit international transmission of text, graphics,
     audio, and video among users on a multitude of separately provided computer networks.

service entirely using their own facilities can profitably enter. This makes a second competition-inhibiting factor relevant. As with electricity distribution, one set of wires can apparently do the work of many. Overbuilding an entire telephone network has seemed wasteful.

A variety of changes in technology have changed this "natural monopoly" aspect in different segments of local telephone service provision. Fiber-optic cables and microwave links can compete with an incumbent's trunk lines between switches or large users. Reduction in the cost of computing make it feasible to provide competitive electronic switching and digitization of telephone traffic. The last aspect of the telephone network to see competition could be the local loops that run between a user's premises and the switches, as these are where the similarities with electricity are most apparent. But cable television lines and wireless telephones (cellular, PCS) have the potentially for economically substituting for the ubiquitous copper wires to our telephones.

Because different components of the local telephone business may become more conducive to competitive entry at different times, section 251(c)(3) of the Telecommunications Act ordered incumbent carriers to offer entrants access to these "network elements" separately. Section 252(d)(1)(A-B) said that charges for these network elements should be "based on the cost (determined without reference to a rate-of-return or other rate-based proceeding) of providing the ... network element," and "may include a reasonable profit." How one is supposed to set cost-based rates, and include a reasonable profit, without examining rates of return remains incomprehensible, at least to this reader.[6]

Despite this mystery, the FCC issued an order in August 1996, which specified seven network elements.[7] More importantly for the stranded costs question is that the FCC prescribed a method for states to use in determining prices for the network elements, called TELRIC, for "total element long-run incremental costs." TELRIC rates are essentially the "forward looking" average variable costs associated with each network element "using the most efficient technology currently available." The FCC would allow "a reasonable share of forward-looking joint and common costs" and have states determine "the appropriate risk-adjusted cost of capital and depreciation rates."[8]

These rates did not last long. The 8th Circuit Court of Appeals issued a temporary and then permanent stay of the pricing portions of the FCC's Interconnection order. The grounds for the permanent stay were that the FCC's promulgation of these pricing rules overstepped its authority over pricing decisions that Congress left to the states.[9] But in justifying its first, temporary stay, the Court

6   I also wonder what a "rate-based proceeding" is. In the alternative, would the FCC charge lobbyists for the costs of its hearings?

7   Network interface devices, local loops, local and tandem switches and software, interoffice transmission facilities, signaling and call-related databases, operations support systems, and operator and directory assistance.

8   In violation of the Telecommunications Act?

9   The Court later refused to allow the FCC to use TELRIC-based element charges as a condition for allowing, claiming that local exchange markets are sufficiently competitive to allow an

found that implementing TELRIC would present a sufficient risk of an unrecoverable economic loss—read "stranded cost"—meeting the "irreparable harm" test for such injunctions. The basis for this claim is that by forcing an incumbent carrier to set element prices based on forward-looking costs using the best available technology, prices will of necessity lie below those based on historical costs.

4. Framework

First in electricity and now in telecommunications, policy decisions justified as means to increase competition are viewed as threatening the ability of incumbent, regulated entities to recover embedded costs of past capital investments. In the electricity industry, the threat of stranded costs arises primarily from the possibility that newly allowed entrants may offer services at lower prices than would the incumbents. On the local telephone side, the threat arises because network element prices charged to new entrants may not be compensatory under the FCC's now-suggested pricing rules.

In both contexts, the laws setting out the relationships between the regulated firms and the regulator regarding stranded costs recovery are unclear. The best evidence a lack of clarity on the electricity side may be the nature and intensity of the stranded cost debate itself. Regulators and legislators treat stranded costs as a question that needs an answer, not one that has already been decided on the basis of prior regulatory or constitutional law. Turning to telephones, the best evidence of the legal indeterminacy of the issue would be the difference in considered opinion between the FCC and the statements of the courts on element pricing policy.[10] My understanding is that numerous state regulators have adopted TELRIC-based prices, despite the lack of an FCC mandate.

The openness of the questions suggests that determining whether electric utilities or incumbent local exchange carriers deserve recovery for stranded costs in these policy contexts requires that gaps in the laws defining the relationships between the regulator and the regulated need to be filled. This, in turn, leads us to view stranded cost recovery policy as an instance of how one should interpret an incomplete contract.[11] The interpretation of a disputed incomplete contract asks for the terms that would have been adopted by the parties were it costless to write and enforce a sufficiently complete contract that would have dealt with the unforeseen contingencies that cause the dispute. From an efficiency perspective, these unspecified terms would be the ones that would have maximized the expected joint profits of the parties, as viewed at the time the contract was written.

This efficiency perspective leads to the consideration of three basic questions, all from the perspective of the time the contract was written:

RBOC to provide long-distance service to its local customers.

10   Defenders of TELRIC have emphasized to me that the Court's eventual opinions have been on jurisdictional grounds, not on the grounds that the rates fail to meet legal tests for being just, reasonable, or compensatory.

11   The following framework is adapted from Brennan and Boyd (1997).

1. Why were the unspecified contingencies not specified in the original
   contract?

The "natural" default interpretation of unspecified contingencies in a contract is
that parties should bear whatever costs accrue to them as a result of those contingencies. This minimizes the cost of writing and monitoring contracts, and avoids
spending time dealing with matters of unlimited scope. For example, if A buys a
house from B and then has to go to the hospital for the flu, it would not make sense
that A could sue B for his health care costs, claiming that such contingencies could
have been included in the contract.

The situation in the stranded cost contexts is a bit different. To some extent one
of the parties to the contract, the government, played some role in enacting the
market-opening policies that have led to the potential for stranded costs. Therefore,
one ought not dismiss claims that the industry should just bear costs following from
initiatives to open markets, as they should have to bear costs related to other
contingencies out of the regulators' hands, e.g., a fall in demand because of less
energy-intensive appliances. The possibility that competition in generation or local
telephone service in the 1990s was too unlikely to be worth incorporating as an
explicit contingency in regulatory franchise contracts entered into in the first half
of the century could explain why the contingency was not explicit. Accordingly,
the government may be obliged to consider competition-related stranded costs
rather than dismiss the incumbents' claims as being outside the purview of the
regulatory scheme.

2. Which party was in the best position to influence the likelihood of
   these contingencies occurring?

An important reason for writing contracts is to control moral hazard. All but the
simplest transactions involve differences in time between the relevant performance
of the two parties. The "second mover" has an opportunistic incentive to renege
on the arrangement, after he has received his benefits and before he has to perform
any costly duties in exchange. When writing contracts, a first principle in assigning
liability for contingencies is a variation of the Learned Hand Rule: Have those who
can mitigate damages at least cost bear the responsibility for them.

Concern over moral hazard on the part of the regulator is a fundamental
underpinning of regulatory policy. Regulated firms are typically vulnerable to
opportunism on the part of the government. Almost by definition of their natural
monopoly status, they typically sink large amounts of unsalvageable physical
capital to provide their service. Once this investment is sunk, the regulator could
turn around and set rates only high enough to cover variable cost. The quasi-con-
stitutional requirement that regulated firms be given a fair opportunity to earn a just
and reasonable return, set out in the mid-20th century regulation cases, is a device
to preclude this opportunism. Without it, regulated firms would be unlikely to be
able to raise capital, and the public would lack the service.

But guaranteeing cost recovery need not lead to efficient outcomes. There can
be opportunism on the other side as well, as regulatory guarantees of cost recovery
could eliminate the regulated firm's incentives to minimize costs. This opens the
door to the possibility that there should be some limits on cost recovery, depending

upon the prudence that the regulated firm exercised.

    3. Which party could have been expected to be able to foresee and adapt
       to those contingencies *ex post* at least cost?

An additional efficiency consideration in setting contractual obligations is to
assign liability for a contingency to the party who can best mitigate the losses if the
contingency occurs. For example, a passenger typically does not hold an airline
responsible for extra hotel expenses if bad weather leads to a flight cancellation.
The passenger is better positioned than the airline to ascertain the most preferable
solution to that unfortunate contingency.[12] In these stranded costs contexts, the
direct question would be whether the regulator or the regulated firm had been in a
better position to adapt to the possibility of competition.

5. Questions

With these summaries of the stranded cost situations and the basic method for
interpreting competition-related cost recovery as a potential breach of an incomplete regulatory contract, we can begin to address the *relative* strengths of the cost
recovery claims in electricity and telecommunications. To do this, we should get
a feel for (a) whether the government or the regulated firms were better able to
adapt to the prospect of market-opening policies, and (b) whether the government
or the regulated firms were most susceptible to moral hazard that an ideal contract
would have prevented.

5.1. Adaptation

Adaptation has two requirements, foresight and flexibility. Without foresight,
the ability to adapt is irrelevant, as the party to the contract has nothing to which to
adapt. Without flexibility, foresight is irrelevant, as there is no way the party can
respond to the contingencies it might foresee.

Since the government enacted the legislation (EPAct, the Telecommunication
Act) and proposed the enabling regulations (FERC Order 888, the FCC's attempted
Interconnection Order), one might presume that it possessed more of the relevant
foresight than the regulated firms. But policy change does not take place in a
vacuum. In both telephones and electricity, it was the result of technological
change and learning from prior regulatory experience. Neither telephones nor
electricity stands out in this regard. In electricity, as reviewed above, open access
policy was a reasonably foreseeable consequence of decreasing scale economies in
generation, falling natural gas prices, and the working of an independent power
generation market under PURPA. In telephony, competition may not have been

---

12   The moral hazard situation above is why one might hold an airline responsible if the
      passenger's delay was due to intentional overbooking. How one should treat mechanical
      problems, which are partly "accidental" and partly a result of the airline's maintenance
      policies, is a good example of a "hard case" where one needs to weigh the airline "moral
      hazard" effects against the passenger's better position to react efficiently to the delay.

quite as foreseeable for long. But the trend of events from the FCC's "Above 890" decision, through MCI's entry into long distance, the divestiture, fiber-optic rings, and cellular radio, would and probably did lead management of the regulated firms to prepare for the prospect of competition policy long before the Telecommunications Act was finally passed.

A second factor should give one pause about holding government liable for stranded cost liability as the party with the best foresight. The primary level of government responsible for regulating utilities and local telephone companies, and for undertaking the direct policies that may produce stranded costs, is the state. States have taken on considerable initiative to promote competition, particularly in electricity, but it was the federal government that set the competition policy wheels in motion. In telephony, TELRIC started out as the FCC's idea, but at this juncture it is the states that are choosing to adopt it as a method for pricing network elements. Even if one were to grant that the federal government had more foresight than the utilities or local telephone companies regarding the advent of competition, it is less than clear that the states possessed a similar advantage.

A stronger case for stranded cost recovery, and a source of some distinction between electric utilities and local telephone companies, may lie not in the area of foresight, but in flexibility. Consider electricity first. With entry in generation looming, one might have expected utilities to cut back on installing capacity in anticipation.[13] However, to some extent utilities were precluded from doing this, most notably by PURPA-mandated requirement to purchase very expensive renewable-fueled power under long-term contract.

On the telephony side, there have been universal service requirements requiring network construction that similarly might not have been undertaken. But in telephony, the stranded cost and entry contexts are different in two fundamental respects. First, this added plant is, virtually by definition, not susceptible to competition. Second, the prime stranded cost exposure that the TELRIC controversy presents involves pricing of network elements. Accordingly, competition policy would be expected to boost demand by competitors for those elements of the telephone network that are not susceptible to competition.

Another dimension of flexibility involves pricing. Both electric utilities and local telephone companies may have been limited by regulation to the extent to which they could price in anticipation of competition. A commonly-voiced argument made in defense of stranded cost recovery is that allowed rates of return did not include a premium to reflect the risk that the incumbent would lose business to entrants following policy decisions to open markets.

5.2. Moral Hazard

To promote efficiency, we should interpret incomplete contracts to assign liability for breach so as to discourage opportunism by one party against the other. Moral hazard in regulated industries is a two-way street. Regulated firms need to

---

13   We should not ignore the possibility that extra capacity might be put in place specifically to deter entry.

be protected from public appropriation of their fixed assets, while the public needs to be protect from having to suffer the adverse consequences of being locked into dealing with a monopolist that is insulated from entry. A particular concern, noted above, is that legal rules to protect the regulated firm against moral hazard by guaranteeing capital cost recovery can reduce or eliminate the firms' incentives to control costs and avoid unnecessary construction.[14]

The most substantial distinctions between the electricity and telephone scenarios may arise when we compare the specific allegations against the regulator. In electricity, state and federal governments have taken advantage of evidence on feasibility of independent generation competition, along with decreasing scale economies, to open power markets. Exposure to stranded costs results from the lost business and lower prices resulting from that decision.

How should an *ex ante* contract have allocated liability to mitigate moral hazard? On the government's side, the concern would be that we want to make regulators bear these costs to discourage them from moving too quickly to open markets. However, few if any believe that government in fact is too prone to reduce the fraction of the economy that falls under its jurisdiction. One could more speculatively add that to the extent regulation substitutes for competition as a means for efficient resource allocation, utilities should find it reasonable to expect the government to adopt competition when feasible.

Utilities may well have had have too much incentive to build capacity in a rate-of-return regulated setting. The Averch-Johnson effect is a one reason to expect overbuilding.[15] More compelling support comes from the absence of an incentive to control costs when revenues are closely tied to them. Moreover, firms rather than regulators are likely to have better information regarding future demand and, thus, are the "least cost" determiners of how much capacity would be necessary. Except when a regulator specifically ordered the capacity decisions, e.g., the PURPA contracts, the responsibility for losses threatened by opening up markets to competition may best lie with the regulated firm.[16]

---

14   For a comparison of the benefits of preventing monopolization against the costs from inducing
      inefficient production, see Brennan (1996).
15   "Fuel adjustment clauses" also may have encourages overbuilding by assuring utilities that
      they would bear no risk regarding the energy costs associated with new plant construction. I
      thank Colin Loxley for suggesting this point.
16   Proponents of stranded cost recovery point out that regulators approve their investments as
      being in prudent and in the public interest. Such oversight is relevant, especially as the
      absence of incentives to minimize costs makes it necessary. However, absent specific
      promises in a regulatory contract, such approval need not include a guarantee of cost recovery
      if competitive entry can take place. Two questions:
           (1) Suppose technological breakthroughs in solar panels that allowed economic
      on-premises generation of electricity to substitute for utility power delivered through the local
      grid. Would utilities be able to get regulators to impose stranded cost recovery charges from a
      resulting fall in prices?
           (2) If one studied speeches by utility executives at the time the potentially stranded
      investments were made, would they say that the regulators "made 'em do it," or would they
      take credit for the expansive vision necessary to embark on these massive generation projects?

The stranded cost context differs in telephones in important respects, because the focus is not on policy change to permit entry, but policy change in how regulated prices are calculated.[17] The need to set network element prices did arise out of a decision to permit entry. But network element prices create an effective price ceiling that would prevent the incumbent from charging prices for its overall services. Such a ceiling could prevent the incumbent from setting prices that it had been led to expect it could on the basis of investment decisions and depreciation policy. The ceiling may be particularly binding on prices for business services, which are more vulnerable to competition and have been the source of cross-subsidies to support residential service and universal service goals (Palmer 1992).

Turning from the effect side to the cause, recall that the central justification for imposing legal requirements on regulators to provide fair opportunities for cost recovery was to counter the incentive that regulators have for opportunistically forcing regulated firms to reduce prices below cost. I have no reason to impugn such intentions to the FCC or state regulators that adopt TELRIC-based rates.[18] However, if such rates are adopted and do turn out to be noncompensatory, the case for some alternative means of compensation for unrecovered costs would be strong.

A number of facts become important, such as the extent to which investment costs have been recovered over time.[19] The theoretical case for stranded cost concern in local telephony may be strong, but the empirical concern could be quite small. The estimates of stranded cost liability should also include above-normal profits from related services, e.g., call waiting, in markets that were essentially open only to the incumbent, and thus could be regarded as part of the reward for having the franchise.

The defense for TELRIC-based rates merits some consideration. The core of the defense is that markets set prices on a forward-looking basis. Simply put, that is true. If capital costs fall at some point of time in a competitive industry, prices from that point onward will fall to a level necessary to recover these lower costs over the expected lifetime of the capital. But one needs to consider how investors would react with that prospect in mind. If the capital cost reduction is correctly anticipated in time to affect investment decisions, firms will cut back investments in advance. This will allow prices to rise in anticipation of the post-innovation price reduction, to generate sufficient returns to recover capital cost.[20]

---

17   Another distinction between the two industries, suggested by some observations by Thomas
       Spavins, is that stranded costs in electricity are purely historical resulting from a "one-shot"
       move from regulation to competition, whereas in telephones cost recovery could be an
       ongoing issue as long as regulators are setting network element prices.
18   I can say from experience on the White House staff that some in the Executive Branch
       regarded RBOC access charges revenues as a pool that could be taken to fund politically
       preferred price reductions.
19   A problem with the stranded cost debate in electricity is that most if not all of the published
       studies estimate exposure by looking at how much revenue utilities would lose with
       competition in generation. The accurate measure would be the current value of the difference
       between the amount investors put up for capital projects and the amount they have already
       recovered in returns over and above operating costs and taxes.
20   Solving for the time path of prices preceding an expected innovation turns out to be a

In regulated contexts, this would show up as accelerated depreciation. In standard regulatory practice, where investments are depreciated on a straight-line original cost basis, depreciation already is accelerated relative to what one would find in a competitive market. In the latter, one would expect real prices to remain constant over time (all else equal), akin to mortgage payments in a zero-inflation era. Original cost depreciation, however, causes nominal prices to fall, with real prices falling even faster in the presence of inflation (Brennan 1991). This implies that investors in regulated firms may turn out to be compensated adequately for the prospect that future rates will reflect new lower cost technology.

If innovations are likely to occur but not likely to be anticipated in sufficient time to bring about price increases in advance, then moving to a method for setting prices on the basis of setting such prices introduces an added risk to investing in a regulated enterprise. To ensure appropriate incentives for investors to put up capital in regulated firms, then, expected rates of return should include a premium for that risk.[21] Whether current rates of return include any premiums over cost, and whether such premiums are adequate compensation for this risk, are questions that the debate over stranded cost recovery will, I hope, clarify over time.

6. Conclusions and Caveats

We began by setting out four simplified possible positions, based on whether one was for or against recovery in the electricity context and for or against recovery in the local telephone context. One can imagine taking the same positions for or against recovery in both contexts, driven by ideological commitments based on simplistic views of the world that regulated firms are the tools of consumer exploitation or the victims of government exploitation. Stranded cost recovery may be the correct thing to do in both the electricity and telephone situations, but that result should come after a careful look at the facts and understanding of the theory. As noted above, such a look could result in advocating recovery in one context but not in another.

After examining each situation and setting out a framework for analysis, two salient factors in the electricity situation and the telephone situation emerge. The first of these has to do with the strength of the claim that the magnitude of the potentially stranded investment was unduly influenced by regulatory mandate. The PURPA "avoided cost" contracts for expensive renewable power are the most compelling example in electricity. However, much of the stranded cost exposure in that industry may well be due to overbuilding based on erroneous demand forecasts—an error for which firms in a competitive economy typically pay. On the telephone side of the story, the volume of potentially stranded costs could be a

surprisingly complex matter, with some paradoxical results, particularly if buyers have fairly inelastic demand are unable to substitute purchases across time.

21   Richard Simnett has suggested to me the possibility that telephone loop costs could increase over time. If so, TELRIC-based rates could create some positive profits for incumbent local exchange carriers, reducing the magnitude and import of any claims for stranded cost recovery.

function of public policy requiring universal service. While that may be a valid concern in rural areas or poor neighborhoods, that is less likely to be a concern in the central business districts and lucrative suburban areas where new entry into local telephone service markets is most likely.

But when we turn to moral hazard, the strength of the case tilts in favor of the telephone companies. The focus of the regulatory change switches from open markets to setting prices. The general need to provide adequate incentives for investment to provide regulated services warrants greater sensitivity in the telephone context to the possibility that regulators will set prices at noncompensatory levels. This could support recovery of embedded costs left stranded by a policy to set network element prices on the basis of forward-looking costs using the most efficient contemporaneous technology.

It is in this sense that box 3 in the initial diagram, where the case for stranded cost recovery may be stronger in the local telephone context than in the electric utility context, is most plausible. But the purpose here is not to settle the stranded cost controversies in each of these situations. Rather, it is to exploit the possibility of a debate between electricity and telephone interests to elicit the relevant facts and frameworks that would be useful for assessing the merits of stranded cost recovery in either situation.

Whether there is any demand for disinterest in the real world of regulatory policy is, alas, another proposition I am unprepared to defend. Policy analysts probably should recognize that, at the end of the day, the link between stranded cost payments and the merits of the case for paying them will likely be attenuated. A stronger factor is likely to be the ability of incumbent utilities to extract rents from regulators and legislators in exchange for limiting their use of legal or political processes to hinder or halt the expansion of retail competition (Brennan and Boyd 1995). In short, stranded cost recovery may be less the result of an assessment of the efficient design of an implicit regulatory contract and more a payoff to expand a state's economy through open competitive markets.

References

Brennan, T. 1991. "Depreciation, Investor Compensation, and Welfare Under Rate-of-Return Regulation," *Review of Industrial Organization* 6: 73-87.

Brennan, T. 1996. "Is Cost-of-Service Regulation Worth The Cost?" *International Journal of the Economics of Business* 3: 25-42.

Brennan, T. and J. Boyd. 1995. "Political Economy and the Efficiency of Compensation for Takings," Resources for the Future Discussion Paper 95-28: Washington, DC.

Brennan, T. and J. Boyd. 1997. "Stranded Costs, Takings, and the Law and Economics of Implicit Contracts," *Journal of Regulatory Economics* 11: 41-54.

Council of Economic Advisers. 1996. *Economic Report of the President*. Washington: Government Printing Office.

Council of Economic Advisers. 1997. *Economic Report of the President*. Washington: Government Printing Office.

Department of Energy. 1998. Comprehensive Electricity Competition Plan, http://www.hr.doe.gov/electric/cecp.htm.

Federal Communications Commission. 1996. The First Report & Order In the Matter of Implementation of the Local Competition Provisions in the Telecommunications Act of 1996, FCC 96-325.

Iowa Utilities Board v. FCC. 1996. Order Granting Stay Pending Judicial Review. 8th Circuit Court of Appeals, Docket No. 96-3321, slip op., filed Oct. 15, 1996.

Linhart, P. and J. Weber. 1997. "On Cost-Based Pricing for Regulation," Telecommunications Policy Research Conference, Alexandria, VA.

Moore, W. 1998. "Identification and Recovery of Stranded Costs for Electric and Telephone Utilities," Rutgers University Western Advanced Regulatory Workshop, Monterey, CA.

Palmer, K. 1992. "A Test for Cross Subsidies in Local Telephone Rates: Do Business Customers Subsidize Residential Customers?" *RAND Journal of Economics* 23: 415-35.

Sidak, G. and D. Spulber. 1997. *Deregulatory Takings and the Regulatory Contract.* Cambridge: Cambridge University Press.

U. S. Congress. 1996. Telecommunications Act of 1996, Pub. L. No. 104-104, 110 Stat. 56.

6

AN ECONOMIC ANALYSIS OF THE STRANDED COST ISSUE FACING ELECTRIC UTILITIES AND POLICYMAKERS TODAY[1]

Colin J. Loxley

1. Introduction

The electric utility industry is moving at a rapid pace towards retail competition and deregulation of the generation (supply) business. One of the major policy questions, which has a potentially enormous economic impact, is the treatment of "stranded costs" (or "stranded assets" as they are also more properly termed). "Stranded costs" result from the fact that the book values of a utility's fixed obligations—physical, contractual, and legal—undertaken under the pre-existing regulatory regime are greater than their market value "going forward" in a competitive environment.

There are several distinct categories of potentially strandable costs. The major categories are:

- Long-term power purchase and fuel contracts;
- Regulatory assets; and
- Utility-owned generation.

There have been numerous estimates of the magnitude of stranded costs, covering an extremely wide range. It would appear that the total magnitude of the problem is potentially in the $200 billion to $300 billion range, with long-term contracts and regulatory assets each lying in the $60 billion to $70 billion range, while credible estimates for utility-owned generation vary from $70 billion to as much as $150 billion.[2]

It is not the intent of this paper to discuss the legal and regulatory arguments

---

1   The opinions expressed in this paper are entirely those of the author and do not reflect in any way those of PSE&G. The author wishes to thank William Moore and Michael Crew for their valuable comments and suggestions.
2   For example, see Federal Energy Regulatory Commission (1994); Moody's Investors Service Research (1995).

surrounding the validity of stranded cost recovery from customers. Instead, I take as a given that utility shareholders should have an opportunity to recover prudently-incurred stranded costs and that such recovery should be associated with lower rates, cost reductions, and efficiency improvements ("mitigation") on the part of the utility, which thereby involve some risk.[3]

This discussion will focus first on some of the structural elements contributing to the creation of stranded costs, because it is clearly objectionable to simplistically classify them as largely due to blunders on the part of utility management, aided and abetted by regulators. Given the magnitude and prevalence of the problem, such an assignment of blame requires a hypothesis of monolithic stupidity which I find untenable.

In reviewing the origins of stranded costs, I find that regulatory policies and accounting, and ratemaking practices, were significant contributors to each of the three major categories, with especial focus on generation-related assets. I suggest that the degree to which the regulatory process created the problem should be taken into consideration in determining stranded cost recovery.

The paper concludes with a discussion of the potential beneficial role of securitization in resolving stranded costs with the minimum loss of economic welfare and efficiency and the crucial challenge of balancing risks in an environment where there is clearly both imperfect and asymmetric information as between regulatory and utility decision-makers.

2. Long-Term Contracts

This category is relatively straightforward. Under the prior regulatory regime, state public utility commissions frequently encouraged or even mandated such long-term contracts as a means of compliance with PURPA[4] and to ensure supply and eliminate price risk. As fuel and power prices have declined over the past decade, these contracts have now become "above-market." In the case of QF contracts, in many states, legislators and/or regulators deliberately set the prices above-market in order to promote the development of independent power generally (often based on "infant industry" arguments) and/or to promote non-conventional sources such as solid waste, landfill gas, geothermal, solar, wind, wood- and coal-waste, etc.[5]

In most cases, the treatment of these costs should be analytically straightforward. These are legally-binding contracts, and courts in several jurisdictions have ruled

---

3   In New Jersey, the Board of Public Utilities (BPU) (1997) stated that utilities should "have an opportunity for a limited number of years, to recover through rates stranded costs associated with generating capacity commitments made prior to the advent of competition." The report makes it clear that rate reduction and expanded customer choice are priorities, however, with stranded costs (especially more recent investments) being subject to stringent verification and prudency review and "mitigation" offset.

4   The Public Utilities Regulatory Policies Act of 1978, which required utilities to purchase power, gave states wide discretion in pricing and contract terms.

5   Examples include New York's "six cent" law, the 10% "adder" in New Jersey to actual avoided costs, and front-end loading of contract prices generally.

that regulatory bodies have little or no discretion or authority to unilaterally force changes on either party. In addition, the utility buyer typically makes no profit on these contracts—they are purely a pass-through of costs incurred. Such contracts may also include so-called "regulatory out" clauses which specifically terminate payments if the regulatory body fails to provide for cost recovery of these expenses.

In most cases, therefore, states have recognized that attempts to force a reduction in these costs threaten to involve them in a legal quagmire with the potential for three-way lawsuits (buyer, seller, and regulator/state). Nonetheless, there have been efforts (in New England and New York, especially) to force cost reductions simply because they represent such a large proportion of the utility's costs (and, therefore, the customers' bill) that meaningful rate reduction is almost impossible if these contracts are unchanged. At the same time, for utilities who are largely power purchasers, any failure to recover these costs would threaten almost immediate bankruptcy.[6]

There is a certain irony in the fact that most states are promoting a restructuring of the industry that would have the utility unbundle or divest its generation and, thereby, create a distribution utility that would become a purchaser of 100% of its supply, while this is precisely the situation in which state regulators have the least amount of leverage and extremely limited ability to reduce overall electric rates.

The way to deal with such contracts is straightforward and applies generally across both regulated and unregulated businesses: the injured party can challenge the contract in court on a number of legal grounds (this has a low probability of success), either before or after abrogating the contact. Or the parties can negotiate a restructuring which, in the case of a high priced purchase, involves a buy-out payment in exchange for either termination of supply or a reduction to market-based prices. In most regions, the wholesale markets and, especially, organized power pools have evolved to the point where generators have no obstacles to selling power independently either into the spot market or via bilaterals.

In the absence of unusual circumstances, the economics of a buy-out are well understood: The appropriate lump-sum payment is based on the discounted value of the future stream of above-market profits that the seller would otherwise have realized. The economic value to be gained lies in the fact that the buy-out payment can typically be financed and amortized over time at a lower rate than the sellers discount value. This is because the seller's discount rate must include a premium for future risk—both operational and legal/regulatory.

Non-utility generation (NUG) contracts have a number of special circumstances, however. On the downside, operational and legal risks have usually either been hedged (e.g., fuel escalators, business insurance, O&M and equipment contracts) or are considered low probability. On the upside, the NUG project cost of debt is typically higher than that of the utility. In addition, most NUG projects are "must-run"/baseload by either physical design or due to the contractual financial

---

6   Vermont, New York (Niagara Mohawk), and New Jersey (Atlantic Electric) provide some
     extreme examples.

incentives or both. Most NUG units run on natural gas and are not economic for baseload operation. There are economic benefits to be gained by making such units dispatchable—i.e., shutting down at night, weekends, or "shoulder" months when the NUG's incremental costs exceed the market price of electricity. The NUG's fuel and steam contracts are often obstacles to a more flexible mode of operation and must also be restructured.

These economic factors suggest that mutually acceptable restructuring of such contracts should be possible, although it is rarely easy. A major issue for the utility and the regulators is one of the transfer of risk. From the utility's perspective, if its contract has strong "regulatory out" language, there is no risk assumed with the contract, which is balanced by no return being allowed. If the utility makes a large lump sum payment to buy-out/ buy-down the NUG project, it faces the regulatory risk of a disallowance of cost recovery should a future commission decide against it. The primary means of ensuring against this would be to securitize the buy-out, supported by the appropriate legislation and an irrevocable regulatory order. This approach serves to minimize the financing cost and thus maximize the savings. If the utility's risk position is unchanged, then the regulator would clearly expect to have all of the net savings passed through to customers, although it would be logical to consider an incentive mechanism for utility management to encourage the appropriate allocation of resources to implement aggressive and innovative approaches to maximizing the net savings.

3. Regulatory Assets

These are a unique construct produced by the accounting model developed for regulated industries. This permits costs to be deferred (and collected over time), if these costs are probable of recovery in the future—which means that the regulatory commission has approved such recovery and that it is (or will be) included in customer rates. While non-regulated businesses operating under Generally Accepted Accounting Principles (GAAP) can also defer some expenses for later periods, these are typically quite limited and most costs must be expensed as and when incurred.

Under "rate-base/rate-of-return" accounting, with periodic test-year rate cases, utilities have an enormous disincentive to incur large "one-time" expenses because of the risk that the regulator will not allow cost recovery. Similarly, regulators are unwilling to allow all such costs into today's rates because they wish to minimize rate increases and delay them into the future. The solution to this joint dilemma was to allow cost recovery over a pre-specified time period, thus minimizing both the level and volatility of rates. This works because utilities have had excellent credit ratings and regulators assured the future revenue stream, thus making these expenditures relatively cheap to finance. Regulatory assets are not usually added to ratebase, so there is no return on them. Unlike other assets, "regulatory assets" only have any value if the utility has customers from whom the regulator permits it to recover these expenses.

Typical "regulatory assets" include:
- Extraordinary property losses from storm or other damage and environmental

clean-up costs, excluding any insurance coverage.

- Unrecovered and abandoned plant and regulatory study costs that would normally be capitalized if carried through to completion, but the utility and regulator agree not to proceed.
- Income taxes that are deferred for recovery through future rates when the tax costs are actually paid.
- Deferred fuel costs which are eligible for recovery through a "true-up" of a fuel adjustment clause.
- DSM costs which are frequently "lumpy" in nature or time and deferred for collection through future rates to spread the costs over the period of expected benefits.
- Pension and other benefits, including the accrual for future other-than pension employee benefits (OPEB) and early retirement costs—normally expensed under GAAP, these are deferred based on the regulator's promise to allow future recovery. OPEB costs for example are allowed a 20 year recovery period.

It is important to recognize that none of these "deferred debits" have any connotation of utility management mistakes or "blunders." They are potentially strandable because of a change in the regulatory model and the accounting that accompanied it. In all cases, past and present customers' bills have been lower than they would have been had these costs been included in rates in full when incurred. In a sense, it can be argued that the regulator decided that consumers discount rates were higher than the utility's interest rate, and thus regulators selected lower rates today in exchange for higher rates in the future. This treatment also led to greater rate stability.

In general, state regulators have recognized that it is not only appropriate but essential to continue to allow recovery of regulatory assets. The bulk of the value is in deferred federal taxes and pensions, and few regulators would see much appeal in reducing rates through defaulting on either of these obligations even supposing it were feasible.

4. Utility-Owned Generation

Estimates of generation-related stranded costs vary widely, from $70 billion to $150 billion, i.e., from 30% to 50% of potential stranded cost. It is important to note that the lower estimates are *net* values, i.e., the potential losses for high-cost utilities are reduced by the potential gains for low-cost utilities (which rarely receive much attention since they also have low rates!).

Stranded assets can be viewed from two perspectives: either as the difference between book value and market value or as the difference between regulated revenues and market revenues. With consistent treatment of tax effects and discount rates, the two approaches give the same results, since the market value is equal to the discounted stream of future net income. That is:

$$\text{Market Value} = \sum_{t=0}^{L} \frac{(P_E \times KWH + P_K \times KW) - (F + O + I)}{(l+d)^t},$$

where

   L = remaining expected life;
   P_E = market price of energy for this unit as operated;[7]
   KWH = energy produced;
   P_K = market price of capacity and ancillary services;[8]
   KW = capacity rating;
   F = fuel cost;
   O = operating cost;
   I = incremental costs, such as capital additions or environmental expenditures;
   d = discount rate.

Book value is adjusted for accumulated depreciation and, if it then exceeds market value, stranded assets (costs) exist. This comparison can be done on either a before-tax or after-tax basis. Additional detail can be added for any potential site value, environmental remediation "clean-up" liability, and "end of life" costs, such as removal less scrap/resale value.

The above equation provides unit-specific stranded asset estimates that can then be summed to arrive at a company's overall exposure. Obviously, these estimates involve significant uncertainty. They depend upon projections of future prices, future costs, and future performance. The issues of the appropriate discount rate and expected life are also likely to be controversial. This "bottom-up" approach to evaluating stranded generation costs can help in understanding why stranded assets are so large.

Much of the public discussion states or implies that they are entirely the result of mistakes, due to the focus on nuclear plants and their high capital costs. This is far from being the case. Current market prices are largely a by-product of the enormous disinflation that has occurred in electric generation over the last ten to fifteen years. If we examine wholesale generation prices in the North-East, for example, we observe that energy prices have declined approximately 50% in nominal terms. In the Pennsylvania-New Jersey-Maryland (PJM) pool, energy prices averaged $41.2/MWH for the period 1982-85, but only $21.9/MWH for the period 1994 through 1997.[9]

This decline has been driven by several key factors. Firstly, it reflects the decline

---

7   A unit's effective energy price depends upon the hourly market prices and when (whether) the
    unit is dispatched or operable. Typically, a production cost model with assumed outage rates
    must be run to determine a unit's energy revenues and fuel costs.
8   Most ancillary services are linked to availability rather than output, and markets for ancillary
    services are still developing in most regions. The combined total of capacity and other
    revenues per kw will be determined by the amount required to keep marginal units in
    operation in the short-run and the costs of new generation in the long-run.
9   PJM prices were calculated as "split savings" billing rates through March 1997 and as the pool
    "market clearing price" for the remainder of 1997.

in fuel prices during this period, particularly natural gas and oil. Secondly, a large surplus of generation capacity came on-line just as demand growth collapsed—particularly following the 1974-75 and 1980-82 recessions, which destroyed the energy-intensive industries of the Midwest and North-East. Much of this capacity was baseload nuclear and coal with low incremental costs, which provided the incentive to market power into neighboring areas and displace higher-cost generation. Thirdly, technological change began to accelerate, especially in turbines, as a by-product of federal defense and aerospace spending and research. This led to the development of efficient, flexible combined-cycle generation for on-peak cycling use, which has rendered much of the older marginal steam-generation obsolete.

The appropriate economic response to these trends in a non-regulated industry would have been two-fold: one, to accelerate depreciation thereby writing down asset values to recognize market realities, and two, to close down or mothball capacity to eliminate the surplus. Unfortunately, the concomitant decline in fuel prices combined with the capital-intensive nature of electric generation meant that short-run marginal costs were still below prevailing market prices, and thus surplus plants were kept in operation. An additional key factor which prevented or limited retirements was the paramount concern for reliability which necessarily requires a significant amount of surplus "reserve" generation.

Similarly, accelerating depreciation was not regarded as a viable option by either regulators or management. Regulators would not approve it because it would require higher rates. Management was reluctant to propose it because ratebase would have fallen, lowering the level of authorized earnings. By the same token, plant retirements would have triggered regulatory "used and useful" concerns.

5. Regulatory versus Tax Accounting

To an unregulated eye, the net plant book values of electric generating units would appear extraordinarily high—after all, the majority of these plants are from 15 to 30 years old. A normal business would have depreciated all or most of the original investment. Unfortunately, the regulatory book lives of most electric generating assets are in the 30 to 40 year range, approximately two to three times the normal business lives.

As mentioned previously, one of the results of the enormous gap between tax and regulatory depreciation is the accumulation of a large deferred tax obligation associated with lower current taxable earnings. Lower current tax payments translate to lower current customer rates. However, the bulk of the impact comes from the lower depreciation allowed for ratemaking purposes.

This has a very substantial leverage in such a capital-intensive industry. For example, a regulatory book depreciation expense of $300 million annually could become $500 to $600 million, the difference of $200 to $300 million representing an overall rate reduction of between 5 and 10%. The use of such extended depreciation periods thus has the effect of benefiting current customers at the expense of future customers. One possible rationale for this behavior was referred to previously, namely that the consumers' discount rate is higher than the utility's cost of capital. However, in this case, where costs are being spread over 40 years, we have clearly seen a political process of intergenerational transfer.

Depreciation accounts are classified by type of equipment, not by a specific asset location, and thus the depreciation for a particular generating unit has to be calculated based upon the equipment (boilers, turbines, etc.) at the plant. As a hypothetical example, a $1 billion (gross plant) nuclear investment made in the mid-1980s would have accumulated approximately $350 million of regulatory depreciation by now, for a net plant book value of approximately $650 million, which is potentially stranded. If tax lives and depreciation had been used, the book value would be less than $300 million.

This problem is exacerbated by the fact that additional capital investments at a plant to repair or replace equipment must also be depreciated over the same extended lives—even if the rest of the plant has a much shorter expected life. Let us suppose that the plant has a remaining life of only five years but needs a boiler rebuilt. Assume the expenditure is economic because the value of the plant's energy and capacity exceeds the fuel and operating costs by enough to return the capital investment over the five-year period. However, the boiler investment has to be depreciated over 30 years, with the result that over 80% of this economic and prudent capital addition will be stranded when the plant is retired.

The end result of using such extended lives for generating assets was, therefore, that depreciation was inadequate to recover the original and on-going investment, thereby understating the true costs of serving customers and producing excessive book values. This would not have been a problem in a stable environment, but the abrupt change of deregulation is now forcing the industry to deal with this problem.[10]

6. Securitization

Securitization is essentially a financing mechanism. Its appeal at the current time is due to the fact it offers access to extremely attractive interest rates on medium term (up to 15-year) debt. It uses legislation as a basis for a guarantee that regulators cannot subsequently change their mind about the revenues required to pay off the debt and interest. It is, therefore, a device for insuring commitment on the part of the regulator.[11] It also insulates the bonds from the risk of bankruptcy by segregating the revenue stream from the utility's other revenues.

This reduction of risk translates to drastically reduced financing costs. Through securitization, it is possible to borrow at, say, 6% and "take out" both utility debt and equity at (roughly) the average cost of capital, say 10 or 11%. The

---

10 Note that while the *magnitude* of stranded assets is due to falling market prices, it is the act of deregulation which *creates* stranded assets. Regulators could have elected to reduce rates and require utilities to purchase new power supplies without any threat to current book values.

11 Regulatory commitment plays an important role, especially during a major change in regulatory policies. See, for example, recent discussions by Crew and Kleindorfer (1996) in the context of incentive regulation.

bulk of the savings come from the equity component, which of course means that the utility will be significantly smaller in equity value and earnings. Because the securitized debt is "partitioned" from the remaining debt and equity, the utility's overall debt ratio can be substantially increased without any offsetting increase in risk and equity return. Clearly there are substantial potential net savings which can then be passed on to customers.

Which elements of stranded costs should be considered for securitization? "Regulatory assets" clearly can and should be securitized from an economic perspective. They are basically "known" quantities and have defined amortization periods. There should not be much controversy about continuing to provide full cost-recovery. Similarly, NUG or other contract buy-out/-down costs should also be securitized in order to maximize economic gains. Again, they are a known quantity and the amortization of the buy-out can be structured to yield immediate net customer savings even in the short-run.

Generation is obviously the controversial area. The uncertainty surrounding market value estimates leads to obvious concern that an irrevocable level of securitization could produce an over-collection of stranded cost by the utility. In several cases this has led to a Faustian bargain where utilities have been forced to sell off extremely valuable hydroelectric and fossil generation in exchange for a promise of 100% stranded cost recovery, principally including nuclear assets.

7. Conclusion

Clearly, the regulator cannot be expected to securitize 100% of an estimated generation stranded cost—although if a minimum estimate could be agreed upon, then securitization at that level would be appropriate. Similarly, a "true-up" process would have all of the usual disincentive effects.

Therefore, the most balanced solution may be to combine securitization of a portion of a reasonable estimate of stranded generation cost, together with a rate-cap mechanism that thereby maximizes the incentives for efficiency and cost reduction, as well as providing an incentive for voluntary asset retirements and sales. Securitization provides a mechanism to ensure regulatory commitment. The reduction in risk facilitates a significant reduction in the cost of capital, thereby producing rate reduction.

The challenge for regulators and utilities in this scenario is the classic one of the regulator being concerned that the utility has better information concerning market values and the opportunities for future cost reduction, while the utility seeks to avoid the potential for a future asymmetric "true- up" in the event that it is successful in mitigating stranded costs.

References

Crew, Michael A., and Paul R. Kleindorfer. 1996. "Incentive Regulation in the United Kingdom and the United States: Some Lessons." *Journal of Regulatory Economics* 9 (No. 3, May): 211-226.

Federal Energy Regulatory Commission. 1994. "Recovery of Stranded Costs by Public Utilities and Transmitting Utilities." Notice of Public Rulemaking (June).

Moody's Investors Service Research. 1995. "Stranded Costs Will Threaten Credit Quality of U.S. Electrics" (August).

New Jersey Board of Public Utilities. 1997. *Restructuring the Electric Power Industry in New Jersey: Findings and Recommendations* (April).

7

PERFORMANCE MEASUREMENT FOR PRICE-CAP REGULATION OF TELECOMMUNICATIONS
Using Evidence from a Cross-section Study of United States Local Exchange Carriers[1]

John R. Norsworthy
Diana H. Tsai

1. Introduction

Price-cap regulation of interstate access charges by the Local Exchange Carriers (LECs), including the Regional Bell Operating Companies (RBOCs), was instituted by the Federal Communications Commission (FCC) in 1991. It replaces rate-of-return regulation in order to secure for the ratepayers some of the benefits of competition in the provision of telecommunications services. An important aspect of the proposed price-cap formula is the productivity growth target (incorporated in the "X factor") that the LECs must achieve in order to obtain higher rates of return than had been authorized under rate-of-return regulation. The rationale is as follows: during the period that a price-cap formula prevails, the LEC is permitted to keep the profits it realizes beyond full operating costs, and a normal rate of return, provided that its prices conform with the cap. At the end of the period, the price cap is to be adjusted to reflect the recent performance of the LEC. The sharing provision in the price-cap plan assigns a fraction of the excess profits earned by the LEC during the period that a given price cap prevails to its customers in the form of rate reductions. For LECs that elect sufficiently high targets for rate reduction, all excess profits may be retained.

The productivity growth target is therefore crucial for all stakeholders in the telecommunications industry. For the customers, a higher productivity target, other

1   The authors gratefully acknowledge the beneficial effects of comments by Michael Crew,
    Steven Friedlander, Richard E. Schuler, Jr., and two anonymous referees.

things equal, means that the LEC must achieve higher gains in efficiency—which translate into a lower cap on rates that the LEC is permitted to charge. For the LEC and its shareholders, a lower productivity target results in a higher price cap, so that a *given* performance in terms of cost reduction and provision of services results in a higher rate of return and after tax profits. For the Interexchange Carriers (IXCs), a lower productivity target and the associated higher price cap means that a higher price may be charged for access by the IXCs to the local telephone network. Access charges constitute between one third and one half of the costs of the IXCs.

An underlying assumption of price-cap regulation is that the regulatory authority does not know the true costs of service provision by the LECs, nor does it know the range of managerial and technological alternatives for cost reduction by the LECs during the period that the price cap will be in force. The theory of price-cap regulation maintains that an appropriately chosen price-cap formula will encourage the LEC to reveal its true costs through the cost reduction activities that it undertakes in its own interests during the period that the price cap prevails (Laffont and Tirole 1993). It is important to note that the favorable consequence of the theory abstracts from two characteristics of the proposed rulemaking context: that quality of service may be reduced to achieve cost reduction, and that the LECs participate in unregulated as well as regulated lines of business that share the many of the same inputs. Both of these factors are important in that they identify incentives for self-interested behavior by the LECs that are not contemplated in the theory of price-cap regulation. There is thus the potential, as well as the incentive, for cross-subsidy from regulated to unregulated activities. It is expected, for example, that the LECs are to be permitted to offer long distance service in competition with the IXCs, even as the IXCs are to be permitted to offer local telephone services in competition with the LECs. The expected competition in this case would not be symmetric if cross-subsidy in fact were to take place (Brautigam and Panzer 1989). The competitive restraint on reduction of service quality by the LECs would not be effective until effective actual competition occurred in the local service market.

To implement price-cap regulation, this study discusses the measures of X factor—the productivity target on which the price-cap formula depends—provisionally using a total factor productivity measurement scheme based on equilibrium-based model and performance-based model. This paper organizes as follows. Section 2 investigates theoretical and practical issues of TFP measurement in the short run disequilibrium framework. The empirical estimable model is depicted in section 3. In section 4, the productivity measures of services by LECs before and after divestiture is examined; and measures of capital quality are reported based on parametric estimates of technological change. Section 5 concludes the paper with a prescriptive summary of empirical performance measures and their role in price-cap regulation.

2. TFP Measurement Issues: Theory and Practice

2.1. Equilibrium and Disequilibrium in Capital Input
In this section, we show the link between the measurement of total factor

productivity (TFP) and the rate of return on capital for the regulated enterprise. In the framework of the variable cost function (VCF) approach, the regulated enterprise is producing an aggregate of services (Y) with three categories of inputs: capital (K), labor (H), and other purchased inputs or "materials" (M). The materials category includes purchased services as well as physical goods. The aggregate output Y comprises local (L), intrastate toll $(T,)$ and interstate access (A) services.

The production function is thus

$$(Y_L, Y_T, Y_A) = f(K, H, M) . \tag{1}$$

For the regulated enterprise, it is not always appropriate to assume that the profits are maximized. Rather, a much more general assumption is preferred: that short run costs of producing the output demanded by customers are minimized. This assumption is consistent with key stylized facts of regulated local telecommunications enterprises: that the capital inputs at any particular point in time need not be at equilibrium levels that would be achieved under conditions of instantaneous adjustment of all inputs to prevailing output demand and input prices, and that the rates at which services are sold are not (necessarily) adjusted by the enterprise to the profit-maximizing level.

The variable cost function, which corresponds to the production function above with the capital input fixed in the short run, is written

$$C_V = g(p_H, p_M, Y_L, Y_T, Y_A, K) , \tag{2}$$

where p_H and p_M are prices of labor and materials respectively.

In this framework, the return to capital is a residual, which is measured as the difference between total revenues, TR, and the cost of the variable inputs, C_V. This residual, called *property income*, PI, is computed as

$$PI = TR - CV = \sum_{r=1}^{R} v_r y_r - \sum_{i=1}^{I} p_i x_i , \tag{3}$$

where y_r is the rth output and v_r is its marginal cost and x_i is the ith variable input and p_i is its marginal product.

For the regulated firm under consideration, $r = L, T, A$ and $i = H, M$.

Thus, the gross return to capital is PI. The gross rate of return to capital based on residual property income is then simply

$$\pi_g = \frac{PI}{K} . \tag{4}$$

This can be called the *residual value* of a unit of (aggregated) capital input. The concept applies only when all capital inputs are expressed as a single aggregate. All rents that accrue to the enterprise, both long-run rents and short-run (or quasi-) rents, positive and negative, are part of π_g. Consequently, in the regulatory context, π_g will include the allowed return *as well as any excess or shortfall*.

The *value* of the capital input *in production* in the VCF model is given by its contribution to production—its marginal product. This can be computed as the *shadow cost of capital*, s_K, from an estimated VCF model as

$$s_K = -\frac{\partial C_V}{\partial K}, \tag{5}$$

which is just (the negative of) the marginal product of capital. It measures the value of the variable inputs that could be saved (hence its negative sign) if one more unit of capital were added to the production process. This shadow cost concept, introduced and elaborated for capital inputs fixed in the short run (Berndt and Fuss 1986), is entirely similar to the shadow cost of limited resource inputs in linear programming.

Generally, the shadow cost of capital will differ from the value of the capital input computed as a residual after costs of other inputs are met. However, when (and only when) production takes place under constant returns to scale, the shadow cost of the aggregate capital input will equal its residual value. Under rate-of-return regulation, it is well-established that the economic forces that would tend to bring the shadow cost of capital into line with its long-run expected user cost are not operative. Even under price-cap regulation, the regulated enterprise must meet all demand that is forthcoming at the posted rates for service. Hence, it can neither adjust output nor raise its price to bring its costs into equality or proportionality with marginal revenue. Furthermore, the *raison d'être* of utility regulation is economies of scale: significantly declining average costs of production over the relevant range of output. However, there is in the literature evidence that, although there are substantial economies of density associated with expansion of traffic on the given network, overall economies of scale in telecommunications are quite close to one.[2] Thus it is a reasonable approximation to suppose that the shadow cost of capital is appropriate for measuring the value of the capital input in the aggregation of total input for price-cap TFP measurement. Under price-cap regulation, this residual value is essentially the administered value of capital that results from the regulatory process: the value that is assessed on the customers of the regulated enterprise, π_g.[3] This value is that which has been determined by default in the price-cap regulatory process to represent the value of the capital input to the ratepayers.

2.2. Measurement of TFP in the Short Run Disequilibrium Framework

The economic theory of productivity measurement specifies that TFP is a ratio of aggregate output to total inputs. The aggregate output index for a productive

---

2   Christensen, et al. (1983) and Nadiri and Shankerman (1981) find economies of scale near one for the Bell System prior to divestiture. Shin and Ying (1992; 1993) and Norsworthy et al. (1993) find cost elasticities near one for the LECs.

3   If robust estimates of the shadow cost of capital could be obtained, they could be consulted in determining the rate of return implicit in the price cap. A shadow price persistently below the long-term user cost would signal overinvestment and hence a downward adjustment in the rate of return and conversely.

enterprise is defined as the weighted sum of the indices of physical outputs, where the weights are the respective marginal costs of production. The aggregate input index for a productive enterprise is defined as the weighted sum of the indices of physical inputs, where the weights are the respective marginal products of the inputs in production of the output (Fisher and Shell 1972). Under special conditions, the prices of inputs are equal to their marginal products. The conditions are that (a) inputs are purchased by cost-minimizing decisionmakers (b) at prices that do not change in response to the quantity demanded. These conditions are met when the purchasers of inputs are cost-minimizing price takers, as in perfectly competitive markets. The conditions are also met when wages and materials prices faced by the short-term cost-minimizing decisionmaker are fixed by prior agreement, as in the case of collective bargaining. The short run cost minimization assumption seems to be a reasonable characterization of the LECs' decisionmaking.[4] Under similarly special conditions, the prices of multiple outputs are equal to their respective marginal costs of production. The conditions are that (a) the level of all outputs are adjusted to maximize the overall profit of the enterprise and (b) that the prices do not respond to the output decisions of the enterprise. These conditions are met when the producers of the outputs are profit-maximizing price takers, also as in perfectly competitive markets. The conditions are also met when prices faced by the enterprise are fixed by prior agreement, and the enterprise adjusts output so as to maximize profits. These conditions are *not* met, even approximately, in the markets for local telecommunications services. While prices (rates) are generally fixed, the LECs are required to provide services to all customers willing to pay the prevailing rates. They do not adjust either prices or output to maximize short-run profits. Consequently the regulatory measurement practice prevailing in the telecommunications industry of using revenue weights to aggregate outputs of the LECs for TFP measurement has no basis in the economic theory of production.

While not consistent with economic theory, the practice of using revenue weights *does* have a rationale. Regulation of utilities must have an empirical basis, and it may be difficult to obtain robust measures of marginal cost econometrically.[5] Further, the asymmetry of cost information between regulators and regulated enterprises could open to new possibilities for moral hazard in cost reporting if self-reported marginal costs, however derived, were to come into widespread use in the regulatory process.[6] At a minimum, more resources would need to be deployed in auditing the cost accounts of the LECs. Moreover, at present, marginal cost measures that can be developed from publicly available data may be difficult

---

4   Cost minimization is shown to be violated in an empirical model when the demand for an
     input exhibits a perverse reaction to price change, i.e., when more of an input is purchased
     when its price rises and other determinants of demand remain the same; or when less of an
     input is purchased when its price falls and other determinants of demand remain the same.
     Norsworthy et al. (1993) tested for such violations of cost minimization in the VCF model of
     the LECs and found very few.
5   Some of these issues are discussed in Nadiri (1996).
6   Laffont and Tirole (1993) discuss the auditing and other moral hazard issues that derive from
     asymmetric information in detail.

to reproduce, depending as they do on state-of-the-art econometric specification and estimation techniques, and upon the software to implement them. Such measures may be useful, however, as *supplements* in appraising the efficiency and pricing performances of the LECs, and the reasonableness of mark-ups allowed by the regulatory process, but they are not sufficiently reliable at present for establishing TFP targets in price-cap regulation.

Using the prevailing practice of revenue weighting of outputs, the level of TFP for the unregulated enterprise in the VCF framework may be measured in quantity terms as

$$TFP = \frac{\sum_{r=L,T,A} u_r y_r}{\sum_{i=H,M} w_i x_i + w_K K}, \tag{6}$$

where

$$u_r = \frac{v_r y_r}{\sum_r v_r y_r} \tag{7}$$

is the revenue share of the rth output y_r, and v_r is its associated unit revenue. The weights are not based on marginal costs. Moreover,

$$w_i = \frac{p_i x_i}{\sum_i p_i x_i - s_K K} \quad \text{and} \quad w_k = \frac{-s_K K}{\sum_i p_i x_i - s_K K}, \tag{8}$$

where s_K is the shadow cost of capital described above.[7] The first expression on the right hand side of equation (6) is aggregate output and the second (in parentheses) is aggregate or total factor input. TFP growth may then be measured as

$$\Delta TFP_t = \sum_{r=L,T,A} \bar{u}_{r,t} \Delta y_{r,t} - \left(\sum_{i=H,M} \bar{w}_{i,t} \Delta x_{i,t} + \bar{w}_{K,t} \Delta K_t \right), \tag{9}$$

where $\bar{u}_{r,t}$ for $r = L, T, A$ are revenue-based weights and $\bar{w}_{i,t}$ for $i = H, M, K$ are cost-based weights. Depending on the computation of the weights, the indices of outputs and inputs may be Fisher Ideal Indices or Tornquist Indices.[8] The $\bar{u}_{r,t}$ and

---

7   Recall that s_K is inherently negative, which requires the negative sign in (7).
8   Diewert (1993) shows the superiority of the Fisher Ideal Index over the Tornquist Index. The Performance Based Model uses the Fisher Ideal Index procedure to aggregate outputs and inputs, rather than the Tornquist Index, which is applied in the USTA model. For prices or quantities near zero, the Tornquist Index is quite ill-behaved; for prices or quantities *at* zero, the Tornquist Index is undefined. Consequently, in the dynamic telecommunications industry, where, prospectively, outputs may appear or vanish, the Fisher Ideal Index is preferable. The

$\overline{w}_{r,t}$ are average weights for adjacent time periods, and Δ denotes year-to-year growth. If, as is conventional, the growth rates are measured in natural logarithms, the first expression on the right hand side of (9) is a quantity index of output growth, and the second a quantity index of input growth.

This measurement procedure requires only minor computational modification to adapt it to the case of the regulated enterprise, although the implications are quite important. The weights for the inputs, $\overline{w}_{i,t}$ and $\overline{w}_{K,t}$ must now be based on expenditures for each input, which is aggregate to the total revenue assessed on the ratepayers. Note that the measures of TFP and its growth depend on prices and quantities of inputs and the unit revenues and quantities of outputs. In order for the TFP measure to be accurate, the quantities of outputs and inputs must be of constant quality or the qualities must be separately measured and incorporated into the TFP measure.

2.3. X-Factor in the Price-Cap Index as an Adjustment to TFP

The X-factor in the price-cap formula is a properly defined measure of the excess of TFP growth of the LECs adjusted for the difference in input prices between the LECs and the national economy, and the difference in productivity between the national economy and the LECs, given the convention of using revenue weights for outputs rather than marginal cost weights. In this section, we establish the relationship between the LEC rate of return and the X-factor in the price-cap formula proposed by the FCC. Next, we show the relationship between the LEC rate of return and the X-factor.

(a) The X-Factor in the Price-Cap Formula

The FCC's proposed formula for adjusting the interstate common line access price-cap index *(PCI)* to be applied to the LECs is written

$$PCI_t = PCI_{t-1}\left[1 + w(\Delta GDPPI - X) + \frac{\Delta Z}{R}\right], \qquad (10)$$

where $\Delta GDPPI$ = percentage change in the GDP deflator between the quarter ending six months prior to the effective date of the new annual tariff and the corresponding quarter of the prior year and X = the productivity factor—the difference between the rate of change in LEC TFP and economy-wide growth in TFP as computed by the Bureau of Labor Statistics, adjusted by the difference in input prices of the LECs and the input prices in the non-farm business sector of the United States. LEC TFP is computed from revenue weights for outputs, price weights for inputs, and the qualities of all outputs and inputs are assumed to remain

Productivity Research Division at the Bureau of Labor Statistics, the source of the TFP measures selected by the Commission for benchmarking the access charges of the LECs, has adopted the Fisher Ideal Index for its computations of major sector productivity and plans its introduction in its manufacturing (two-digit) sectoral measures. In its order in the Price Cap Performance Review, FCC Order 97-159, the FCC specifies that the Fisher Ideal Index should be used as the measurement standard for productivity growth in the X-Factor.

constant. ΔZ = dollar effect of current regulatory changes when compared to the regulations in effect at the time that the PCI was updated to PCI_{t-1} measured at the base period rate of operations. R = base period quantities for each rate element i, multiplied by the price for each rate element i at the time the PCI was updated to $P\ C_{t-1}$. $w = (R + \Delta Z)$ divided by R. PCI_t = the new (adjusted) PCI value. PCI_{t-1} = the immediately preceding PCI value.[9]

The g adjustment in the above expression is not applied to other baskets. The X factor can be developed readily from the fundamental objective of the price cap: that prices of telephone services should rise no faster than an index of output prices for the economy as a whole, $\Delta GNPPI$. This objective can be expressed as

$$\frac{PCI_t}{PCI_{t-1}} \leq (1 + \Delta GNPPI - X) , \tag{11}$$

wherethe X factor is

$$X = \Delta TFP_{LECs} - \Delta TFP_n + (\Delta IP_{LECs} - \Delta IP_n) \tag{12}$$

and the subscript n denotes the national economy. The X factor includes a *target* rate of TFP growth, definted as an excess above national TFP growth, and an input price differential. The X factor may be selected by the LECs to trigger various levels of sharing of profits above a standard rate of return. As presently implemented in the price-cap plan for interstate regulated by the FCC, selection of the lowest X factor by a LEC requires that all profits above the target level be shared with customers of the LECs in the form of rate reductions. The highest X factor requires no sharing. In the present plan, there are intermediate ranges of the X factor that require partial sharing. The sharing provision has the objective of encouraging the LECs to choose a higher X when their prospects for profitability are high, and a lower X when their prospects are lower.

The X factor may be specific to the basket of services to which the *PCI* applies. The baskets proposed to be recognized and separately capped are: common line interstate access, traffic-sensitive switched interstate access elements; special access (trunking, etc.), and interstate interexchange services.[10] At issue is whether the TFP computation on which the X factor is to be based should be *actual* performance by the LECs measured according to the disequilibrium model or a theoretical performance by the LECs *assumed* by the U.S. Telephone Association model (Christensen 1995). The disequilibrium approach depends entirely on measured quantities describing current performance of the regulated company. The USTA approach *assumes* that the capital investment of the LECs is optimal, and thus specifies a user cost of capital based on that assumption. In each case, the same measures of other inputs and of output are used.

Based on *measured* performance of the LECs—the disequilibrium approach—

---

9   This formulation is taken directly from NECA (1995) Section 61.45, pp. 20-21.
10   National Exchange Carriers Association (1995), sec. 61.42, pp. 16-17.

the productivity component of the X factor in period t computed from equation (9) is

$$TFP_t^M = \sum_{r=L,T,A} \bar{u}_{r,t}\Delta y_{r,t} - \left(\sum_{i=H,M} \bar{w}_{i,t}\Delta x_{i,t} + \bar{w}_{K,t}\Delta K_t \right), \tag{13}$$

where the weight for the growth of the capital input is computed from the realized rate of return s_K as discussed above. Based on the theoretically optimal performance of the LECs—the USTA approach—the productivity component of the X factor in period t is then

$$TFP_t^S = \sum_{r=L,T,A} \bar{u}_{r,t}\Delta y_{r,t} - \left(\sum_{i=H,M} \bar{w}_{i,t}\Delta x_{i,t} + \bar{z}_{K,t}^*\Delta K_t \right), \tag{14}$$

where the weight for the growth of the capital input is computed from the ex ante user cost of capital, incorporating a rate of return and associated user cost of capital that is not specified at present. Most important, the rate of return underlying equation (14) is not tied to actual performance of the LECs. Thus, if the LECs choose a high depreciation rate with the rate of return defined as in the USTA model, the growth in capital input will receive a higher weight, and, with other elements in the computation of the X factor remaining the same, the X factor will be lower.[11] As the theory of regulation now recognizes, the regulated enterprise should be expected to act in its own interest concerning the use and revelation of information about its costs of operation that is not shared with the regulatory authority.

(b) Rate of Return for LECs and TFP

The realized rate of return for the LEC is simply the ratio of property income less allowable depreciation to the value of the capital input, which is different from the realized regulatory rate of return in three main ways. These concern depreciation, capital gains or losses, and the assets included in the rate base. Economic depreciation includes the economic values of loss of function, obsolescence (to the extent that it is not captured in the change in the asset price in the capital gains term), and discards from the stock of capital. Regulatory depreciation is applied at stipulated rates to the physical assets. These regulatory depreciation rates may attempt, explicitly or implicitly, to account for the factors that determine economic depreciation, but they are also influenced by other factors. The regulatory rate of return may allow for capital gains or losses, but only implicitly. Only part of the financial assets of an enterprise are typically entered in the rate base for calculation of the rate of return, although some interest costs are allowed as part of operating costs. Finally, assets values are generally measured at historical cost.

Thus, the regulatory rate of return before applicable taxes, for period T, denoted

---

11   In its order in the Price Cap Performance Review, FCC Order 97-159, the FCC specifies that the short-run approach to measuring the return to capital should be applied productivity growth measurement for the X-Factor. The sensitivity of the user cost of capital to the depreciation rate, the rate of return, and other determining factors is shown in Norsworthy and Tsai (1998, ch. 3).

ρ_T, can be written

$$\rho_T = \left[\frac{(TR - C_V^*) - \delta_R p_{A,T} \cdot A_{h,T-1}}{A_{h,T-1} + \theta F_{T-1}} \right] (1 - \tau), \qquad (15)$$

where δ_R is regulatory depreciation, $A_{h,T-1}$ is the book value of physical assets, CV is the adjusted variable cost of production, F_{T-1} is the current value of financial assets, at tax rate τ, and θ is the proportion of financial assets allowed into the rate calculation. (The value of θ may be zero in some regulatory jurisdictions (Norsworthy and Tsai 1998, ch. 3).)

The link to the total factor productivity computation is straightforward. Property income, $TR - C_V^*$, is just the difference between revenues and variable cost. In the price-cap context, TR is the revenue from the target basket of services, and C_V^* is the variable cost of production. In most cases, the quantity $TR - C_V^*$ will vary in the same direction as TFP, because TFP is a ratio of outputs to inputs, while TR is the value of output and C_V^* is the value of variable inputs.

3. The Empirical Cost Model

3.1. Regulatory Uses

This section reports a cross-section econometric model of production to measure performance for eleven local exchange carriers (LECs) in United States from 1981-1990. There are several ways that information from such a model can be used for regulatory purposes. A major attraction of the price-cap incentive regulation scheme is that the regulator need not know the costs of the regulated company. However, as Laffont and Tirole (1993) point out, the efficiency of the price-cap scheme depends upon how closely the menu offered to the company spans the range of cost alternatives that the company actually faces. Exogenous information from a model that identifies marginal costs of producing various services can narrow the range of the productivity targets in the X-Factor menu and result in less rent accruing to the company under the price-cap scheme. In the first round of the FCC's regulation of interstate access charges, for example, five of the seven RBOCs chose the highest X-Factor target, and another petitioned to change to the higher target after the scheme was underway. Clearly, the FCC had underestimated the productivity growth potential of the RBOCs.[12]

If the estimated levels of TFP emerging from the model are judged to be

---

12   The X-Factor had been established by the FCC based primarily on cost data and analyses supplied by the companies themselves. The playing out of the first phase of price-cap regulation illustrates beautifully the value of asymmetric information to the companies. In the subsequent round, five of the seven RBOCs selected the highest X-Factor target again, even though the target menu has been raised. In the most recent round, the FCC set considerably higher targets.

sufficiently accurate, individual targets for the regulated companies might be set, based on their deviations from best practice, whether price caps or some other regulatory scheme were used. For example, in the study described here, New York Telephone was found to be at once the highest cost and the most profitable of the 11 large LECs studied. An individually specified target for this case would seem to be defensible.

Moreover, as noted above, TFP measures based on marginal cost aggregation of output will generally differ from those based on revenue weights. Use of marginal cost-weighted TFP would result in generally lower (and harder to reach) productivity targets. But use of the marginal cost weights depends upon the regulators' faith in both the data supplied by the regulated companies and in the econometric methods yielding the marginal cost measures. At present, the best use of econometric results may be to narrow the range of the options offered in the incentive regulation scheme, price-cap or otherwise. MacDonald et al. (1994) discuss limitations of price-cap regulation and alternatives to it in state regulatory proceedings.

3.2. Model Description

The model is estimated using iterative three-stage least squares, a generalized least squares estimator. All equations allow for company specific effects. Annual effects by year are included for the years 1981-90. The estimated dependent variables in the model are: Variable Cost; Quantity of Labor Input (Employment); Quantity of Non-Capital Purchased Inputs (Materials); Revenue from Local Services; Revenue from Toll Services; Revenue from Access Charges (1984 and later).

The specification of outputs and inputs of the Large LECs model follows.

Output

y_l	Local services: local call minutes
y_t	Toll services: total call minutes less local call minutes
y_a	Access line: total access lines (residential, business, public)

Revenues

r_l	Local: total local revenue
r_t	Toll: total toll revenue
r_a	Access: access revenues (after 1983)
g_p	Gross Profit: total revenues - total operating expenses

Capital and Technology

k_s	Switching: Total central office (C.O.) switches
z_d	Digital Switching: number of digital central office switches
z_a	Analog Switching: number of analog C.O. switches
z_o	Other Switching: number of electromechanical C.O. switches
k_x	Transmission: Total miles of interoffice cable
z_f	Fiber: Miles of fiber optic cable, k_x
z_c	Copper: Miles of copper cable, k_x

Variable Costs: Labor and "Materials"

C_v Variable Costs: Total Operating Expenses

v_e Employment costs: Compensation including social security taxes

q_e Employees: Full-time + 1/2 part-time workers

p_e Compensation per employee: v_e/q_e

v_m Cost of materials and purchased services: Total Operating Expenses – Employee Compensation

p_m Price index for "Materials" from input-output study. Same for all LECs

q_m "Real" materials input: v_m/p_m

The restricted translog variable cost function for all LECs is given by

$$\ln CV = a_o + S_i a_i \ln p_i + \tfrac{1}{2} S_i S_j a_{ij} \ln p_i \ln p_j$$

$$+ \sum_m b_m \ln y_m + \tfrac{1}{2} \sum_m \sum_n b_{mn} \ln y_m \ln y_n$$

$$+ \sum_r b_r \ln k_r + \tfrac{1}{2} \sum_r \sum_s b_{rs} \ln k_r \ln k_s$$

$$+ \sum_i \sum_m b_{im} \ln p_i \ln y_m + \sum_i \sum_r b_{ir} \ln p_i \ln k_r$$

$$+ \sum_m \sum_r b_{mr} \ln y_m \ln k_r \tag{16}$$

$$\text{for } i,j = e,m$$
$$m,n = l,t,a$$
$$r,s = s,x$$

First-degree homogeneity in prices is imposed by

$$\sum_i a_i = 1 \qquad \sum_i a_{ij} = \sum_j a_{ij} = 0 \qquad \text{for all } i,j$$

$$\sum_i b_{im} = 0 \qquad \sum_i b_{ir} = 0 \qquad \text{for all } i,m,r.$$

The restricted variable cost function also requires

$$\sum_m b_{mn} + \sum_r b_{rs} = 0 \qquad \text{for all } m,n,r,s$$

$$\sum_m b_{im} + \sum_r b_{ir} = 0 \qquad \text{for all } i,m,r.$$

These restrictions are imposed on the parameters of the variable cost function and on the demand and revenue equations derived therefrom.

Variable input demand equations[13] are derived from the restricted variable cost function:

$$q_i = \left(\frac{CV}{p_i}\right) \cdot s_i , \tag{17}$$

where s_i, the share of input i in variable cost, is derived from equation (16) using Shepard's Lemma under conditions of variable cost minimization.

$$S_i = \frac{\partial \ln CV}{\partial \ln p_i} = a_i + \sum_m b_{im} \ln y_m + \sum_r b_{ir} \ln k_r . \tag{18}$$

The model is formulated as a pooled time series-cross section model, comprising 11 LECs for the period 1981-90. This specification requires independent error terms for each equation for each year and for each company. Consequently, estimable specifications for the variable cost function and the input demand equations are written

$$\ln CV = g(\cdot) + \sum_t \eta_{ct} + \sum_u \varepsilon_{cu} + e_c$$

$$q_i = \left(\frac{CV}{p_i}\right) \cdot s_i + \sum_t \eta_{it} + \sum_u \varepsilon_{iu} + e_i , \tag{19}$$

where η_{at} is the fixed effect error term for equation a in year t, $t = 1981, ..., 1989$, $a = c,e,m$; ε_{au} is the fixed effect error term for LEC u in equation a, where $u = IL,MI,NY,NE,NJ,PC,PN,SC,SO,SW$.

For each equation, Mountain Telephone in 1990 is the "base" observation. Thus, the year and LEC errors represent deviations from this base. The fixed effects for the years and for the LECs are averaged to zero. The generalized least squares (GLS) estimation procedure incorporates the assumption that the η_{at}, ε_{au}, and e_a are independently normally distributed and serially uncorrelated, with zero means and finite variances.

For this multiple output restricted variable cost function model, the revenue equation for output y_m can be shown to be

$$r_{mm} = \frac{\partial TR}{\partial y_m} = \frac{\partial CV}{\partial y_m} + mu_m , \tag{20}$$

where mu_m is a markup over the marginal cost of y_m (Norsworthy and Jang 1992,

---

13   Estimation of the demand functions for the variable inputs is a more efficient procedure than estimation of the share equations, because the share equations are not stochastically independent: only $n-1$ share equations may have independent error terms because $\sum_i s_i = 1$ (McElroy 1987; Norsworthy and Jang 1992, ch. 3).

ch. 12). This markup by definition (independent of any behavioral assumption) has two components. One component is associated with non-constant returns to scale (denoted A), and the other with the share of gross return. Under conditions of constant returns to scale, the marginal cost of each output is constant, so that average variable cost and marginal cost are equal. It can be shown that under non-constant returns to scale,

$$A = CV \left(1 - \frac{1}{\sum_m \frac{\partial \ln CV}{\partial \ln y_m} + \sum_r \frac{\partial \ln CV}{\partial \ln k_r}} \right). \tag{21}$$

Thus, for output y_m and gross return $G = TR - CV$,

$$mu_m = h_m A + g_m G, \tag{22}$$

where h_m and g_m are estimated parameters that partition A and G respectively among the three outputs. Consequently,

$$\sum_m h_m = \sum_m g_m = 1. \tag{23}$$

The quantity A and the associated parameters h_m play only a technical role in the model. However, the attribution of gross profit to local and toll service revenues and to access charges measured by the g parameters is potentially interesting for regulatory policy. Finally, the unit revenue equations are specified

$$ur_{mm} = \left(\frac{CV}{y_m} \right) \cdot \frac{\partial \ln CV}{\partial \ln y_m} + u_m A + g_m G \text{ for } m = l,t,a. \tag{24}$$

Estimable revenue equations are derived from (24) by addition of the error terms required by the time series-cross section model. Instead of the fixed effects formulation applied to error components of the cost function and input demand equations, it proved more appropriate to apply a random effects formulation in the revenue equations. In the light of potentially differing perceptions of equity under different regulatory regimes, it seemed appropriate to test a specification permitting the g_m parameter to shift through time and across the LECs. In practice, this specification gave a far better fit for the revenue equations than the fixed effects formulation. Thus, the estimable unit revenue equations are written

$$r_m = CV \cdot \frac{\partial \ln CV}{\partial \ln y_m} + h_m A + g_m (G + \eta_m G + \varepsilon_m G) + e_m \quad m = l,t,a, \tag{25}$$

where the random effects error components are reflected in the shift in g_m.

Thus, we estimate the six equations given in (19) and (25) using the generalized (GLS) procedure iterative three stage least squares. Two variants of the model were estimated to show the effects of adjusting for quality change deriving from advances in switching and interoffice transmission technology. The hypothesis of no quality change is rejected by a substantial margin. Only the results for the model with quality change were reported here.

In each estimated equation, the error components specification is implemented using dummy variables to capture the intercept shifts (equations (19)) and the slope shifts associated with the pooled time series-cross section specification. In particular, the error components of equation (19) become

$$\sum_t h_{at} = \sum_t a_t d_t \quad \text{all } t \neq 1990$$

$$\sum_u e_{au} = \sum_u a_u d_u \quad \text{all } u \neq MT \tag{26}$$

$$a = c,e,m,$$

where d_t is a dummy variable denoting time period t; d_u is a dummy variable denoting company u; a_t, a_u are estimated intercept shift coefficients corresponding to the mean error components of t and u.

For the revenue equations, the error components (random effects) associated with the allocation of gross profit G become

$$\sum_t h_{at} = y_t d_t$$

$$\sum_u e_{au} = y_u d_u, \tag{27}$$

where d_t and d_u are as above and y_t, y_u are slope shift coefficients for variable G corresponding to the mean error components of t and u.

In a dummy variable formulation of the error components, the fixed effects specifications of equation (19) can be viewed as a special case of the more general random effects model where the independent variable associated with the shift is constant. (There is some loss of efficiency in this approach when a conventional GLS estimator such as iterative three-stage least squares is applied).

For estimation, we assume that h_{at} is independently normally distributed with mean m_{ha} and variance s_{ht}^2 for $a = c,e,m,l,t,a$, also that l_{au} is independently normally distributed with mean m_{lu}^2, for all a, u and that e_a is independently normally distributed with mean $m_a = 0$ and variance s_a^2 for all a. Further, we require that

$$\sum_\alpha \mu_\eta \alpha = \sum_\alpha \mu_\varepsilon \alpha = \sum_\alpha \mu_\alpha = 0.$$

Each of the error components is assumed to have zero mean across all equations. Variances of each error component are assumed to be equal across all equations, but not across error components.

4. Empirical Evidence: Productivity and Capital Modernization Performance of Large LECs

An advantage of cross-section econometric results for regulation of telecommunications is that it provides information about the comparative performance of the particular company being regulated, as well as the marginal costs and marginal products required for incentive schemes based on TFP changes. This information may be useful in establishing specific targets for the regulated firm concerning, e.g., modernization of equipment and general targets for productivity growth or reduction in costs per access line based on performance of other firms. The results of parameters estimation and model characteristics are shown in the appendix.

4.1. Performance of Local Exchange Carriers (LECs) Before and After Divestiture

Table 1 shows the pattern of markups over marginal cost from the pre-divestiture and post-divestiture periods for each of the LECs. These markups over marginal cost provide some insight into the motivations of the LECs, and perhaps into the phenomenon of regulatory capture as well. The measurement of the markups reported does not depend upon particular assumptions about demand elasticities or competitive conditions in the output market. The general pattern is that the markups for local service rise after divestiture. Markups for toll services also change considerably after divestiture: they decline for almost all LECs. This result is easily understood: the LECs provide only intraLATA long distance calls after divestiture, whereas before divestiture, all toll services were provided through the LECs. The markup on toll services declined substantially after divestiture because the product mix has changed and because the LECs (may have) anticipated increasing competition such as is now emerging, with several states authorizing by-pass of the local network for intraLATA toll calls. Much of the predivestiture revenue from tolls was of course replaced by access charges.

Access to the local network is a monopoly of the LEC; it is not surprising that the markup component of the price of access should be so high relative to its marginal production cost. The cost of producing services is largely a capital cost, using capital shared with other regulated services: local and intraLATA toll. Each of these effects—decreasing markups on intraLATA toll service and high markup for access to the local network by the long distance service providers—is consistent with the expectation that the LECs will pursue their own private objectives under regulation. It is perhaps surprising that regulatory authorities were apparently so permissive in authorizing what seem to be predatory access charges.[14] Such pricing may have been thought necessary to lubricate the transition from AT&T ownership

---

14   Optimal access charges and the incentive intervention to encourage them are addressed in
      Laffont and Tirole (1993, ch. 5). However, the history of the long distance-local rate structure
      may partially explain the pattern. Before divestiture, there was a conscious regulatory policy
      of using long distance revenues to subsidize local service. After divestiture, this pattern was
      continued in the structure of interstate access charges. See Norsworthy and Berndt (1996).

Table 1. Average Markups of Prices of Services over their Marginal Costs			
	Service	1981-83	1984-90
Average For	LOCAL	9.66035	7.97179
All LECs	TOLL	16.16586	-1.87762
	ACCESS	0.00000	4.54079
Illinois	LOCAL	10.72170	7.48168
Bell	TOLL	13.35216	-5.52373
	ACCESS	0.00000	6.11726
Michigan	LOCAL	7.11158	7.27850
Bell	TOLL	16.96187	0.22699
	ACCESS	0.00000	1.77124
New England	LOCAL	10.72829	9.43151
Telephone	TOLL	17.07365	-0.18073
	ACCESS	0.00000	2.38844
New Jersey	LOCAL	10.63709	8.54003
Bell	TOLL	9.57913	0.09926
	ACCESS	0.00000	1.53425
New York	LOCAL	14.58609	10.44690
Telephone	TOLL	17.17097	-7.26801
	ACCESS	0.00000	9.38968
Pacific	LOCAL	6.00915	7.13666
Bell	TOLL	13.95124	1.33819
	ACCESS	0.00000	3.01034
Pennsylvania	LOCAL	7.87383	5.39401
Bell	TOLL	13.24890	-1.56750
	ACCESS	0.00000	3.13197
So Central	LOCAL	7.63207	6.23399
Bell	TOLL	24.76644	-1.17253
	ACCESS	0.00000	6.48423
Southern	LOCAL	9.46889	7.51201
Bell	TOLL	18.49454	-2.30251
	ACCESS	0.00000	6.64771
Southwestern	LOCAL	9.10046	7.62387
Bell	TOLL	18.01147	-1.69092
	ACCESS	0.00000	4.97147
Mountain	LOCAL	12.39468	10.61059
Bell	TOLL	15.21411	-2.61235
	ACCESS	0.00000	4.50216

at divestiture and to finance modernization of switching capital to accommodate equal access to long distance carriers,[15] but rising local charges suggest that the LECs have adequate alternative revenue sources. The practice of subsidizing a monopolized local service with revenues from a competitive service (interstate access) clearly distorts the allocation of resources and the social welfare at present.

The markups on intraLATA toll services are almost all negative, suggesting that local and access charges are subsidizing intraLATA tolls. If this is true, a partial remedy may be to permit competition in local service as prescribed in the Telecommunication Reform Act of 1996. The current regulatory efforts to encourage competition in provision of intraLATA long distance service otherwise may be subverted by the subsidy implicit in the strategic pricing practices of the LECs as authorized in state jurisdictions.[16]

The markups of unit revenues over marginal costs for local and intraLATA toll calls and access to the network demonstrate unequivocally the exploitation of their recently acquired monopoly power by the LECs. Those markups also suggest that the regulatory authority has been rather permissive in authorizing the rate structure that prevailed in the late 1980s, as though there were a consensus that long distance charges should continue to subsidize local service. However, part of the pattern— the uniform reduction of intraLATA toll charges below marginal costs—is unlikely to have been part of a subsidy plan generally accepted by regulators. Rather, it probably reflects the behavioral assumption made explicit in Laffont and Tirole (1993): that the regulated enterprise will attempt to exploit its information advantage concerning costs of producing services. In this case, the objective of the LECs is likely to have been to reduce prices in the area where potential competition loomed: intraLATA long distance service. These results suggest that the theory of optimal regulation, with its recognition of information asymmetry and of the self-seeking motivation of the regulated firm, should indeed be adopted in framing regulatory practice. Local predators are scarcely more benign than global ones, quite apparently.

4.2. Productivity Measurement for Incentive Regulation

Table 2 shows the differential effects of marginal cost and revenue weighting of output on TFP growth measures for 11 LECs. The growth rates differ considerably according to whether marginal cost or revenue weights are applied. Generally, revenue weights give higher rates of growth, generally by three to four percent per year for the 1981-1990 period, but by considerably less—about 1.5 percent per year—in 1984-1990. When more detailed time periods are examined, there are cases where marginal cost weights give higher growth rates.[17] As noted above, review of productivity performance after relatively short periods is to be expected under price-cap regulation; consequently, distortion and consequent bad results of regulatory decisions may result from use of revenue-weighted productivity measures for incentive regulation.

---

15   Modernization was powerfully assisted by increases in authorized depreciation at the LECs in the late 1980s. See FCC, *SOCC* for 1986-1990.

16   However, see the discussion below concerning separation of common carrier services from other telecommunications services provided by the LECs.

17   For example, New York Telephone shows about 4 percent higher average annual growth based on marginal cost weights in 1988-90.

Table 2. Total Factor Productivity Growth: Average Annual Rates for 11 Large LECs			
	TFP Basis	1981-1990	1984-1990
	MC WTS	0.023536	0.023467
All LECs	REV WTS	0.061952	0.038122
	MC QADJ	0.017299	0.016082
	MC WTS	0.053513	n/a
Illinois	REV WTS	0.055922	n/a
Bell	MC QADJ	0.048793	n/a
	MC WTS	0.017605	0.018637
Michigan	REV WTS	0.066895	0.042664
Bell	MC QADJ	0.014676	0.015591
	MC WTS	0.013212	0.015100
New England	REV WTS	0.061631	0.045962
Telephone	MC QADJ	0.008591	0.008892
	MC WTS	0.013661	0.011511
New Jersey	REV WTS	0.051531	0.028084
Bell	MC QADJ	0.007684	0.007066
	MC WTS	0.039358	0.031009
New York	REV WTS	0.056870	0.029551
Telephone	MC QADJ	0.031929	0.022174
	MC WTS	0.046813	0.054860
Pacific	REV WTS	0.080369	0.069431
Bell	MC QADJ	0.039405	0.045259
	MC WTS	0.013050	0.008328
Pennsylvania	REV WTS	0.055407	0.024737
Bell	MC QADJ	0.004198	-0.00050
	MC WTS	0.011694	0.010147
South-central	REV WTS	0.058627	0.026899
Bell	MC QADJ	0.002183	-0.00256
	MC WTS	0.021078	0.020082
Southern	REV WTS	0.063167	0.032138
Bell	MC QADJ	0.010043	0.005677
	MC WTS	0.023699	0.033433
Southwestern	REV WTS	0.061883	0.046796
Bell	MC QADJ	0.019712	0.028396
	MC WTS	0.007414	0.004675
Mountain States	REV WTS	0.046912	0.041022
Bell	MC QADJ	0.005003	0.001666
Note: MC WTS: marginal cost weighted TFP REV WTS: revenue weighted TFP MC QADJ: marginal cost weighted TFP adjusted for changes in quality of capital			

To inform the regulatory process, a first-stage investigation of these differences would be to separate TFP growth into components due to economies of scale, economies of scope, modernization of equipment, and the residual contribution of factors not included in the model. Economies of scale have two components in telecommunications: economies of density, associated with increasing density of traffic on a given network, and economies of size, associated with expansion of the network. Preliminary realization of this agenda can be based on the empirical model whose results are discussed here. However, TFP differences signal differences in unit cost reduction. The economic logic of the Laffont-Tirole framework, as well as common sense, suggest that differences in management practice and in regulatory oversight may account for part of the differing productivity performance records of the LECs. Deeper studies of these issues as comparative cases might also improve the information base for regulatory authorities.

Also significant from a regulatory perspective is that TFP, when measured properly using marginal cost weights, rises at an average annual rate of 2.3% for all LECs in both time periods. Revenue-weighted TFP, however, rises at an annual rate of 6.2% for all LECs. The reason for this result is that revenues overvalue access services (compared to the marginal cost of access services), and the growth there artificially inflates measured growth of aggregate output. The marginal cost-weighted TFP performance is only about 1.3% better than (properly measured) TFP growth in the aggregate United States private business sector. Productivity offsets in current incentive plans for the LECs are based on revenue-weighted measures of TFP and thus are higher than would result from marginal cost-based TFP. This difference in measurement method is important for consistent regulation because competition, actual and potential, as well as future technological advance, are likely to bring revenues closer to proportionality with marginal costs. This will have the effect of bringing revenue-based TFP closer to marginal cost-based measures, which in turn will make revenue-weighted TFP targets less achievable. To implement such targets could lead to the necessity for renegotiating rates allowed under incentive plans or scrapping incentive regulation altogether. While this unanticipated stringency may serve initially to wring some of the fat out of the LECs, the longer-term prospect is for an uncertain regulatory environment, and hence ineffective regulation.

5. Conclusions

The prospect for using properly measured TFP directly in price-cap regulation of the LECs depends upon many factors. Revenue-weighted TFP levels and growth rates are quite far from the corresponding marginal cost-based measures that are called for by economic theory. It is clear that conventional indices of asset prices understate the growth in quality of capital equipment. The shortcomings of GDP-based benchmarks for productivity growth are discussed in Norsworthy et al. (1993). Application of the present PCI formula may reduce service quality, increase moral hazard in reporting and auditing, and set off a flurry of pleas for rate adjustment at state and regional regulatory authorities. However, it is also clear that properly measured TFP, if based on audited cost data, can reduce uncertainty about comparative performances of the LECs and RBOCs in terms of levels and growth of TFP. Moreover, it can narrow the uncertainty in the formulation of an effective menu of price-cap targets. The marginal cost-based TFP measures are reliably associated with total cost per access line, more so than the revenue weighted measures. However, it must be acknowledged that cost models are sensitive to specification changes.

The LECs have opportunities for their exercise of monopoly power to the disadvantage of customers and competitors, and they may be expected to use asymmetric information concerning production costs and technology to their advantage. Recent selections of X-Factors by the RBOCs surprised many ob-servers, including possibly the regulatory staff at the FCC. Most (five of seven) RBOCs chose the highest target growth rates (5.3 percent per year) in order to be permitted to retain excess earnings that would have been capped or shared if lower targets were chosen. This general pattern of surprise is a strong indicator of asymmetric information. It is also evidence the price-cap approach is successful, in that it induces the RBOCs to reveal part of the cost information through their choices of the X-Factor—the target rates of efficiency improvement. Both logic and the empirical evidence on markups over marginal cost assert the new locus of monopoly power in telecommunications: the local area network. In a mixed competitive environment—one that permits the LECs to compete in provision of some services while enjoying monopoly in others, the LECs can and do exploit this power. The mere *threat* of competition will do little to diminish exercise of this power because it derives from the expensive-to-duplicate fixed capital linking relatively low intensity users to the entire range of telecommunications services. Competition will focus at the other end of the spectrum: the high intensity users, where there are economically feasible technological alternatives to conventional wire and cable connections. In the near term, the effective subsidy of unregulated service by regulated service seems unavoidable, as does predatory pricing of access services by the LECs. This perception of the motivation of the regulated enterprise underlies incentive regulation. The fact is that price-cap regulation, while it eliminates some incentives to distort the competitive result, creates some new ones and reinforces others. An important source of distortion is introduced when the LECs are permitted to pursue both regulated and unregulated business under the same corporate umbrella. If a separation is not enforced, there are strong incentives for the LECs to exercise their monopoly power in several ways.

Appendix. Estimation Results of Empirical Cost Model for 11 Large LECs

The estimation results for the production revenue model for the large LECs are shown in tables A1-A7. The chief findings revealed in that table are (a) the relatively high explanatory power of the equations, (b) the substantial variations across LECs and the years before divestiture, and (c) the serial correlation revealed in the Durbin-Watson statistics.

The estimated model coefficients are shown in several groups to clarify the explanation of them. The first group is the structural coefficients of the model, of

Table A1. Parameters of Restricted Variable Cost Model: 11 LECs Common Parameters — All Equations			
Parameter Name	Estimated Value	Standard Error	t-statistic
AE	.373102	.023210	16.0750
AEM	-.041473	.013737	-3.01899
AM	.626898	.023210	27.0097
BA	.301837	.067388	4.47909
BL	.341740	.075780	4.50962
BT	.327427	.088682	3.69214
CS	.667870E-05	.045016	.148364E-03
CX	.859571E-03	.149952	.573232E-02
BEA	.088596	.023500	3.76997
BEL	.034121	.031589	1.08017
BET	-.063968	.026166	-2.44465
BES	-.058222	.028023	-2.07762
BEX	-.014634	.026349	-.555384
BAL	-.077820	.029273	-2.65840
BAT	.022294	.029742	.749583
BAS	-.047965	.014338	-3.34540
BAX	.151808	.025728	5.90050
BLT	-.080284	.026099	-3.07614
BLS	-.042619	.021556	-1.97709
BLX	-.041326	.024984	-1.65410
BTS	.012859	.018902	.680288
BTX	-.094473	.020750	-4.55297
BSX	.093038	.045431	2.04789
QXF	.039764	.351792	.113031
QSD	.304973	.140068	2.17733
QSO	-.049172	.847563E-02	-5.80163

which appear in two equations or more. The remaining groups are company and year shifts specific to particular equations—the cost function, the variable input demand equation, and the revenue equations associated with each output.

Gauged in terms its explanatory power, the model fits the data quite well. All equations exhibit R^2s of .90 or better. Serial correlation among equation residuals is relatively high, which could bias the estimated standard errors and hence t-statistics. However, the coefficient estimates themselves are not biased by serial correlation in the residuals. Consequently, these coefficients, and the quantities inferred from them—total factor productivity, marginal costs, elasticities of substitution, capital quality, etc.—are unbiased. As a result, the levels and differences among these inferred quantities are not biased, although the statistical significance of the differences cannot be reliably determined.

The company fixed effects in the cost function—the c_u coefficients—are mixed in sign, showing otherwise unexplained variation in costs. These shifts are all measured against Mountain Telephone (MT). The model shows generally higher variable costs for New York Telephone than other companies, even after adjustment for differences in output levels and the service network, differences in switching and transmission capital, and differences in the use of labor and materials.

A.1. The Structural Coefficients

The structural coefficients of the model represent average characteristics across all LECs. The a_e coefficient is the average cost share of employment across all LECs for all time periods: about 37 percent of variable costs are employment costs, and 63 percent are therefore materials" costs—i.e., the cost of other purchased inputs. *AEM* is the parameter governing substitution between employment and materials, the low value indicates weak substitutability.

The *BA*, *BL*, and *BT* coefficients are the cost elasticities weights of the outputs: local service has the largest component of variable cost, .342. The service network has a component of .302. The cost elasticity of toll service is .327. The coefficients *CS* and *CX* measure the contribution of capital to the reduction of variable costs. These coefficients are quite small and not significantly different from zero. This is not surprising for two reasons. First, except in the case of substantial underinvestment when capital severely constrains production—here, the delivery of telecommunication services—the restricted variable cost function (RVCF) model may fail to capture what is primarily a peak-load rather than average load constraint. Second, there is the well-known (though less widely documented empirically) Averch-Johnson (1962) effect—the tendency for rate-of-return regulated enterprises to over-invest in capital assets. Some of our current work (Norsworthy and Tsai 1994) suggests that dynamic models of production capture the capital effect much better than the static RVCF model. (It is doubtful that changing the specification of capital quality would affect the result substantially, because a number of different specifications were tested, and yielded similarly low estimates of *CS* and *CX*.)

The remaining second-order coefficients relate input to outputs (*BEA*, *BEL*, *BET*); outputs to each other (*BAL*, *BAT*, *BLT*); inputs and outputs to capital inputs (*BES*, *BAS*, *BAX*, *BLS*, *BLX*, *BTS*, *BTX*); and capital inputs to each other (*CSX*). The employment coefficients and materials coefficients have equal magnitudes (and equal standard errors) and opposite signs, from the homogeneity conditions. The second-order materials coefficients are thus not shown. Similarly, the second-order square coefficients (*BAA*, *BLL*, etc.) for outputs and capital inputs are determined via restrictions from other coefficients in the model. The *BEA* coefficient is positive and indicates that increases in the service network and in local usage generate relatively more requirements for labor than for materials. Increasing toll traffic has a negative effect on the employment-materials mix (*BET* is negative). The positive value of *BES* indicates that additions to switching capital generate a relatively greater employment requirement.

The *BAL* coefficient is negative, which indicates (minor) economies of scope between network maintenance and local usage. That is, as the network and local usage expand together, costs rise less than proportionately. A one-percent increase both in the number of access lines in service network and in local traffic results in a .977 percent increase in variable costs. Network and toll services show diseconomies of scope, since *BAT* is positive. The effect is about twice that of the diseconomies between network and local traffic. The negative coefficient *BAS* shows economies from increasing the number of access lines compared with the number of central office switches. This effect may derive from the fact that recently-installed central office switches serve a larger number of access lines than earlier models. The coefficient *BAX* is positive, meaning that increases in the number of access lines generates a slightly-less-than-proportional increase in required interoffice transmission capacity. This effect probably reflects the fact that the installation of access lines was contemporary with installation of new interoffice fiber cabling. The capacity of the fiber cable is of course greater than the copper cabling it replaces.

Local and toll traffic show rather strong economies of scope—*BLT* is -0.08—which is hardly surprising since they share the same local network. Local traffic expansion requires a much less than proportional increase in switching capacity (*BLS* in negative) and a more than proportionate increase in interoffice transmission capacity (*BLX* is positive). Increasing toll traffic has opposite effects from local traffic on capital requirements. Finally, expansion of switching capacity is accompanied by less than proportional added requirements for interoffice transmission capacity (*BSX* is .831).

The quality adjustment coefficients for capital show the increase in effective capital input of increasing the proportion of fiber in total interoffice cable miles (*QXF*), increasing the proportion of digital central office switches, and decreasing the proportion of non-electronic (other) switches (*QSO*). Thus, increasing fiber optic interoffice cable miles by one percent leads to a very small percent increase in effective interoffice transmission capacity. This unexpected effect may result from the fact that interoffice cable capacity is not binding, i.e., does not affect the capacity to produce output. The coefficients measuring quality change in switching equipment conform more closely to expectations: digital electronic switches are about 30 percent more effective than analog electronic switches (*QSD*). The base case is omitted from the quality adjustment expression to avoid linear dependence of the switch technology indication. The coefficient for other switches, *QSO*, is negative, indicating lower performance than analog and digital switches.

These quality adjustment factors for the capital input are determined not only from the direct role of capital in cost reduction measured by the *CS* and *CX* coefficients (which, as we noted, are near zero) but also from interaction with each of the variable inputs and each of the outputs. The capital quality adjustment terms for each type of capital appear in each equation, and thus we expect the coefficients to be reasonably well identified. It should be noted that all of the coefficients in this first table are the averages for all LECs for all years, after adjustment for company- and year-specific effects.

A.2. The Cost Function

Table A.2 shows the coefficients specific to the cost function, and the statistics associated with the equation estimation. The intercept coefficient, *A0*, represents

Table A2. Parameters of Restricted Variable Cost Model: 11 LECs Cost Function			
Parameter Name	Estimated Value	Standard Error	t-statistic
A0	3.45941	.059246	58.3909
C81	.091411	.059414	1.53853
C82	.116768	.054489	2.14297
C83	.016042	.044110	.363678
C85	-.124300	.038773	-3.20587
C86	-.146526	.039874	-3.67472
C87	-.165796	.042279	-3.92144
C88	-.061815	.047402	-1.30406
C89	-.065591	.052205	-1.25642
C90	-.125439	.053949	-2.32515
CIL	-.132485	.116869	-1.13362
CNJ	-.346223	.189375	-1.82824
CMI	-.166591	.062588	-2.66170
CNE	.044962	.061812	.727405
CPC	-.018691	.068556	-.272635
CPN	-.182718	.106052	-1.72291
CSC	.104704	.074180	1.41149
CSO	.018798	.042931	.437873
CSW	.903060E-02	.081132	.111307
CNY	.408228	.092476	4.41444
Mean of dependent variable = 3.33241			
Std. dev. of dependent var. = .463610			
Sum of squared residuals = 1.47858			
Variance of residuals = .013442			
Std. error of regression = .115938			
R-squared = .942174			
Durbin-Watson statistic = .268468			

the log of variable cost for Mountain Telephone in 1984; other C coefficients are shifts from this base value after adjustment for those factors included in the model. Note, however, that these costs exclude depreciation and other fixed costs associated with capital. Total factor productivity (the level, not the growth rate) is a better measure of efficiency than variable cost. Hence, for example, C81 with a value of .0914 denotes an average shift for all LECs of that amount from the base value in 1984. The value of -.1325 for CIL means that the log of average variable cost for Illinois Bell is .1325 lower than for Mountain Telephone. In general, costs fall sharply during the first three years, than are flat from 1984 to 1987 (but below 1990), rise in 1988, and decline thereafter. The rise in 1988 may also indicate that some accounting changes have not been detected. The company shift coefficients show that the other large LECs have lower variable costs of production than New

Parameter Name	Estimated Value	Standard Error	t-statistic
Table A3. Parameters of Restricted Variable Cost Model: 11 LECs Employment Demand Function			
EIL	1.77150	.582262	3.04244
EMI	1.12884	.438244	2.57582
ENE	.842292	.437443	1.92549
EPC	2.26627	.952716	2.37875
EPN	.483221	.485731	.994832
ESC	.285690	.560044	.510120
ESO	1.04817	.711436	1.47332
ESW	.999269	.796589	1.25443
ENJ	2.72074	.599895	4.53536
ENY	-.625888	.969656	-.645474
E81	1.33148	.609702	2.18382
E82	.380847	.571109	.666855
E83	.905335E-02	.472354	.019166
E85	-.409654	.391876	-1.04537
E86	-.621548	.393007	-1.58152
E87	-.434914	.403337	-1.07829
E88	-1.93047	.446578	-4.32282
E89	-2.06039	.480352	-4.28933
E90	-1.48801	.498470	-2.98515
Mean of dependent variable = 13.7618			
Std. dev. of dependent var. = 7.23465			
Sum of squared residuals = 141.977			
Variance of residuals = 1.29070			
Std. error of regression = 1.13609			
R-squared = .976260			
Durbin-Watson statistic = .588992			

York Telephone; the New York Telephone shift coefficient is the largest, with a value of .4082.

A.3. Input Demand Equations

The equation statistics for the cost function show very good fits and evidence of serial correlation. Tables A.3 and A.4 shows the coefficients specific to the employment and materials demand functions. Company shift results are especially interesting: most LECs—the exceptions are South Central and Southwestern Bell—have substantially larger demand for labor when other factors are accounted for. Table A.4 shows that exactly the reverse is true for "materials"—i.e., other purchased inputs. So it is a materials-for-labor trade-off that we observe. This may reflect the somewhat higher than average wage rate at New York Telephone, but the difference seems to be larger than the small measured substitution effect would bring about. The fact that we are using the same material price index for all LECs

Table A4. Parameters of Restricted Variable Cost Model: 11 LECs Materials Demand Function			
Parameter Name	Estimated Value	Standard Error	t-statistic
MIL	-.598724	.699053	-.856478
MMI	-.834134	.563911	-1.47919
MNE	.054893	.572683	.095853
MNJ	-2.67364	.732182	-3.65161
MPC	-2.38248	1.05909	-2.24956
MPN	.733347	.604385	1.21338
MSC	1.11818	.662163	1.68868
MSO	-1.09282	.751373	-1.45443
MSW	-1.16121	.868767	-1.33662
MNY	3.92314	1.09329	3.58837
M81	-2.05246	.695122	-2.95266
M82	-1.09077	.686553	-1.58876
M83	-.946901	.649421	-1.45807
M85	-.664018	.523407	-1.26865
M86	-.278157	.520648	-.534252
M87	-.253761	.529148	-.479565
M88	1.59593	.559782	2.85099
M89	2.02451	.588840	3.43813
M90	1.22827	.612001	2.00698
Mean of dependent variable = 16.6409			
Std. dev. of dependent var. = 7.99131			
Sum of squared residuals = 292.043			
Variance of residuals = 2.65494			
Std. error of regression = 1.62940			
R-squared = .965449			
Durbin-Watson statistic = .403497			

may partially explain this finding, but probably not all the substantial shift that we observe.

Through time, employment declines, particularly in the early years, and material usage increases, although the pattern seems to be reversed for 1988 and 1989. The equation statistics show considerable evidence of serial correlation and an extremely good fit for the materials equation. The model explains almost 97 percent of the variation in materials input when year and company effects are taken into account. This result gives us more confidence about using the common materials price index. The fit of the employment equation is almost as good. However, it was not possible to adjust employment and the corresponding wage bill for capitalized labor.

A.4. Revenue Equations

Coefficients and equation statistics for the revenue equations are shown in tables

Table A5. Parameters of Restricted Variable Cost Model: 11 LECs Local Revenue Equation			
Parameter Name	Estimated Value	Standard Error	t-statistic
H1	.088850	2.32635	.038193
G1	.838296	.081139	10.3316
G1IL	-.073928	.089839	-.822890
G1MI	-.074508	.095431	-.780756
G1NE	-.233440	.071606	-3.26006
G1NJ	-.237680	.112800	-2.10709
G1PC	-.428992	.064012	-6.70174
G1PN	-.158193	.094146	-1.68029
G1SC	-.373121	.063141	-5.90936
G1SO	-.194108	.060949	-3.18478
G1SW	-.279791	.064319	-4.35005
G1NY	-.139599	.069380	-2.01210
G181	.148814	.061259	2.42926
G182	.148356	.056772	2.61321
G183	.075218	.049860	1.50859
G185	.127755	.052650	2.42649
G186	.133292	.050868	2.62032
G187	.151911	.052891	2.87216
G188	.197822	.062195	3.18069
G189	.307222	.070540	4.35529
G190	.469053	.083283	5.63206
Mean of dependent variable = 20.7505			
Std. dev. of dependent var. = 9.92519			
Sum of squared residuals = 439.542			
Variance of residuals = 3.99584			
Std. error of regression = 1.99896			
R-squared = .959459			
Durbin-Watson statistic = .197742			

A.5 and A.6. These equations are particularly interesting because they make it possible to associate contributions to the gross return to the LECs with local and toll revenues and access charges and to compare these patterns across LECs. The parameters G_1 and G_2 capture these effects, with company and year offsets captured in the shift parameters—G_{1t}, G_{2t} for year effects and G_{1u}, G_{2u} for company effects in the local and toll equations. Adding up constraints on the gross return relating to total revenue, determine the G coefficients of the access revenue equation:

$$G_3 = 1 - G_1 - G_2$$

$$G_{3t} = G_{1t} - G_{2t}$$

Table A6. Parameters of Restricted Variable Cost Model: 11 LECs Toll Revenue Equation			
Parameter Name	Estimated Value	Standard Error	t-statistic
G2IL	-.118095	.097767	-1.20793
G2MI	.368585	.098038	3.75963
G2NE	.257522	.076941	3.34701
G2NJ	.167159	.127527	1.31078
G2PC	.438457	.067083	6.53601
G2PN	.049110	.102599	.478656
G2SC	.273969	.062168	4.40690
G2SO	.118855	.061675	1.92713
G2SW	.271347	.063736	4.25735
G2NY	-.244286	.068019	-3.59141
G281	1.04324	.070364	14.8265
G282	1.09930	.066636	16.4971
G283	1.13607	.061984	18.3284
G285	-.186164	.049499	-3.76096
G286	-.208369	.049566	-4.20384
G287	-.207110	.051060	-4.05622
G288	-.344819	.062370	-5.52864
G289	-.523234	.073802	-7.08968
G290	-.641443	.085995	-7.45907
Mean of dependent variable = 11.4861			
Std. dev. of dependent var. = 9.47446			
Sum of squared residuals = 383.535			
Variance of residuals = 3.48668			
Std. error of regression = 1.86727			
R-squared = .960988			
Durbin-Watson statistic = .640743			

Table A7. Parameters of Restricted Variable Cost Model: 11 LECs Access Revenue Equation			
Parameter Name	Estimated Value	Standard Error	t-statistic
H2	1.21281	2.49316	.486453
G2	-.081529	.090776	-.898129
Mean of dependent variable = 9.91949			
Std. dev. of dependent var. = 9.02192			
Sum of squared residuals = 414.494			
Variance of residuals = 3.76813			
Std. error of regression = 1.94117			
R-squared = .953668			
Durbin-Watson statistic = .319336			

$$G_{3u} = G_{1u} - G_{2u} \ .$$

The coefficient G_1 indicates that Mountain Telephone derived about 70% of its gross return G—total revenue less operating expenses, thus the gross return includes depreciation costs—from local revenues in 1990. Of the remaining gross return, about 20 percent came from toll charges and the balance from access charges. The other large LECs, with the exception of Illinois Bell, got considerably less gross return from local revenues and more from toll revenues.

The H parameters have the effect of distributing the correction for non-constant returns to scale. However, because the scale coefficient is quite close to 1, this coefficient plays a small role despite its size. As with G_3, the H_3 coefficient is determined by the adding up restriction:

$$H_3 = 1 - H_1 - H_2 \ .$$

References

Averch, H., and L.L. Johnson. 1962. "Behavior of the Firm Under Regulatory Constraint." *American Economic Review* 52:1052-1069.

Berndt, Ernst R., and Melvyn A. Fuss. 1986. "Productivity Measurement With Adjustments for Variations in Capacity Utilization and Other Forms of Temporary Equilibrium." *Journal of Econometrics* 33:7-29.

Brautigan, R., and J. Panzer. 1989 "Diversification Incentives under Price-Based and Cost-Based Regulation." *Rand Journal of Economics* (autumn).

Brown, R.S., and L.R. Christensen. 1981 "Estimating Elasticities of Substitution in a Model of Partial Static Equilibrium: An Application to U.S. Agriculture 1947 to 1974." In *Modeling and Measuring Natural Resources Substitution*, edited by Ernest R. Berndt and Barry Field.

Christensen, L.R. (USTA, U.S. Telephone Association). 1995. "Letter To: FCC, Federal Communications Commission." Feb 1.

Christensen, L. R., Schoech, P. E., and Meitzen, M. E. 1994. "Attachment 6. Productivity of the Local Telephone Operating Companies Subject to Price Cap Regulation. USTA, U. S. Telephone Association." FCC Docket 94-1, USTA Comments.

Christensen, L.R., D.C. Christensen, and P.E. Schoech. 1983 "Econometric Estimation of Scale Economies in Telecommunications." In *Econometric Analysis of Telecommunications*, edited by L. Courville, A. de Fontenay and R. Dobell. North-Holland.

Denny, M., and M.A. Fuss. 1983. "General Approach to Intertemporal and Interspatial Productivity Comparisons." *Journal of Econometrics* 23:315-330.

Duncan, G.M. 1990. "Measuring Capacity, Marginal Cost, and Firm Specific Total Productivity Changes From a Panel of Firms Facing Random Demand and Heterogeneous Technical Change." GTE Laboratories.

Federal Communications Commission. 1997. Order 97-159. Fourth Report and Order in CC Docket No. 94-1, Price Cap Performance Review for Local Exchange Carriers, CC Docket No. 94-1 and Second Report and Order in CC Docket no. 96-262, Access Charge Reform. Adopted: May 7; Released: May 21.

Federal Communications Commission. 1994. "Price Cap Performance Review for Local Exchange Carriers; First Report and Order." Washington, D.C.: FCC, Federal Communications Commission. CC Docket No. 94-1, FCC 95-132.

Federal Communications Commission. 1995 "Price Cap Performance Review for Local Exchange Carriers; Fourth Further Notice of Proposed Rulemaking." Washington, D.C.: FCC, Federal Communications Commission. CC Docket 94-1, FCC 95-395.

Federal Communications Commissions. 1993. "Industry Analysis Division. Trends in Telephone Service." Washington, D.C.

Federal-State Joint Board. 1993. "Monitoring Report." FCC Docket No. 87-339.

Fisher, F.M., and K. Shell. 1972. *The Economic Theory of Price Indexes*. New York: Academic Press.

Fuss, Melvyn, and Leonard Waverman. 1993. "Efficiency Principles for Telecommunications Pricing: Fairness for All." The National Conference on the Future of Telecommunications Policy in Canada, Toronto, Ontario.

Gordon, R.J. 1990. *The Measurement of Durable Goods Prices*. Chicago: Chicago University Press.

Harper, M.J., Ernst R. Berndt, and David O. Wood. 1989. "Rates of Return and Capital Aggregation Using Alternative Rental Prices." In *Technology and Capital Formation*, edited by Dale W. Jorgenson and Ralph Landau, pages 331-372. Cambridge, MA: MIT Press.

Hulten, Charles R., and Frank C. Wykoff. 1981. "The Measurement of Economic Depreciation." In *Depreciation, Inflation, and the Taxation of Income Capital*, edited by Charles R. Hulten and Frank C. Wykoff, pages 81-132. The Urban Institute.

Jorgenson, Dale W. and Yun, Kun-Young. 1991. *Tax Reform and the Cost of Capital*. New York: Oxford University Press.

Kraushaar, J. 1991. *Report on Quality of Service for the Bell Operating Companies*. Federal Communications Commission. July.

Kraushaar, J. 1990. *Fiber Deployment Update*. Industry Analysis Division Common Carrier Bureau. Federal Communication Commission.

Kwoka, J.E., Jr. 1991. "Productivity and Price Caps in Telecommunications." In *Price Caps and Incentive Regulation in Telecommunications*, edited by Michael A. Einhorn. Kluwer Academic Publishers.

Laffont, J.-J., and J. Tirole. 1993. *A Theory of Incentives in Procurement and Regulation*. MIT Press.

MacDonald, James C., John R. Norsworthy, and Cecile W. Fu 1994. "Incentive Regulation in Telecommunications: Why States Don't Choose Price Caps." In *Incentive Regulation of Industry*, edited by Michael Crew. Kluwer Academic Publishers.

Nadiri, M.I., and M. Schankerman. 1981. "The Structure of Production, Technological Change, and the Rate of Growth of Total Factor Productivity in the U.S. Bell System." In *Productivity Measurement in Regulated Industries*, edited by T.G. Cowing and R.E. Stevenson. Academic Press.

Nadiri, M.I. 1996. "The Measurement of Productivity Growth for Interstate Access Services," Appendix C in Reply Comments of AT&T, CC Docket 94-1, 4th Further Notice of Proposed Rulemaking.

National Economic Research Associates 1994. "Economic Performance of the LEC Price Cap Plan." USTA Comments Attachment 5, FCC Docket 94-1, 4th Further Notice of Proposed Rulemaking.

NERA-National Economic Research Associates. 1994. *Historical Productivity Growth In The U.S. Telecommunications Industry*. White Plains, NY: NERA (National Economic Research Associates).

Noam, E. 1990. "The Quality of Regulation in Regulating Quality: A Proposal for an Integrated Incentive Approach to Telephone Service Performance." In *Price Caps and Incentive Regulation in Telecommunications*, edited by M.A. Einhorn. Boston: Kluwer Academic Publishers.

Norsworthy, John R. 1996. "Analysis of Total Factor Productivity Methods for Measuring the X-Factor of the Local Exchange Carriers' Interstate Access Services," Appendix A in *Comments of AT&T, Docket CC 94-1, Price Cap Performance Review of Local Exchange Carriers,* January 11.

Norsworthy, John R. 1996. "Responses to Issues for Comment." Appendix B in *Comments of AT&T, Docket CC 94-1, Price Cap Performance Review of Local Exchange Carriers,* January 11.

Norsworthy, John R., and Ernst R. Berndt. 1996 "Response to Comments of Local Exchange Carriers on Methods for Measuring the X-Factor for Their Interstate Access Services." Appendix B in Reply Comments of AT&T, CC Docket 94-1, 4th Further Notice of Proposed Rulemaking, March.

Norsworthy, John R., and S.L. Jang. 1992. *Empirical Measurement and Analysis of Productivity and Technological Change: Applications in High Technology and Service Industries.* North-Holland.

Norsworthy, John R., S.L. Jang, James C. MacDonald, Diana H. Tsai, Cecile Fu, and Yi Jing. 1993. "Measurement of Productivity and Marginal Costs for Incentive Regulation of Telecommunication Services." Troy, NY: Center for Science & Technology Policy: Rensselaer Polytechnic Institute.

Norsworthy, John R., and Diana H. Tsai. 1994. "Internal Adjustment Costs in a Short/Long Run Model of Production: A Dynamic Model of U.S. Manufacturing." Presented at the Annual Conference of Canadian Economic Association, Calgary, Alberta, June.

Norsworthy, John R., and Diana H. Tsai. 1998. *Macroeconomic Policy as Implicit Industrial Policy: Its Industry and Enterprise Effects.* Kluwer Academic Publishers.

Shin, Richard, and John Ying. 1992. "Unnatural Monopolies in Local Telephone." *Rand Journal of Economics* 171-183.

Shin, Richard, and John Ying. 1993 "Costly Gains to Breaking Up: LECs and the Baby Bells." *Review of Economics and Statistics* 357-361.

Spavins, D.T., and J. Lande. 1990. "FCC-Industry Analysis Div. Supplemental Notice of Proposed Rulemaking." Filed as Appendix: *"Total Telephone Productivity in the Pre and Post-Divestiture Periods."* Washington, DC: Federal Communications Commission.

Taylor, William E., Study Director. 1992. *An Assessment of the Draft New York Telephone Company Potential Performance Gains Study.* Cambridge, MA: National Economic Research Associates.

Triplett, Jack E. 1989. "Price and Technological Change in a Capital Good: A Survey of Research on Computers." In *Technology and Capital Formation,* edited by Dale W. Jorgenson and Ralph Landau. Cambridge, MA: MIT Press.

Tsai, Diana H., and John R. Norsworthy. 1996. "Measuring the Effects of Macroeconomic Policy in Industry Econometric Models: Toward Assessment of Industrial Policy." *Journal of Policy Modeling* 18(3): 289-333.

Walker, K.L. 1990. "Directions in Optical Fibers." *AT&T Technical Journal* 11-12.

8

COMPUTABLE GENERAL EQUILIBRIUM MODELS AND ELECTRICITY CO$_2$ EMISSIONS[1]

Yoonyoung Kang
Menahem Spiegel

1. Introduction

In recent years, there has been growing concern that the likelihood of significant global warming by the middle of the next century is linked to increasing human activities. This increase in human activity is expected to affect the global climate change through growing atmospheric concentration of greenhouse gases (GHGs).[2] The Intergovernmental Panel on Climate Change (IPCC) estimates that, at the current rate of increase of GHGs, the mean global temperature will rise at a rate of about 0.3°C per decade. Such a rise in temperature, i.e., global warming, could have serious impacts on economic activity and society at different localities. As a result, an increasing number of policy makers have begun to consider various methods of slowing global warming by curbing the emissions of GHGs. Most consideration has been given to human-made emissions of CO$_2$ which results mainly (about 75%) from the burning of fossil fuels. The phasing out of the CFCs under the Montreal Protocol and current uncertainty about the source and the controllability of methane have diverted most policy considerations to the need to curb human-made CO$_2$ emissions. Therefore, controlling (reducing) CO$_2$ emissions has become the subject of many UN-organized conferences and conventions. The least-cost implementation policy has become a central research objective.

The models most often used to estimate the economy-at-large (macroeconomic)

---

1   Comments and suggestions made by Michael Crew and Linda Brennan on an earlier version of this paper are gratefully acknowledged. The paper benefited from the presentation at the Research Seminar on October 24, 1997.

2   The main greenhouse gases are carbon dioxide (CO$_2$), methane, chlorofluorocarbons (CFCs), and nitrous oxide.

expected cost of controlling the rate of CO_2 emissions belong to the basic group of the Computable General Equilibrium model (CGE). In general, the CGE models provide a reliable analytic tool to estimate the macroeconomic effects of microeconomic changes. This model is extremely valuable for analyzing situations where the output and commodity prices of a large number of industries are affected. Most often CGE models are used in policy analysis. Where they provide a framework to evaluate the impact and cost of implementing different policies. Although the early uses of CGE models were in the field of environmental policy analysis, more recently, the CGE models have been widely used in many different occasions and in many varied fields of economics and business.[3]

There are two main objectives for this paper. The first, to provide an overview of the basic characteristics of the Computable General Equilibrium model (CGE). The second, to present examples of the traditional use of the CGE model for analyzing the impact of environmental regulation in general and its implications for the electric utility industry in particular.

As an analytical instrument, the basic and most useful objective of the Computable General Equilibrium (CGE) model is to provide a framework for analyzing major policy changes which are expected to affect a large number of interconnected industries or the economy as a whole. The CGE model is extremely useful in analyzing the macro effects, and therefore it is widely used in cases where a change in policy is not of limited and isolated impact but where the quantities and the prices of a large number of commodities are affected. CGE models are especially effective when industries are interconnected. Such interconnection among the different industries arises when they all use the same (affected) input or a substitute of the affected input. Similar interconnection arises when the different industries sell their output in the same (affected) markets.

Environmental policy and regulations in general and air regulation in particular serve as a good example of the interconnectivity discussed above. In particular, air regulation, which implies controlling certain byproducts of the production process, might affect many industries using similar technology (e.g., internal combustion) or using similar input (sulfur-rich coal.) A variety of recent environmental regulations on air, water, and solid waste disposal come to mind.

The main concern of Mr. Yoonyoung Kang in his dissertation entitled: "CO_2, Energy and Economy Interaction; A Multi-Sectoral, Dynamic, Computable General Equilibrium Model for Korea"[4] (hereafter Kang (1997)) was to analyze the expected economic impact of the Korean environmental regulation. This was done by the application of CGE models and simulating the long-term growth of the Korean economy with and without the regulation.

---

3   For recent applications of the CGE model, see Waters et al. (1997) for tax applications. For
     international trade applications, see Kildegaard (1996.) For public economics applications, see
     Nechyba (1996.) For regional science applications, see Hoffmann et al. (1996.) For monetary
     economic applications, see Altig et al. (1995.)
4   This study, Kang (1997), is the most important source for this paper, and it is frequently cited
     here for illustrations.

In his study, Kang (1997) explores and estimav the national economic cost, in terms of lost Gross Domestic Product (GDP), to the Korean economy stemming from the attempt to control CO_2 emissions.[5] Using the CGE model, Kang (1997) analyzes a set of different policy instruments that might be useful. Since combustion is an important source of CO_2 emissions, policies intended to reduce emissions will usually result in higher energy prices. Several policies were assumed to take place in order to achieve the same emission objective and to compare the outcomes of their deployment. The alternative policy instruments which were analyzed in Kang (1997) are: a) Carbon tax, b) Energy tax, c) Ad valorem tax, and d) Emissions standard.

Using the CGE model, the experiments simulate the impact of CO_2 control policy on main macroeconomic variables and economic growth, sectoral allocation of production, and the effect on energy market. For analysis and comprehensive assessment of the effects of environmental regulations, interaction among industries must be scrutinized. To estimate the national cost requires a complete specification of supply and demand relationships of all the affected industries, as well as a detailed representation of many other aspects which were affected directly or indirectly. The major empirical finding of Kang (1997) is that the most cost-effective policy instrument that can be used to achieve the policy objective is the appropriate Carbon Tax.

2. An Overview of the Computable General Equilibrium (CGE) Model

The important advantage of using the CGE model is that it brings together the interactive economic behavior and decision making of many (independent) economic agents who operate in many interrelated markets. The economic decision makers are grouped into the following four sectors (or groups) of (similar) agents: the producers, the consumers, the government, and the foreign sector.

The economic behavior of the participant in each sector is described in detail below. Since homogeneity of agent within a group is assumed, in many instances references below are made to the representative agent. The aggregate decision of these agents is reflected in determining the market prices and quantities of goods and services and in the relevant factor market.

The current model used has a recursive dynamic in which saving decisions in one period affect future economic outcomes through the accumulation of productive capital. The model is simulated over the 1990-2010 period and is calibrated on exogenous growth rate of population and on neutral technical progress in energy use. Given the recursive structure of the model, evolution over time can be described as a sequence of single-period static temporary equilibria.

---

5   Although possible, CGE models have not been used to evaluate the benefit of environmental regulation. The literature and research work reviewed here are mainly estimates of cost side only. Therefore, the discussion is limited to quantifying costs of different regulation while disregarding their potential benefit.

2.1. The Producers

Producers' decisions and activity are assumed to derive from the objective of profit maximization. Since the impact of the environmental regulation might differ substantially across industries, producers are divided into industry groups. Most often this division is done according to the two-digit Standard Industrial Classification (SIC).[6] Producers in each industry are assumed to produce a single homogeneous product. The output produced by the industry is sold to final consumers, to other industries where it is used as an input, and to the foreign market.

In each sector, the single output is produced using capital, labor, intermediate goods and services, and energy inputs (coal, oil, gas, and electricity). It is generally assumed that the inputs used are purchased in a competitive market at a unique market clearing price. At any given period, the total supply of primary inputs (capital and labor) are usually predetermined by activity of the previous period. For tractability, a linear production technology (constant return to scale technology) is employed. The quantities of inputs demanded are selected by producers through a process of cost minimization given the sector's output demand and the relative prices.

With constant returns to scale production technology, the derived competitive market supply functions are perfectly elastic at unit cost. The constant unit cost (or output price) is a function of the input prices: price of capital, price of labor, price of energy, and prices of other raw materials. With a constant output price, the quantity of output traded is determined by the demand (and the competitive profit is zero). In the general equilibrium framework, since each sector supplies its output to final consumption and as inputs to other sectors, output prices—which are the cost of input for other sectors—and the optimal combination of inputs must be determined simultaneously in all sectors.

The total demand for the primary inputs labor and capital originates from the producers. The amount of capital supplied to the capital services transaction market is determined by the net capital stock that is transferred from the previous year. This stock of capital depends on last year's investment (saving) and the fixed capital depreciation rate. It is generally assumed that capital is a homogenous factor and that all demanders use the same capital market. Therefore, capital input is assumed to be perfectly mobile across sectors. As a result, the rental rates of capital will be the same across sectors. The sum of capital rental payment is the household capital income.

2.2. The Consumers' Demand for Final Goods

Households' behavior is assumed to derive from maximizing their utility functions given the goods' prices and their budget constraints. For the sake of simplicity, it assumed that all households are identical, so only the representative household will be considered. For clarity, the household consumption decision making can be

---

6   Jorgenson and Wilcoxen (1993b) consider a desegregated model of 35 industries, while Kang (1997) considers only 18 industries corresponding to the two-digit Standard Industrial Classification of Korea.

viewed as a multistage process. At the first stage, the household allocates its budget between consumption goods and saving (investment) goods. At the second stage, the household allocates its consumption expenditures among the different consumption goods. At the next stage, the household decides for each good how much to consume out of domestically produced output and how much consume from imports.

Household income is generated from labor and from non-labor income. The periodical income is generated by the sale of its endowed capital and labor inputs in the labor and in the capital markets. The household, through the financial market, also receives/pays interest from/to foreign consumers on its international investments/borrowing. The existence of active government also implies that the household's disposable income is the sum of incomes from all sources minus income taxes paid on capital and labor (possibly at different rates.)

2.3. The Government

The government is an important participant in modern economies. The government, on the one hand, is a demander in the markets for final good. On the other hand, the government spends part of its resources on transfer (lump-sum) payments to households. The main source of resources is from taxes. The government levies taxes of the following kinds: environmental taxes, labor income taxes, capital income taxes, indirect taxes on domestically-produced goods, and tariffs (of different rates) on imported goods. In the general equilibrium framework, tax revenues are endogenous in the model as they depend on the economic activity.

On the expenditure side of the government budget, there are two main items: lump-sum transfer payments made by the government to households and government purchases of goods and services. As the goods purchased by the government can be goods which are domestically produced or imported, in this model we must allocate the government expenditures of each product to these two sources. This allocation of government expenditures between domestic goods and imported goods is done according to a log-linear utility function. In this model, the government might run a budget deficit, a surplus, or a balanced budget. It is most common to assume that the government deficit as a fraction of total budget is fixed in real terms at the first (benchmark) year value. More difficult is the question of what should be done with the revenue of the environmental tax. The two possible treatments of the environmental tax are:

1. all the revenue is redistributed as transfers;
2. the revenue is part of general revenue, not transfers.

2.4. The Foreign Sector

In the foreign trade sector, there are two important components: imports (foreign supply of goods) and exports (foreign demand for domestic goods). Imposing the modified small-country assumptions implies that the import supply curve and export demand curve are perfectly elastic at their respective world prices. That is, any amount of any good can be bought or sold at its exogenous given world price measured in foreign currency. Therefore, the quantities of the imported goods are determined by the domestic demand, which depends on the relative prices of imported and domestic products.

It is common to use the Armington (1969) approach which assumes that imported products are an imperfect substitute for similar domestic commodities. Exported goods and domestically-consumed goods are treated as perfect substitutes. Thus, a country can import and export the same good at the same time. The exchange rate is assumed to be related to government policy (managed exchange rate, i.e., exogenous to the current model). In addition to the exchange rate policy, the government might impose tariffs on imported goods and grant subsidies on exported goods. Due to the assumed fixed (not flexible) exchange rate, the trade accounts in the country's balance of payment might not be balanced. In such a case, the trade account is balanced by international capital inflow (or outflow). This capital flow will account for changes in the stock of foreign assets either by borrowing or lending. Change in capital assets will imply a flow of periodical interest payments or receipts.

3. Equilibrium in the CGE

The equilibrium concept for the CGE model is that all endogenous variables concerning prices and quantities are simultaneously determined. This solution can be viewed as a simultaneous intersection of all demand and supply curves in each and every product market. Such an equilibrium solution of the CGE model is characterized by a set of prices of final goods and prices of the primary factors, which equates the quantities supplied to the quantities demanded in each and every market. When conditions for uniqueness of solution hold, only one vector exists of prices at which all demand and supply decisions by the optimizing behavior of each agent in the economy are mutually compatible.

Macro-closure Rule: The reconciliation of the macroeconomic financial balances in a CGE model is known as the "macro-closure rule." It means that aggregate investment is equal to aggregate saving.[7] In a simple situation, this capital formation and government savings (budget deficit or surplus) and trade deficit can be incorporated in the household decision making so that the macro-closure rule will be maintained. Therefore, in each period, the net saving is equal to net investment, where net saving is the sum of private savings minus depreciation plus net public (government) saving plus net capital inflow (from current account).

In the CGE model, there are two kinds of time-related equilibria: the static one-period (or benchmark) equilibrium and the dynamic equilibrium. The benchmark refers to the first- period equilibrium, while the dynamic is the extrapolation from this first period for a certain predetermined time span into the immediate future following the benchmark.

3.1. The Benchmark Equilibrium in the CGE
The initial period of the CGE model is referred to as the benchmark period. The

---

7   For details, see Dewatripont and Michel (1987).

first step in solving a CGE model is to solve its equilibrium values for that first period (and then for the dynamic part, to extend it into the future).

A major source of data and information needed for solving the static benchmark equilibrium is the Social Accounting Matrix (SAM.) This is an important source, as it assembles and provides information about the important actors in the economy: composition, production, and distribution of output at the perimeter. The SAM is based on national input-output information of the economy and augmented by industrial transactions and international transactions. Therefore, the SAM represents the mapping of the flow of funds in the economy.

The SAM provides the initial picture of the *generation, transmission, and distribution* of income. It consists of several accounts, representing production, factor inputs, institutions, and the rest of the world. By convention, the rows and the columns represent the income and expenditure accounts. As the SAM provides the picture of the flow-of-funds, the total expenditures of any one column must equal the sum of the receipts of the corresponding row. The accounts of producers correspond to the producing sector in the input-output account. Each producer (sector), down its column, pays all its revenues to other producers, households, and the government and sells its output in the domestic market and abroad along its row. (The value added is paid to the owners of factors of production and to the government.) The household account shows its income sources and how the household disposes of its income. The capital account acts like an investment bank; it collects all the savings and spend them on investment goods.

Parameterization: The initial set of parameters of the model are derived by solving the model for the first period under the important constraint that the solved equilibrium values derived from the model are exactly the same as those in the SAM.

The Parameters and Calibration: Due to the difficult estimation process, it is common practice in CGE modeling to "fix" key parameters on the basis of empirical evidence, and the other parameters are calibrated adjusted to reproduce the benchmark-year data.[8]

The basic equilibrium prices searched for by the solution algorithm are the rental value of capital goods, the wages, and the prices of goods, including coal, oil, and gas. In the environment policy experiment, the solution algorithm computes, in addition, the carbon, the energy, or the ad valorem tax needed to satisfy the constraint on carbon emissions. The inflation rate is exogenously projected for the model. No monetary sector exists. All demand and supply functions are assumed to be homogeneous of degree zero in nominal variables. Thus, only relative prices determine quantities. (It is assumed that all prices are equal to one in the base year.)

---

8   The main drawback in the calibration of the values of the benchmark year is that the calibration process distortion and random errors of the benchmark year are internalized as basic components, thus affecting the parameters and becoming an important part of the results. Jogenson and Wilcoxen (1990) use an econometric estimation rather than calibration.

3.2. The Dynamic Equilibrium

The flow of time is expressed by growth or contraction of base-year stocks of two primary factors: labor and capital. Agents are assumed to be myopic, basing their decisions on static expectations about prices and quantities. (This assumption implies that events—such as pre-announced carbon-taxes—do not have any influence on agents' decisions and market outcomes until they actually occur. The alternative hypothesis is perfect foresight. Both alternatives are inconsistent with actual economic outcomes over time.)

The intertemporal linkage equations are defined to update the exogenous variables and parameters. These equations will provide all the exogenous variables needed for the next period by the CGE model, which is then solved for a new equilibrium. The model is solved forward in a dynamically recursive fashion, with each static solution depending only on current and past variables. Therefore, the development of the economy over time is characterized by a sequence of period-related, but intertemporally uncoordinated, flow equilibria.[9] The dynamics originate from a capital accumulation process and labor force growth exogenously determined (and only secondarily determined by the lagged structure used in behavioral equations).

Capital Accumulation: In the dynamic setting, a standard accumulation function for the national capital stock such as: $K_t = (1 - \delta_t) K_{t-1} + I_{t-1}$ might represent the amount of available capital stock (K_t) in period t. This level is determined by the capital stock of the previous period $(t - 1)$ plus the net capital accumulation of that period (i.e., public and private investment minus depreciation).

Labor Force Growth: Assuming a constant rate of growth of the labor force and zero unemployment, the periodical labor supply increases at the same rate.

4. The Structure of the Estimated CGE Model for the Korean Economy[10]

For all the calculations, the Generalized Algebraic Modeling System (GAMS) has been used to solve the non-linear optimization problem of the basic model and also for simulations of the potential trajectories. These were solved as a sequential dynamic model with capital accumulation resulting from savings. The summary of the model structure is as follows.

4.1. The Main Economic Components

There were two regions in the model, Korea and the rest of the world, where the rest of the world was treated as exogenous (not a *world* general equilibrium model). The production structure of the eighteen industries (and products) was repre-

---

9   As in most dynamic CGA models, convergence to a balanced growth path is not guaranteed, but can be imposed through a suitable calibration of the parameters of the model. The resulting path is not necessarily unique, since there may be several ways to calibrate the model in order to ensure convergence.

10   For further details concerning the CGE model and its estimation, see Kang (1997).

sented by a Joint Leontief-CES-Cobb-Douglas production function with constant returns to scale technology.

The 18 industries were:

1. Agriculture	10. Metal products
2. Mining	11. Manufacturing
3. Food Tobacco	12. Construction
4. Textile	13. Transportation
5. Pulp paper	14. Services
6. Chemicals basic	15. Coal
7. Chemicals products	16. Oil Products
8. Stone & Clay	17. Electricity
9. Iron & Steel	18. Gas Utility

The inputs used were: labor, capital, energy, and other intermediate material inputs. The labor and capital were homogeneous inputs and are mobile among industries. While labor supply and labor growth were exogenous, capital stock was endogenously determined through the capital accumulation process. Labor and capital were traded on the domestic market only and were immobile between Korea and the rest of the world.

The final demand was dependent on a log-linear utility and income of the representative consumer and on the relative prices. Excess demand and supply for goods was accommodated by the rest of the world.

Government activity was represented by the budget accounts. The government revenues were from direct income taxes, indirect commodity taxes, tariffs on imported goods, and environment taxes. The world prices for commodities produced abroad were exogenous. A modified small-country assumption and product differentiation were included.

The environmental issue was CO_2 emissions and domestic air pollution affecting global warming, which arise from the combustion of fossil fuels. It was assumed that the air pollution occurred in fixed proportions of the level of use.

This objective of pollution reduction could be achieved either by input substitution of labor and capital and/or by substitution between fuel inputs and/or by reducing the output of polluting industries. In an attempt to promote such a reduction, in the model estimated, the following monetary and non-monetary incentives were applied:

1. Taxes on fossil fuels at a uniform rates (an *ad valorem* tax) or energy related; and

2. Economy-wide or industry-specific emission standards.

The model was first solved for the so-called, Business-as-Usual scenario (or BaU). Next, the model was solved for the exact same time periods, with the constraint that the CO_2 emissions were controlled at the target level. Finally, the results of the models employing the emissions control policy variables were compared to the BaU solution, which served as a reference equilibrium solution. Some of these results are discussed below.

Table 1. Summary Results of the Business-as-Usual Scenario[a]			
	1990	2000	2010	Growth rate 90/10 (%)
Industry production Trillion won	417.15	748.31	1276.44	5.75
Share (%)	100	100	100	
Industry Share (%)				
1. Agriculture	5.3	5.3	5.0	5.49
2. Mining	0.4	0.4	0.4	4.90
3. Food	6.8	6.9	6.7	5.74
4. Textile	7.6	6.5	5.6	4.12
5. Pulp & Paper	1.2	1.1	1.1	5.69
6. Industrial Chemicals	1.1	1.3	1.5	7.27
7. Chemical Products	5.2	5.4	5.6	6.16
8. Stone & Ceramics	1.9	2.0	2.0	5.92
9. Iron & Steel	4.6	4.4	4.3	5.44
10. Non-ferrous metals	0.8	0.7	0.7	5.21
11. Manufacturing	18.2	19.2	20.7	6.41
12. Construction	10.5	10.7	11.0	6.00
13. Transportation	3.8	3.7	3.6	5.56
14. Services	28.7	28.5	27.9	5.60
15. Coal	0.6	0.5	0.4	4.35
16. Oil (refinery)	1.8	1.8	1.8	5.78
17. Electricity	1.4	1.4	1.4	5.79
18. Gas	0.2	0.2	0.2	5.32
[a]Source: Kang (1997)				

5. Results from CGE Model for Korea[11]

5.1. The Dynamic Solution for BaU

To obtain a meaningful estimate of the economic impact of a given emission abatement policy, we must first identify the base (or the alternative) situation against which all the results will be compared. This base line case is called the Business-as-Usual (BaU). The BaU scenario represent the estimated trajectory of the CGE equilibrium values for the Korean economy if no emissions abatement action were used to control CO_2 emissions. The model as a whole and the calculated equilibrium values refer to the twenty years period 1990-2010. [12] The benchmark year or the base year is 1990 and the last (terminal) year of the experiment, i.e., the

---

11   If not mentioned otherwise, the numerical results reported in this section are from Kang (1997).
12   This time period was selected so as to conform with discussions at the UN conferences. All
       results reported here refer to the single abatement policy objective which is achieving in 2010
       the CO_2 emission level of 1990.

Table 2. Demand for Fossil Fuel by Sector in the Business-as-Usual Scenario[a]				
	1990	2000	2010	Growth rate 90/10 (%)
Coal demand				
Million TOE	36.616	63.634	106.677	5.49
Share (%)	30.37	30.44	30.84	
Oil demand				
Million TOE	82.929	143.673	236.366	5.38
Share (%)	68.79	68.72	68.33	
Gas demand				
Million TOE	1.017	1.758	2.862	5.31
Share (%)	0.84	0.84	0.83	
Total energy demand				
TOE	120.56	209.07	345.59	5.41
Share (%)	100	100	100	
Industry Share (%)				
1. Agriculture	1.9	1.7	1.5	4.42
2. Mining	0.2	0.2	0.2	3.94
3. Food	0.7	0.7	07	5.26
4. Textile	1.0	0.9	0.7	3.82
5. Pulp & Paper	0.4	0.3	0.3	5.12
6. Industrial Chemicals	5.0	5.7	6.4	6.67
7. Chemical Products	1.6	1.6	1.7	5.82
8. Stone & Ceramics	3.1	3.2	3.3	5.77
9. Iron & Steel	6.9	6.6	6.5	5.11
10. Non-ferrous metals	0.4	0.4	0.4	5.01
11. Manufacturing	1.8	1.8	2.0	6.02
12. Construction	3.1	3.2	3.2	5.66
13. Transportation	10.5	10.3	10.0	5.15
14. Services	7.8	7.7	7.5	5.18
15. Coal	10.3	9.2	8.3	4.31
16. Oil (refinery)	25.5	26.1	26.8	5.67
17. Electricity	5.6	5.9	6.2	5.90
18. Gas	2.1	2.0	2.0	5.18
19. Residential	12.3	12.4	12.4	5.45
[a]Source: Kang (1997)				

year by which the target of emissions control needs to be met, is 2010. For political and other reasons, the benchmark year could be changed to 1995 or 2000. Some of the calculations were using these as the benchmark.

Table 1 presents the results for CGE model for the BaU scenario for the benchmark year of 1990 and the future target year is year 2010. Using the above stated assumptions about the population growth and the assumptions about the capital accumulation, this equilibrium values derived for this scenario are in line

Table 3. CO_2 Emissions in the Business-as-Usual Scenario[a]				
Year	1990	2000	2010	Growth rate 90/10 (%)
Emissions (mill. ton)	66.22	116.02	193.70	5.51
Industry Share (%)				
1. Agriculture	2.77	2.55	2.25	4.43
2. Mining	0.36	0.32	0.27	3.94
3. Food	1.01	1.01	0.97	5.27
4. Textile	1.49	1.26	1.07	3.82
5. Pulp & Paper	0.52	0.50	0.48	5.13
6. Industrial Chemicals	7.49	8.35	9.35	6.69
7. Chemical Products	2.47	2.54	2.65	5.89
8. Stone & Ceramics	6.16	5.29	5.49	5.84
9. Iron & Steel	12.19	11.62	11.34	5.14
10. Non-ferrous metals	0.62	0.59	0.58	5.08
11. Manufacturing	2.60	2.71	2.88	6.05
12. Construction	4.53	4.61	4.66	5.66
13. Transportation	15.38	14.92	14.34	5.15
14. Services	11.80	11.53	11.18	5.23
15. Coal	0.22	0.18	0.16	3.82
16. Oil (refinery)	1.34	1.37	1.39	5.71
17. Electricity	9.11	9.52	9.97	5.99
18. Gas	0.69	0.68	0.66	5.27
19. Residential	20.24	20.44	20.30	5.53
[a]Source: Kang (1997).				

with the past growth rate of the Korean economy, predicting an annual average growth rate of the industrial production of 5.75%.[13] As part of the total GDP, the production of the electricity sector is expected to grow at a similar annual rate of 5.79%. The share of industrial output produced by the electricity industry is expected to stay constant at about 1.4%.

Table 2 presents the demand for fossil fuel by the different industrial sectors. These values are derived from the calculated CGE equilibria. The total demand for fossil fuel consumption over the 20-year period is expected to quadruple. The share of the electricity industry is 5.6% of the total demand at the beginning of the period (1990), and this share is expected to grow to 6.2% of the total demand by the end of the period (2010). For the same period, the expected annual growth rate of demand for fossil fuels by the electric utility industry is expected to be about 5.9%. Thus, the predicted rate of growth of the demand for fossil energy of the electric

---

13   Recent information suggests the near future economic growth of the Korean economy might
      be significantly smaller than its recent trend.

utility industry is among the fastest growing demands.

Note that, while the electric utility industry produces only about 1.4% of the industrial output, its annual consumption of fossil fuel is about four times as large, about 5.6%. This relationship reveals, once again, that the electric utility industry is relatively highly intensive in consuming fossil fuels. Most of this fossil fuel is used by the electric utility industry for the purpose of internal combustion. With the slow pace of technological development in this industry, one would expect that the current technology and the phenomenon of high intensity in consuming fossil fuel is most likely to persist. This high intensity of fuel consumption will have its implication on the intensity of electric utility in emissions of CO_2, as we will be seen below.

Table 3 presents the distribution of CO_2 emissions by industry. Under the BaU scenario, the total amount of CO_2 emission is expected to grow from 66.22 million cubic tones in 1990 at an annual rate of 5.51% to 193.70 million cubic tons twenty years later in year 2010. The share of the electric utility industry in the total CO_2 emissions is about 9.11% at the beginning of the period, and it is predicted to rise to 9.97% of the total CO_2 emissions by the end of the period. Under the BaU scenario, the electric utility industry is expected to be among the fastest growing industries in terms of CO_2 emissions. Given that we are in the environmental sensitive age, one would therefore expect that the electrc utility industry will be closely monitored and controlled for emissions.[14]

5.2. The Impact of The Different Emission Control Instruments

In general, the expected economic impact of the introduction of CO_2 emissions control policies is an increase in the prices of energy inputs which will bring about an increase in the output prices which will lead to the end result of a reduction of the output produced by the affected industries. First, we consider the economic impact on the general level—the economy at large as it is measured by the GDP—and then we will consider the specific impact on the electric utility industry.

Different potential policy instruments were considered. As each of these instruments generates a different set of incentives to the decision makers, their reactions will differ and, therefore, the predicted economic impact will differ as well. When the objective of the environmental authority was to achieve in year 2010 the CO_2 emissions level of 1990, the following four instruments were considered as alternative policy instruments:

1. Carbon tax policy;
2. Energy tax policy;
3. Ad valorm tax policy;
4. Technical and operational standards.

For each of the above instruments, the CGE model was solved with the additional objective of using the minimum amount of the instrument (one at a time) which will ensure that in year 2010 the CO_2 emission level be equal to that of 1990.

---

14   In addition, the emissions are concentrated at a few production sites, which eases regulation
      enforcement and inspection.

Table 4. The Impact of Alternative Emission Control Policies[a]

Policy	Carbon tax	Energy tax	Ad valorem	Standard
Sector output				
Coal	-84.6	-82.5	-96.5	-61.2
Oil (refinery)	-86.7	-87.4	-99.9	-65.0
Electricity	-24.0	-24.1	-33.8	-67.9
Gas	-23.5	-31.3	-94.4	-66.0
Commodity Price				
Coal	1258.7	1086.5	745.8	-5.1
Oil (refinery)	394.9	421.2	752.1	-0.9
Electricity	103.1	105.5	254.0	40.8
Gas	290.6	338.7	435.2	-3.8
Fossil energy demand				
Coal	-85.5	-83.6	-96.7	-61.5
Oil (refinery)	-86.9	-87.6	-99.9	-65.0
Electricity	-44.9	-43.6	-73.0	-66.3
Gas	-28.0	-34.8	-92.8	-66.2
Residential	-92.0	-91.9	-93.8	-67.5

[a]Source: Kang (1997).

In terms of GDP level, we compare here the predicted output when using one policy instrument to the predicted output under BaU scenario. First, when comparing the GDP at the year 2010, the decrease in GDP when using the carbon tax is about 15.08%; when using the energy tax, the decrease in GDP is 15.46%; when using the ad valorem tax, the decrease is 20.37%; and when using the standards, the decrease in GDP is 41.33%.

In terms of the annual growth rate of the GDP, a very similar picture is revealed. When comparing the predicted annual growth rate of BaU to the predicted annual growth rate when the policy instruments are being employed, we observe that, as a result of the carbon tax, the annual rate of growth of GDP will drop by 2.10% (compared to BaU). When the policy instrument employed is the energy tax, the decrease in the predicted annual gowth rate is 2.14%. When the instrument is the ad valorem tax, the decrease is 3.17%; and when the standards are employed, the decrease is 5.67%.

From these and other comparisons of the economic (GDP) cost of the different policy instruments, it is clear that the least damage to GDP will occur if the policy instrument used is the carbon tax.

Table 4 summarizes the impact of the different emissions control policies instruments on the output prices of the electric utility sector and the other energy related sectors: Coal, Oil refinery, and Gas. For the electric utility industry, the use of the carbon tax or the energy tax will result in a similar (predicted) output level in year 2010. Compared with the predicted output under the BaU, the use of these emission control instruments will result in a (relative) decrease in output of 24%. The use of the ad valorem tax will result in a 34% decrease in the output of the electric utility sector. The use of standards as a policy instrument will result in a

Table 5. Alternative Target Dates for Emission Control by Carbon Tax Policy[a]			
Emission level	1990 level	1995 level	2000 level
Sector output			
Coal	-84.6	-77.6	-65.7
Oil (refinery)	-86.7	-79.9	-67.9
Electricity	-24.0	-16.3	-9.4
Gas	-23.5	-13.1	-5.0
Commodity Price			
Coal	1258.7	643.2	283.6
Oil (refinery)	394.9	208.1	97.2
Electricity	103.1	54.6	25.2
Gas	290.6	153.6	71.1
Fossil energy demand			
Coal	-85.6	-78.9	-67.2
Oil (refinery)	-84.7	-80.2	-68.2
Electricity	-41.1	-37.2	-27.9
Gas	-29.9	-17.4	-8.4
Residential	-90.4	-83.6	-68.4
[a]Source: Kang (1997).			

68% decrease in output.

The predicted price of output in the electric utility industry for year 2010 (relative to the BaU) is 103% if the carbon tax is used as the emission control instrument. The price will be 106% higher in the case of the energy tax and only 41% higher in the emission standards case.

As it came up in recent international negotiations, the targeted level of annual CO_2 emissions was vigorously debated. It is clear that the higher the level of annual emissions accepted by the international community the lower will be the economic cost to the individual country (and to the individual industry) of adjusting to that level. Table 5 presents the economic costs of adjusting to different levels of allowed annual CO_2 emissions. As the agreed level of emissions is higher (i.e., further into the future) and when the policy instrument used is the carbon tax, the output loss (compared with the BaU) in year 2010 will be smaller the higher is the agreed upon level. That is, the loss of output in the electric utility industry will be 24% if the 1990 emissions level is adopted, 16% if the 1995 emission level adopted, or only 9% if the emissions level adopted corresponds to year 2010. Very similar results are revealed for the prices and demand for fossil fuels.

6. Concluding Remarks

This paper reports the simulation results from a CGE model for the Korean economy in general and the electric utility industry in particular. These results reflect the expected economic cost (impact) of implementing a variety of CO_2 emissions reduction policy instruments. In the simulation, the following policy instruments were considered: carbon tax, energy tax, ad valorm tax, and technical and operational standards. The range of tax and non-tax policies needed in order to achieve a certain environmental objective and their implied economic cost of abatement vary significantly across the policy instruments tested.

The main result is that, when the objective is to reduce the CO_2 emissions, using any policy instrument will result the in economic cost of lost output. The least-cost policy instrument which supports the desired environmental outcome is the implementation of a direct carbon tax on all sources of energy used. Using this policy instrument will also result in the lowest level of output loss and the smallest distortion in the relative price of energy and other inputs. Other policy instruments, if used, will cause a larger decrease of output accompanied with a total larger price increases.

References

Amano, Akihiro. 1990. "Energy Prices and CO_2 Emissions in the 1990s." *Journal of Policy Modeling* 12 (3): 495-510.

Armington, P. 1969. "A Theory of Demand for Products Distinguishing by Place of Production." *IMF Staff Papers* 16: 159-78.

Altig, David E., Charles T. Carlstrom, and Kevin J. Lansing. 1995. "Computable General equilibrium Models and Monetary Advice." *Journal of Money, Credit and Banking* 27(4 (part 2), November): 1472-1493.

Bergman, Lars. 1988. "Energy Policy Modeling: A survey of General Equilibrium Approaches." *Journal of Policy Modeling* 10(3): 377-399.

Bergman, Lars. 1990. "Energy and Environment Constraints on Growth: A CGE Modeling Approach." *Journal of Policy Modeling* 12(4): 671-691.

Bergman Lars. 1991):. "General Equilibrium Effects of Environmental Policy: A CGE Modeling Approach." *Environmental and Resource Economics* 1: 67-85.

Bliitzer, Charles R., and Richard S. Eckaus. 1986. "Energy-Economy Interactions in Mexico: A Multiperiod General Equilibrium Model,." *Journal of Development Economic* 21: 259-281.

Bliitzer, Charles R., Richard S. Eckaus, Lahiri Supriya, and Alexander Meeraus. 1994. "A General Equilibrium Analysis of the Effects of Carbon Emissions Restrictions on Economic Growth in a Developing Country." In *Applied General Equilibrium and Economic Development*, edited by J. Mercenier and T. N. Srinivasan. Ann Arbor: University of Michigan Press.

Conrad, Klaus, and Iris Henseler-Unger. 1986. "Applied General Equilibrium Modeling for Long-Term Energy Planing in Germany." *Journal of Policy Modeling* 8(4): 531-549.

Conrad, Klaus, and Michael Schroder. 1993. "Choosing Environmental Policy Instruments Using General Equilibrum Models." *Journal of Policy Modeling* 15(5&6): 521-543.

Dervis, K., Jaime De Melo, and S. Robinson. 1982. *General Equilibrium Models for Development Policy.* A World Bank Research Publication, Cambridge University Press.

Dewatripont, M., and G. Michel. 1987. "On Closure Rules, Homogeneity, and Dynamics in Applied General Equilibrium Models." *Journal of Development Economics* 26 (1 June): 65-76.

Dixon, Peter B. 1990. "A General Equilibrium Approach to Public Utility Pricing: Determining Prices for Water Authority." *Journal of Policy Modeling* 12(4): 745-767.

Gunning, Jan Willem, and Michael A. Keyzer. 1995. "Applied General Equilibrium Models for Policy Analysis." In *Handbook of Development Economics,* Vol. III, edited by J. Behrman and T. N. Srinivasan. Elsevier Science B.V.

Hoffmann, Sandra, Sherman Robinson, and Shankar Subramanian. 1996. "The Role of Defense Cuts in the California Recession: Computable General Equilibrium Models and Interstate Factor Mobility. *Journal of Regonal Science.* 36 (No. 4, November): 571-595.

Intergovernmental Panel on Climate Change (IPCC). 1990. "Policy Makers Summary of Scientific Assessment of Climate Change." New York: WMO and UNEP.

IPCC. 1992. "1992 IPCC Supplement: Science Assessment."

Jorgenson, Dale W., and Peter Wilcoxen. 1990. "Intertemporal General Equilibrium Modeling of U.S. Environmental Regulation." *Journal of Policy Modeling* 12(4): 715-744.

Jorgenson, Dale W., and Peter Wilcoxen. 1993a. "Reducing U.S. Carbon Dioxide Emissions: An assessment of Different Instruments." *Journal of Policy Modeling* 15(5&6): 491-520.

Jorgenson, Dale W. and Peter Wilcoxen. 1993b. "Reducing US Carbon Emissions: An Econometric General Equilibrium Assesment." *Resources and Energy Economics* 15(1): 7-25.

Kang, Yoonyoung. 1997. "CO2, Energy and Economy interactions; A Multisectorial, Dynamic, Computable General Equilibrium Model for Korea." PhD Dissertation, Energy Management and Policy, The University of Pennsylvania.

Kildegaard, Arne. 1996. "Liquidity, Risk, and the Collapse of the Mexican Peso: A Dynamic CGE Interpretation." *Southern Economic Journal.* 63 (No. 2, October): 460-472.

Nechyba, Thomas. 1996. "A Computable General Equilibrium Model of Intergovernmental Aid." *Journal of Public Economics.* 62 (No. 3, November): 363-397.

Waters, Edwards C., David W. Holland, and Bruce A. Weber. 1997. "Economic Impacts of a Property Tax Limitation: A Computable General Equilibrium Analysis of Oregon's Measure 5." *Land Economics* 73(No. 1, February): 72-89.

9

CUSTOMER RESPONSE TO REAL-TIME PRICES IN THE ENGLAND AND WALES ELECTRICITY MARKET:
Implications for Demand-Side Bidding and Pricing Options Design Under Competition

Robert H. Patrick
Frank A. Wolak

1. Introduction

Dissatisfaction with the performance of cost-of-service regulated or government-owned electric utilitieshas led to dramatic changes in the market structure and rules governing the operation of electricity industries in the United States and worldwide. These restructuring efforts seek to introduce competition to provide incentives for efficient pricing, investment, and operation. The predominant view is that competition is feasible for structurally or functionally separated firms generating (wholesale) and/or supplying (retail) electricity, while transmission and distribution services are most efficiently provided by firms facing alternative (to cost-based) forms of regulation (e.g., price caps). An example of this view is the England and Wales (E&W) electricity market which was established in 1990 and has served as a model for restructuring worldwide.

Electric utilities face substantial challenges and opportunities as a result of evolving regulatory structures designed to increase competition in electricity generation and supply.[1] In order to adapt to this new environment, electric utilities must increase the level of customer satisfaction and lower their cost of service.[2] Remaining viable in this new environment will require utilities to develop comprehensive strategies aimed at matching profitable service options to diverse customer needs. Knowledge of electricity demands at the customer-level is critical to success

---

[1]   See, for example, Energy Information Administration (1996).

[2]   See, for example, Stewart (1997), which presents an overview of some of these issues and the views of Duke Power's CEO, William H. Grigg.

in the evolving competitive business environment.

This chapter presents some of the results and implications of estimates of customer-level demands developed in Patrick and Wolak (1997a,b). Patrick and Wolak estimate the customer-level demands for electricity by large and medium-sized industrial and commercial customers (with peak demands of at least 100 kWs) purchasing electricity according to half-hourly spot prices from the England and Wales (E&W) electricity market. Data from a Regional Electricity Company (REC) in this market, Midlands Electricity plc (MEB),[3] over the years 1991-1995 was used to quantify half-hourly customer-level demands under MEB's real-time pricing program—what MEB calls a Pool Price Contract (PPC). Under this pricing option, customers are charged according to half-hourly spot prices set in the E&W electricity market—the "pool selling price" (PSP). A large portion of the PSP for each half-hour of a day is known from the day-ahead perspective, but only known with certainty thirty days *ex post* of actual consumption. PPC customers also face a demand charge (termed a "triad charge" in the E&W market) on the average kWs consumed during the three half-hours coincident with the largest E&W transmission system demands, subject to the constraint that these three half-hours are separated by at least ten days. Triad charges can only be known in March of each fiscal year, after actual electricity consumption has occurred.[4]

The econometric model developed and estimated in Patrick and Wolak (1997a,b) quantifies the extent of intertemporal substitution in electricity consumption between pricing periods within days due to changes in the E&W pool prices, and distinguishes between the demand-altering effects of changes in pool prices and changes in the triad charges. The resulting model can be used to measure the demand altering effects arising from the imposition of arbitrary time-varying and consumption-dependent pricing structures. This model provides crucial input into a utility's program for the design of market-based strategies for enhancing customer and utility benefits in increasingly competitive electricity markets. In particular, the econometric model can be used to estimate customer-level electricity loads, revenues from electricity supply, and customer benefits under alternative rate structures; to generate the own-price and cross-price elasticities which can be used in rate simulation and optimization programs; and to provide customer-level demand relationships essential in the design of pricing options to attract and maintain customers in a market with competing suppliers, while insuring that the costs of each customer's consumption are covered.[5]

These demand models can also be used by electricity retailers to formulate

---

3   Midlands Electricity plc is the name of the privatized firm serving the area formerly served by
     the Midlands Electricity Board. MEB continues to be used as the acronym for Midlands
     Electricity plc due to customer familiarity.
4   Fiscal years in the E&W market run from April 1 through March 31 of the next year.
5   The costs of serving a customer are natually heavily dependent on the customer's consumption
     path (see the pool prices below for example). Since the customers prior (as well as current and
     future) consumption path may be unobservable (depending on metering capabilities and
     access to information on the consumer), it is easy to envisage situations where the customer's
     consumption could be subsidized by a pricing policy offered.

demand-side bids into a competitive wholesale electricity market. Demand-side bidding is important in order to introduce a price response into the price-determination process in markets such as the E&W (which uses a perfectly inelastic day-ahead demand forecast in determining each half-hour's market price). As discussed in Wolak and Patrick (1997), the magnitude of the within-day price-response in the aggregate electricity demand used to set prices on a half-hourly or hourly basis by an electricity market is a major determinant of both the mean and time series behavior of market clearing prices. The existence of a substantial price response in the aggregate demand that sets the market clearing price will also reduce the variability of these prices throughout the day relative to the case of little or no price response in this demand, because a price-responsive demand implies less capacity will be called upon to generate in response to higher bids by generators (regardless of whether these high prices are due to market power). This underscores the importance of accurately measuring the response of customer-level electricity demand to within-day price changes and incorporating this information into the within-day aggregate demand function that sets the market clearing prices for electricity in a competitive electricity market.

If the RECs and other suppliers purchasing from the E&W market are able to predict accurately the response of demand to within-day price changes for their customers on the PPC, they can use this information to formulate their demand-side bid functions.[6] If a REC is able to entice more of its customers to face prices for electricity which reflect the current *PSP* from the E&W market for that half-hour, given accurate estimates of the price-responsiveness of these customers, the REC can then formulate an aggregate demand-side bid function which has a relatively larger price response. Consequently, the combination of a greater number of customers subject to prices that move with the half-hourly *PSP* and more accurate measurements of the price-responses of these customers will allow more aggressive demand-side bidding into the E&W pool. Substantial amounts of demand-side bidding by RECs will result in a half-hourly demand function for electricity which implies significant reductions in the amount demanded as the price of electricity increases. The more price-elastic this demand, the greater is the extent to which higher bid prices will translate into reductions in the quantity of electricity demanded rather than increased market clearing prices (with little change in the quantity demanded). As emphasized by Wolak and Patrick (1997), the current operation of the E&W market illustrates the sort of price volatility that can occur if the demand setting the market price is very price inelastic and only a small fraction of the total electricity consumed in any half-hour is sold to final customers at prices that vary with the half-hourly *PSP*. Consequently, accurate measurement of the within-day price response of its customers is an important necessary ingredient for any electricity retailer to demand-side bid aggressively and, therefore, build sig-

---

6   Inacurate demand-side bidding would lead to a higher half-hourly *UPLIFT* component of the PPC. *UPLIFT*, the component of the *PSP* which is determined after demand is realized. The largest portion of the *PSP* is known the day prior to consumption. Wolak and Patrick (1996a; 1997) provide more detail.

nificant price-responses into the market price-setting process.

Potential benefits to RECs and their customers from significant demand-side bidding include reduced magnitudes and variability of market prices. Moreover, if RECs and/or other suppliers can encourage fixed-price customers to shift usage away from or conserve electricity during peak demand periods, not only will losses be avoided by serving the fixed-price customers when pool prices are greater than the contracted fixed rates, savings can also accrue due to lower transmission demand charges which are paid by RECs on their aggregate system demand coincident with the E&W market transmission system peaks.

In Patrick and Wolak (1997a,b), we analyzed five of the 263 (five-digit British Industrial Code (BIC)) industries making up the set of MEB spot pricing customers from April 1, 1991 through March 31, 1995. We are currently in the process of estimating electricity demand models for the remaining industries. As reported in our 1997 papers, we are able very precisely to estimate mean customer-level own- and cross-price elasticities of demand which vary across half-hours within the day as well as with the magnitude of the prices and quantities consumed. Although we find a substantial amount of heterogeneity across industries in the within-day pattern of their half-hourly own- and cross-price elasticities of demand for electric-ity, these patterns appear consistent with the production processes of the industries. The pattern of own- and cross-price elasticities throughout the day also vary substantially across half-hours for each industry. Although these elasticities may seem small in absolute value, given the large amount of price variation that characterizes the E&W market, there is significant potential to shift a sizeable amount of load away from high-priced load periods within the day. Consequently, shifting more customers to pool or similar pricing contracts is a very promising way build sufficient price-responsiveness into the aggregate demand determining the market-clearing price each pricing period. The results for our modeling exercise for the water supply industry (BIC 17000) is used as an example for illustrative purposes in this chapter.

The remainder of this chapter proceeds as follows. In the next section, we briefly present some background on the electricity industry structure in E&W and describe the pool price determination process and MEB's PPC. Section 3 provides a description of the MEB data and other data used to estimate the model. Section 4 illustrates why, given the rules of the E&W market, industry-level price and demand data cannot be used to estimate the price responsiveness of customers to these half-hourly market prices. This underscores the necessity of our customer level approach to estimating the structure of electricity demand under real-time market prices. This section is followed by a discussion of the price elasticity estimates for the water supply industry in Section 5. Section 6 contains brief examples of how the econometric model might be used to compare alternative pricing structures and to implement demand-side bidding. This chapter closes with a discussion of future research on designing pricing options under competition.

2. The Price Determination Process in the England and Wales Electricity Market

This section summarizes the industry structure and describes the pool price determination process in the England and Wales electricity market. This is followed by a discussion of the PPC. Understanding the pool price determination process is necessary to appreciate the specification of our model for day-ahead electricity demand under a PPC.[7]

2.1. Industry Structure

March 31, 1990 marked the beginning of an evolving economic restructuring of the electric utility industry in the United Kingdom. This process privatized the government-owned Central Electricity Generating Board and Area Electricity Boards and introduced competition into the generation and supply sectors of the market. In England and Wales, the Central Electricity Generating Board, which prior to restructuring provided generation and bulk transmission, was divided into three generation companies and the National Grid Company (NGC). National Power and PowerGen took over all fossil fuel generating stations, while nuclear generating plants became the responsibility of Nuclear Electric. The twelve RECs were formed from the Area Electricity Boards, which provide distribution services and electricity supply to final consumers. NGC provides transmission services from generators to the RECs and manages the pool, coordinating the transmission and dispatch of electricity generators.

Prices for transmission and distribution services from NGC and the RECs are restricted to grow no faster than the percentage change in the economy-wide price level, measured by the Retail Prices Index (RPI), less an X-factor adjustment for productivity increases. RECs are required, with compensation for distribution services provided, to allow competitors to transfer electricity over their systems. The RECs' electricity supply prices for all customers were regulated, until the 1994/95 fiscal year, by RPI - X + Y, where Y is an adjustment factor which passes-through unexpected costs the REC incurs, as well as purchased electricity costs, and transmission and distribution services. Since the beginning of the 1994/95 fiscal year, supply to non-franchise customers has not been regulated, since these customers have the option of choosing their supplier from any of the 12 RECs as well as National Power or PowerGen directly. Supply services provided by the RECs are regulated by RPI-X+Y for all franchise customers (i.e., those that do not have a choice of their electricity supplier). On March 31, 1994, the 1 MW limit for a customer to be classified as non-franchise was reduced to 100 KW. This size restriction on customer peak demand will be phased out during the 1998 fiscal year, when even residential customers will have the option to choose a supplier (i.e., all electricity consumers become non-franchise).[8]

---

7   Wolak and Patrick (1996a; 1997) provide details on the pool and operation of this market.
8   The Regulator has decided to phase in the relaxation of this size restriction during 1998 to permit more time for the transition. All customers in the E&W market are planned to be able

2.2. Pool Price Determination Process

Generators offer prices at which they will provide various quantities of electricity to the E&W pool during each half-hour of the following day. These prices and quantities submitted by generators are input into the general ordering and loading (GOAL) program at NGC to determine the merit order of dispatching generation and reserve capacity. The lowest price generating capacity is dispatched first, although system constraints may cause deviations in this order, in the sense that higher-priced units may be "constrained to operate" to maintain system integrity. NGC computes a forecast of half-hourly system demands for the next day. The system marginal price (SMP) for each half-hour of the next day is the price bid on the marginal generation unit required to satisfy each forecast half-hourly system demand for the next day. The SMP is one component of the price paid to generators for each MWh of electricity provided to the pool during each half-hour.

The Pool Purchase Price (PPP), the price paid to generators per MWh in the relevant half-hour is defined as $PPP = SMP + CC$, where the capacity charge is $CC = LOLP \times (VOLL - SMP)$. LOLP is the loss of load probability,[9] and VOLL is the value of lost load. SMP is intended to reflect the operating costs of producing electricity (this is the largest component of PPP for most of the half hour periods). VOLL is set for the entire fiscal year to approximate the per MWh willingness of customers to pay to avoid supply interruptions during that year. VOLL was set by the Regulator at 2,000 £/MWh for 1990/91 and has increased annually by the growth in the Retail Prices Index (RPI) since that time.[10] The LOLP is determined for each half-hour as the probability of a supply interruption due to the capacity made available by the generators being insufficient to meet expected demand. The PPP is known with certainty from the day-ahead perspective.

For each day-ahead price-setting process, the 48 load periods within the day are divided into two distinct pricing-rule regimes, referred to as Table A and Table B periods. The pool selling price (PSP) is the price paid by RECs purchasing electricity from the pool to sell to their final commercial, industrial, and residential customers. During Table A half-hours the PSP is

$$PSP = PPP + UPLIFT = SMP + CC + UPLIFT.$$

UPLIFT is a per MWh charge which covers services related to maintaining the stability and control of the National Electricity System and costs of supplying the

---

to choose their electricity supplier by the end of 1998 fiscal year under the current plan, although there have been a number of delays and revisions of previous plans for the under 100 kW market.

9   LOLP is calculated for each half-hour with PROMOD and other computations outlined in the *Pooling and Settlement Agreement for the Electricity Industry in England and Wales, Schedule 9-The Pool Rules*, using NGC's day-ahead half-hourly demand forecast and generators' availability and other operational parameters. Wolak and Patrick (1997) provide additional detail and the implications of this procedure for determining the LOLP.

10   The VOLL was 2187.00 £/MWh from April 1, 1991; 2285.00£/MWh from April 1, 1992; 2345.00 £/MWh from April 1, 1993; 2389.00 £/MWh from April 1, 1994; 2458.00£/MWh from April 1, 1995 through March 31, 1996.

difference between NGC's forecast of the day's demands and the actual demands for each load period during that day and, therefore, can only be known at the end of the day in which the electricity is produced. These costs are charged to electricity consumption only during Table A periods in the form of this per MWh charge.

The *ex ante* and *ex post* prices paid by suppliers for each megawatt-hour (MWh) are identical for Table B half-hours, i.e., *PSP = PPP* for Table B periods. The determination of Table A versus Table B half-hours is as follows. Table A is in effect for those half-hour periods during which the expected system excess capacity is within 1000 MW of the excess capacity during the peak half-hour of the previous day. Excess capacity is the amount of capacity offered by generators in any half-hour less the amount of this capacity actually used to fill demand in that period. Expected excess capacity during each half-hour period of the next day is defined as the maximum capacity generators offer to make available to the pool less expected demand as forecast by NGC. If the expected excess capacity in any half-hour period of the next day is within 1000 MW of the benchmark excess capacity from the relevant previous day's system peak, then the half-hour is classified as Table A and *UPLIFT* charges are added to the per MWh *PPP* during this half-hour to arrive at the *PSP*. Thus, the only energy price uncertainty from the day-ahead perspective is the *UPLIFT* component of the *PSP*, which is only known *ex post* and only applies to the Table A half-hours.[11]

By 4 PM each day, the Settlement System Administrator (SSA) provides Pool Members, which includes all of the RECs, with the *SMP*, *CC*, *LOLP*, and identity of the Table A and B pricing periods.

2.3. MEB's Pool Price Contract

The PPC was first offered at beginning after March 31, 1991 to allow consumers with peak demands greater than 1 MW to assume the risks of pool price volatility and therefore avoid the costs associated with hedging against this price volatility. Under the PPC, wholesale electricity costs for both energy and transmission services are directly passed through to the customer. For traditional pricing contracts, the REC absorbs all the wholesale price risk associated with the *PSP* and retails electricity to final consumers according to fixed and deterministic prices (i.e., they do not vary with the *PSP*).

The peak demand size limit on customers given the option to choose their supplier as well as purchase according to a PPC was reduced to 100 KW in 1994, coinciding with the same limit change in the definition of franchise customers.

---

11   To insure that "fixed" costs are not congregated in a few periods, thereby driving up the relative prices in these periods, there is an upper bound on the number of Table B periods each day. From 21:00 hours (the start of the schedule run) to 05:00 hours, a maximum of seven of the sixteen pricing periods can be classified as Table B. From 05:01 to 05:00 hours at least 28 of the 48 pricing periods must be Table A pricing periods. From 05:01 to 12:00 hours (the end of the schedule run), a maximum of 5 Table B pricing periods are allowed. If the initial calculations produce more than the allowed number of Table B periods, the Table B periods associated with the minimum expected excess capacity are changed to Table A periods, until the constraint on the number of Table B periods is binding.

Over the six months following March 31, 1998, this size limit will be phased out so that there will no longer be franchise designations, the entire supply segment of the electricity market will be open to competition and any customer willing to pay the cost of installing meters capable of recording half-hourly consumption will have the option to pay for electricity according to pool prices.

MEB had 370 commercial and industrial customers (of approximately 500 customers with demands over 1 MW) purchasing their electricity according to a PPC for the year April 1, 1991 through March 31, 1992, the first year of the program. This number of customers on the pool price contract remained stable over the following two years, although approximately one-fourth of the customers each year are new. For the year of April 1, 1994 to March 31, 1995, when the pool price contract was first offered to relatively smaller consumers—those with greater than 100 KW peak demand—a number of commercial customers, as well as smaller industrials, were then given the option to purchase electricity according to pool prices. Approximately 150 customers in this size class signed up for the Pool Price contract for the year 1994-1995. Table 1(a) gives the number of customer/year pairs in each BIC class (by two-digit BIC code), as well as a general description of the types of industries contained in each class, for our sample. For many of the industries listed by two-digit BIC code in table 1(a), we are able to estimate less aggregated industry-level electricity demands, which is indicated by the industries listed in table 1(b). Table 1(b) lists BIC class and activity designations for the five specific industries analyzed and presented in Patrick and Wolak (1997a,b).

The expected *PSP*s for all 48 half-hourly intervals beginning with the load period ending at 5:30 am the next day until the load period ending at 5:00 am the following day are faxed to all pool price customers immediately following the REC's receipt of the *SMP*, *CC*, and identity of the Table A and Table B periods from NGC. Figure 1 contains a sample of the fax sent to PPC customers.[12] The REC develops forecasts of the *UPLIFT* component of the *PSP* for Table A half-hours and provides these with the 48 half-hourly *SMP*s and *CC*s. The *PSP* reported in this fax is equal to the *PPP* in Table B periods and the sum of the REC's estimate of the *UPLIFT* and the *PPP* in Table A periods. The actual (*ex post*) *PSP* paid by electricity consumers on the PPC for Table A periods is known 28 days following the day the electricity is consumed. The actual or *ex post PSP* is equal to the *ex ante PSP* for Table B periods because the *UPLIFT* is known to be zero in these load periods.

Customers on PPCs also pay a demand charge. This £/MW triad charge is levied on the average capacity used by each PPC customer during the three half-hour load periods during the fiscal year ("triads") in which the load on the England and Wales system is highest, subject to the constraint that each of these three periods is separated from the others by at least ten days. The precise triad charge is set each

---

12   Note that the load period numbering scheme that appears on this FAX differs from the one we use throughout the paper. We assign load period 1 to be load period 11 as it is defined on the Pool Price FAX, so that load 1 to 48 by our convention corresponds to load period 11 to 48, 1-10 on the Pool Price FAX, to reflect the actual order in which the load periods occur during the operation of the day-ahead market and appear on the Pool Price FAX.

Table 1(a). Two-Digit 1980 BIC Codes and Total Number of Customer-Year Pairs

BIC	Description	Total Customer Years
14000	mineral oil processing	11
16000	prod. & dist. of electricity, gas, & other forms of energy	9
17000	water supply industry	31
22000	metal manufacturing	138
23000	extraction of minerals not elsewhere specified	31
24000	manufacture of non-metallic mineral products	180
25000	chemical industry	44
31000	manufacture of metal goods not elsewhere specified	427
32000	industrial plant and steelwork	75
33000	manufacturing of office and data processing equipment	10
34000	electrical and electronic engineering	70
35000	manufacture of motor vehicles and parts thereof	66
36000	manufacture of other transport equipment	13
37000	instrument engineering	5
41000	food, drink & tobacco manufacturing industries	55
42000	sugar and sugar by-products	52
43000	textile industry	29
45000	footwear and clothing industries	1
46000	timber and wooden furntiture industries	31
47000	manufacture of paper & paper products; printing & publishing	73
48000	processing of rubber & plastics	72
49000	other manufacturing industries	130
61000	wholesale distribution (except in scrap & waste materials)	58
63000	commission agents	22
64000 & 65000	retail distribution	67
66000	hotels and catering	4
67000	repair of consumer goods and vehicles	2

Table 1(b). Five 1980 BIC Code Industries Used in Analysis

BIC	Description	Customer Years
17000	water supply industry	31
22200	steel tubes	37
22460	copper, brass, and other copper alloys	22
24890	ceramic goods	19
31600	hand tools and finished metal goods	15

Time Ending	Period No.	FORECAST PPU FOR : 10/10/94 AND 11/10/94				Final PSP for 12/9/94 & 13/9/94
		SMP	Capacity Payment	Uplift	PSP	
5:30	11	0.992	0.000	0.000	0.992	0.954
6:00	12	0.997	0.000	0.000	0.997	0.955
6:30	13	1.003	0.000	0.000	1.003	0.994
7:00	14	1.670	0.000	0.245	1.915	1.586
7:30	15	2.857	0.008	0.248	3.113	1.913
8:00	16	3.835	0.042	0.257	4.134	1.981
8:30	17	4.000	0.060	0.260	4.320	1.993
9:00	18	4.000	0.081	0.268	4.349	1.996
9:30	19	3.835	0.071	0.265	4.171	2.144
10:00	20	3.835	0.072	0.266	4.173	2.682
10:30	21	3.835	0.066	0.265	4.166	2.684
11:00	22	3.835	0.063	0.264	4.162	2.686
11:30	23	3.835	0.059	0.263	4.157	2.688
12:00	24	2.999	0.051	0.261	3.311	2.688
12:30	25	2.999	0.036	0.256	3.291	2.684
13:00	26	2.999	0.024	0.253	3.276	2.144
13:30	27	2.992	0.011	0.249	3.252	2.139
14:00	28	2.660	0.006	0.247	2.913	2.137
14:30	29	2.660	0.003	0.246	2.909	2.137
15:00	30	2.992	0.003	0.246	3.241	1.977
15:30	31	2.660	0.002	0.246	2.908	1.977
16:00	32	2.660	0.003	0.246	2.909	1.978
16:30	33	2.660	0.011	0.249	2.920	2.750
17:00	34	2.992	0.018	0.251	3.261	2.753
17:30	35	3.193	0.024	0.253	3.470	2.751
18:00	36	3.193	0.044	0.259	3.496	2.748
18:30	37	4.280	0.120	0.280	4.680	1.976
19:00	38	4.700	0.150	0.285	5.135	1.971
19:30	39	4.700	0.128	0.282	5.110	1.971
20:00	40	4.280	0.046	0.258	4.584	4.042
20:30	41	3.193	0.008	0.248	3.449	4.042
21:00	42	2.176	0.002	0.246	2.424	4.042
21:30	43	1.987	0.001	0.245	2.233	1.970
22:00	44	1.919	0.000	0.245	2.164	1.970
22:30	45	1.670	0.000	0.245	1.915	1.970
23:00	46	1.670	0.000	0.245	1.915	1.841
23:30	47	1.670	0.000	0.245	1.915	1.586
0:00	48	1.000	0.000	0.000	1.000	1.441
0:30	1	0.998	0.000	0.000	0.998	0.992
1:00	2	0.997	0.000	0.000	0.997	0.960
1:30	3	1.081	0.000	0.000	1.081	0.960
2:00	4	2.495	0.000	0.245	2.740	0.960
2:30	5	2.495	0.000	0.245	2.740	0.960
3:00	6	2.495	0.000	0.245	2.740	0.960
3:30	7	2.495	0.000	0.245	2.740	0.960
4:00	8	1.670	0.000	0.245	1.915	0.960
4:30	9	0.998	0.000	0.000	0.998	0.960
5:00	10	0.998	0.000	0.090	0.998	0.960

Figure 1. Sample Pool Price Contract Day-Ahead Fax

year by NGC (subject to their RPI-X price-cap regulation). The triad charge faced by these PPC customers was 6,150 £/MW for fiscal year 1991/92; 5,420 £/MW for 1992/93; 10,350 £/MW for 1993/4; and 10,730 £/MW for 1994/95.

There are various mechanisms that RECs can use to warn their PPC customers of potential triad periods. *Triad advance warnings* are generally faxed to consumers on Thursday nights and give the load periods during the following week that the REC feels are more likely to be triad periods. *Triad priority alerts* are issued the night before the day that the REC considers the probability of a triad period to be particularly high. These alerts also list the half-hours most likely to be triad periods. To mitigate the incentive for RECs to issue triad priority alerts, the regulatory contract allows a maximum of 25 hours of priority alerts each fiscal year. Actual triad charges have only occurred in the four-month period from November to February. Table 2(a)-(d) lists all triad advance warnings, priority alerts, and actual triads periods for our sample.

The actual price for service paid by PPC customers also contains various other factors which do not depend on the pool price. Customers on fixed rates face similar charges. These are the distribution use of system charges, corrections for the transmission and distributions losses (which are fixed percentage markups on each MWh sold and therefore do not affect the ratio of the price a customer pays for electricity in one load period relative to another), and a 17.5% value-added tax (VAT). The distribution use of system charge is composed of a standing charge per month (the monthly connect fee), the availability charge which is multiplied by the line capacity, and the per MWh delivered charge which has two different values for night and day.

The REC initially marketed the PPC by advising eligible (potential) customers that they could most likely reduce their electricity costs with the PPC regardless of whether they could manage their load or not (because of the risk premium built into the REC's fixed-price contracts). Insurance against price increases was also offered

Table 2(a). Advance Warnings, Priority Alerts, and Realized Triads Fiscal Year 1991/92			
Date	Advance Warnings	Time Periods for Priority Alerts	Triads
11/21/91			25
11/26/91	24,25		
12/3/91	24,25		
12/4/91	24,25		
12/5/91	24,25		
12/9/91	24,25		
12/10/91	24,25	24,25	
12/11/91	24,25	24,25	25
12/12/91	24,25	24,25	
1/6/92	24,25		
1/7/92	24,25		
1/8/92	24,25		
1/9/92	24,25		
1/13/92	24,25		
1/14/92	24,25	24,25	
1/15/92	24,25	24,25	
1/16/92	24,25	24,25	
1/21/92		24,25,26	
1/22/92		24,25,26	
1/23/92	24,25,26	24,25,26	25
1/28/92		25,26	
2/3/92	25,26		
2/10/92	25,26	25,26	
2/11/92	25,26		
2/18/92		25,26	
Total hours	20.5	13.5	1.5

Table 2(b). Advance Warnings, Priority Alerts, and Realized Triads Fiscal Year 1992/93			
Date	Advance Warnings	Time Periods for Priority Alerts	Triads
11/17/92			25
11/26/92		24,25	
12/3/92	24,25	24,25	
12/7/92	24,25		
12/8/92	24,25	24,25	
12/9/92	24,25	24,25	24
12/10/92	24,25	24,25	
12/14/92	24,25		
12/15/92	24,25	24,25	
12/16/92	24,25	24,25	
12/17/92	24,25	24,25	
1/4/93		24,25	25
1/5/93	24,25	24,25	
1/6/93	24,25	24,25	
1/7/93	24,25	24,25	
1/11/93	24,25		
1/12/93	24,25	24,25	
1/13/93	24,25	24,25	
1/14/93	24,25		
1/19/93	24,25	24,25	
1/20/93	24,25		
1/21/93	24,25		
1/25/93	24,25,26	25,26	
1/26/93	24,25,26	25,26	
1/27/93	24,25,26		
2/1/93	24,25,26		
2/2/93	25,26	25,26	
2/3/93	25,26		
2/4/93	25,26		
2/8/93	25,26		
2/9/93	25,26		
2/10/93	25,26	25,26	
2/11/93	25,26	25,26	
Total hours	31	20	1.5

by the REC the first year they offered the PPC, as PPC consumers were given the option to "fallback" to paying for electricity according to their previous rate structure. PPC customers choosing this fallback option were only allowed to pay according to their prior rates the first year, provided the customer would commit to the PPC a second year and would then pay according to pool prices during the second year of the program. All but 70 customers during 1991/92 accepted this option of paying according to their "fallback" (prior) rate structure. All other customers in 1991/92 and all customers that select the PPC since then have been

Table 2(c). Advance Warnings, Priority Alerts, and Realized Triads Fiscal Year 1993/94			
Date	Advance Warning	Time Periods for Priority Alert	Triad
11/9/93	24,25		
11/10/93	24,25		
11/11/93	24,25	24,25	
11/15/93	24,25	24,25	
11/16/93	24,25	24,25	
11/17/93	24,25	24,25	
11/18/93	24,25	24,25	
11/22/93	24,25	24,25	
11/23/93	24,25	24,25	
11/24/93	24,25	24,25	
11/25/93	24,25	24,25	
11/29/93			24
12/13/93	24,25	24,25	
12/14/93	24,25	24,25	24
12/15/93	24,25	24,25	
12/16/93	24,25	24,25	
1/5/94		24,25	
1/6/94	24,25	24,25	
1/17/94	24,25	24,25	
1/13/94	24,25	24,25	
1/18/94	24,25	24,25	25
1/19/94	24,25	24,25	
2/2/94		25,26	
2/3/94		25,26	
2/14/94	25,26	25,26	
2/15/94	25,26	25,26	
Total hours	22	23	1.5

obligated to pay according to pool prices. We omitted the customers with fallback options from our demand analysis because they did not actually purchase electricity according to the pool price, but the set of prices (either the pool price or the previous year's fixed price contract) that yields the lowest annual electricity bill.

3. Data

The REC provided data on the half-hourly consumption of all of its PPC customers from April 1, 1991 through March 31, 1995. We also collected the information contained on the faxes sent to each PPC customer the day before their actual consumption occurs. This fax contains the *ex ante* half-hourly forecasted *PSP* for the sample period—*SMP* + *CC* + Forecasted *UPLIFT* Charge. As noted earlier, the forecasted *UPLIFT* is estimated by the REC, whereas the actual value of *UPLIFT* is only known 28 days from the day in which the electricity is actually sold. We also collected information on the actual value of *UPLIFT* for our sample

Date	Advance Warning	Time Periods for Priority Alert	Triad
11/28/94	24,25		
11/29/94	24,25	24,25	
12/5/94	24,25	24,25	
12/6/94	24,25	24,25	
12/7/94	24,25	24,25	
12/8/94	24,25	24,25	
12/12/94	24,25	24,25	
12/13/94	24,25	24,25	
12/14/94	24,25	24,25	25
12/15/94	24,25	24,25	
12/19/94	24,25	24,25	
12/20/94	24,25	24,25	
12/21/94	24,25	24,25	
12/22/94	24,25	24,25	
1/3/95	24,25	24,25	
1/4/95		24,25	25
1/10/95		24,25	
1/11/95	25	25	
1/12/95	25	25	
1/18/95	24,25	24,25	
1/19/95	24,25	24,25	25
1/25/95		24,25	
1/26/95		24,25	
1/30/95	25,26		
1/31/95	25,26		
Total hours	20	21	1.5

Table 2(d). Triad Advance Warnings, Priority Alerts, and Realized Triads Fiscal Year 1994/95

period. Table 3 gives the sample means and standard deviations for the various components of the *PSP* for each fiscal year during our sample.

As discussed in Wolak and Patrick (1997), a notable feature of the behavior of *PSP* is its tremendous variability, even over very short time horizons. For our sample period, the maximum ratio of the highest to lowest *PSP* within a day is 76.6, whereas the sample average of this ratio is 4.1. The maximum ratio of the highest to lowest *PSP* within a month is 107.5 and the average of this ratio over all months in our sample is 11.0. Finally, the maximum ratio of the highest to lowest *PSP* within a fiscal year is approximately 117.8.

The England and Wales total system load (TSL) exhibits dramatically less volatility according to this metric. For example, the maximum ratio of the highest to lowest TSL within a day is 1.89 and the average over all days in the sample is 1.49. Within a month, the maximum of the highest to lowest TSL is 2.38 and the average over all months in the sample is 2.04. For the time horizon of a fiscal year, the maximum ratio of the highest to lowest TSL is 3.08. Consistent with this difference in volatility, the TSL can be forecasted much more accurately at all time

Table 3. Sample Means and Standard Deviations of Components of *PSP*			
	Year	Mean	Std Dev
SMP	1	19.52	4.10
CC	1	1.29	8.76
UPLIFT	1	1.61	2.31
PSP	1	22.42	12.72
SMP	2	22.64	4.24
CC	2	0.17	1.70
UPLIFT	2	1.39	1.12
PSP	2	24.19	5.75
SMP	3	24.16	6.71
CC	3	0.28	2.97
UPLIFT	3	2.18	1.62
PSP	3	26.62	8.76
SMP	4	20.78	12.28
CC	4	3.22	24.49
UPLIFT	4	2.38	4.53
PSP	4	26.38	35.08

horizons than the *PSP*. In making this comparison, we define forecasting accuracy as the standard deviation of the forecast error as a percent of the sample mean of the time series under consideration.

As discussed in Wolak and Patrick (1997), the major source of the large values of the *PSP* over the years shown in figure 2 is the *CC*, which is known with certainty on a day-ahead basis. In addition, large values of the *UPLIFT* tend to occur in the same load periods within the day that large values of *CC* occur, which makes forecasting *UPLIFT* relatively easier. Nevertheless, the two largest components of the *PSP* are known to the customer before consumption choices are made for the following day, and the remaining component is forecastable with considerable

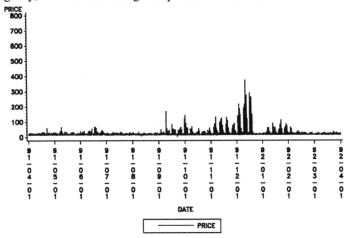

Figure 2(a). Price 1991-1992

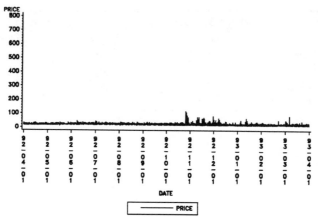

Figure 2(b). Price 1992-1993

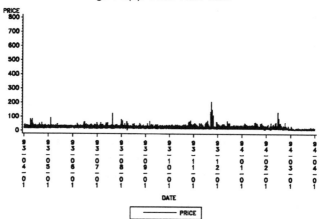

Figure 2(c). Price 1993-1994

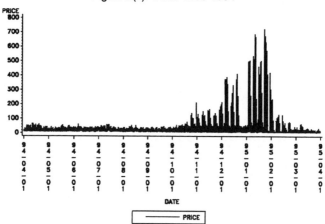

Figure 2(d). Price 1994-1995

accuracy. For example, the sample mean over our four years of data of the difference between the REC's *ex ante* forecast of *UPLIFT* and the actual *ex post* value of *UPLIFT* is 0.07 £/MWh with a standard deviation of 1.16. The mean absolute deviation of the difference between the REC's *ex ante* forecast of *UPLIFT* and the actual *ex post* value of *UPLIFT* is 0.56 £/MWh with a standard deviation of 1.02. Comparing these magnitudes to the annual means of the *PSP* given in table 3, which are on the order of 25 £/MWh, shows that the uncertainty between the *ex ante* and *ex post* values of *PSP* is small.

4. The Impossibility of Using Aggregate Data to Estimate Price Responsiveness

As noted in Section 2, the market rules governing the price determination process in the E&W market do not use the actual market demand to set the SMP and CC, the two major components of the PSP.   These prices are set using a perfectly inelastic (with respect to price) forecast of the half-hourly market demand for the next day. In addition, for the vast majority of final customers, the price they pay for electricity does not vary with movements in the PSP for the entire fiscal year. Consequently, any attempt to estimate a relationship between the PSP for given half-hour and the total system load for that half-hour will not recover the true relationship between final demand and the half-hourly market price, because few customers are paying for electricity during that half-hour at the PSP or even at a price that varies with the PSP throughout the day, month or year.

Comparing the time path of PSP to the time path of total system load bears this logic out. Figure 2 plots the half-hourly *PSP* in (£/MWh) for the more than 17,000 prices for each fiscal year during our sample period. Figure 3 plots the half-hourly TSL in gigawatts (GW) of capacity used for each fiscal year in our sample period. The highest values of *PSP* within a fiscal year tend to occur during the four-month period from November to February. These are also the months when there is an enormous amount of price volatility within the day and across days. The pattern

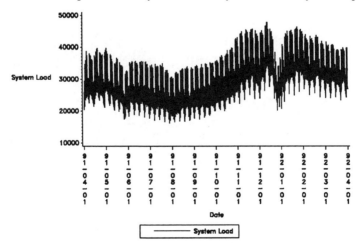

Figure 3(a). System Loads 1991-1992

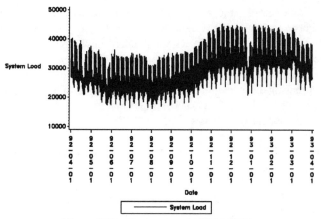

Figure 3(b). System Loads 1992-1993

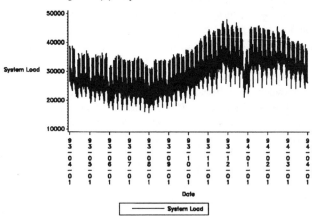

Figure 3(c). System Loads 1993-1994

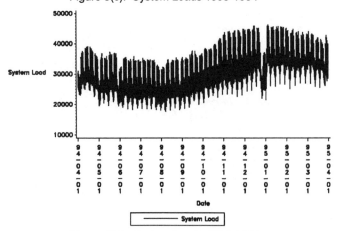

Figure 3(d). System Loads 1994-1995

and the magnitude of the volatility differs markedly across the four fiscal years. All of the price graphs are plotted using the same scale on the vertical axis to illustrate this point.

Compared to the four graphs in figure 2, the four graphs in figure 3 indicate the very predictable pattern of TSL across days, weeks, and years. In particular, the total demand in a single day in one year is very similar to the demand in that same day in the previous year. The cycle of demand within a given week is similar to the cycle of demand within that same week in another year. Similar statements can be made for the cycles in TSL within months across different years.

The difference between the four price graphs and the four TSL graphs illustrates a very important implication of the operation of the E&W market which does not allow a meaningful price-response to be recovered from co-movements in TSL and the *PSP*. Despite the large differences in the patterns of *PSP* movements across the four years, there is no discernable change in the pattern of TSL across the four years. This occurs because the vast majority of business customers, and all residential customers, purchase power on fixed-price contracts set for the entire fiscal year. These customers do not face any within-year price changes or even within-day price changes which depend on within-year changes in the *PSP* that might trigger a within-day demand response.

Each of the 12 RECs and other suppliers offer several fixed-price options to electricity consumers. For residential customers, RECs offer a small number of different standard price contracts, e.g., the single-price for all load periods contract, or a two-price contract (separate prices for day and night load periods). For business customers, each REC offers several standard price contracts, but particularly for large customers who can choose their supplier from any of the 12 RECs or any of the generators or other suppliers, price contracts are often negotiated on a customer-by-customer basis. Consequently, for the same half-hour period, there are hundreds and potentially even thousands of different retail prices that different customers throughout the E&W system are paying for electricity. In addition, movements in the *PSP*, or in any of its components, generally have no effect on the movements in these contract prices for the duration of the contract period, usually a fiscal year. The lack of responsiveness of TSL to changes in *PSP* does not imply that individual customers do not respond to price changes. This lack of responsiveness is indicative of the fact that only a very small fraction of final customers purchase electricity at the half-hourly *PSP*, with the remaining vast majority purchasing electricity on the fixed-price contracts described above.

An important consequence of virtually no customers purchasing electricity at the half-hourly *PSP* is that it makes little, if any, economic sense to estimate an aggregate demand curve for electricity involving *PSP* or *PPP* as the price variable and TSL as the quantity demanded variable to recover a price-response. Movements in the half-hourly or the daily average *PSP* or *PPP*, which identify the aggregate price response, are irrelevant to the vast majority of electricity consumers who instead face prices that are unrelated to any within-year movements in the *PSP* or *PPP* for the entire fiscal year. Consequently, a price response recovered from regressing the current value of the TSL on the *PSP* for that load period is likely to be extremely misleading about the true potential aggregate price response because only between 5 and 10 percent of TSL is purchased at *PSP* and the remaining is purchased according to prices that are invariant to changes in the *PSP* for an entire fiscal year.

To estimate the within-day electricity demand response to within-day changes in the *PSP* requires a sample of customers actually purchasing electricity at prices which move with changes in the half-hourly *PSP*. PPC customers are ideally suited to this task because the within-day relative prices that they pay for electricity in any load period within the day are those obtained from the *PSP*.

5. Estimated Price Elasticities for the Water Supply Industry

In this section, we present the price elasticity estimates for the water supply industry. Patrick and Wolak (1997a,b) provide the complete modeling analyses and results for all the industries in table 1b. The remaining industries in table 1a are currently being examined.

The own-price and cross-price elasticities of demand for any day and load period can be computed from the Patrick and Wolak (1997a,b) estimated model. Because prices and demands are extremely variable over the course of the year and within the day, there is considerable variability both within the day and across days in these own- and cross-price elasticities. In addition, these elasticities also vary across days due to movements in four weather variables. To facilitate the interpretation of the water supply industry demand model, we present the computed sample mean own-price and cross-price elasticities and the upper and lower 95 percent confidence bounds on these sample mean elasticities.

This water supply industry must pump substantial amounts of water into its storage and sewage-treatment facilities once or twice a day, so that it has the ability to shift this activity to the lowest-priced load periods within the day at very short notice. As expected, there is a considerable amount of heterogeneity in the within-day own-price responses. Figure 5 plots the sample mean own-price elasticities and their upper and lower 95% confidence bounds as a function of the load period for the water supply industry. The sample mean own-price elasticities are very precisely estimated. Although during the usual peak total system load periods 20 to 26, i.e., beginning at 2:30 PM and ending at 6:00 PM, we find a uniformly small mean own-price elasticity. For the load periods immediately preceding and immediately following this time period, the mean own-price elasticity is over 0.20 in absolute value and gets as large in absolute value as 0.27 in load period 10, the period from 9:30 to 10:00 AM. The mean own-price elasticity is also very large for the load period beginning at 11:00 AM, taking on a value of -0.142. Given the amount of price volatility in the *PSP* and the expected demand charge, this within-load-period own-price elasticity of demand is very large. Recall the enormous volatility in the *PSP* shown in figure 2 and the volatility in the expected demand charge given in figure 4. In particular, it would not be unusual to have values of expected prices across days for the same load period that differ by a factor 20 or 30, which would imply a sizeable reduction in the within period demand. Table 4 gives the sample mean and standard deviation of expected half-hourly prices for our four years of data. For some load periods, the standard deviation of

Table 4. Sample Mean and Standard Deviation of Load Period Level Expected Prices					
Load Period	Mean Price £/MWH	Standard Deviation	Load Period	Mean Price £/MWH	Standard Deviation
1	16.4041	4.672	25	65.4332	139.679
2	16.5361	5.068	26	46.9099	67.86
3	17.0682	5.188	27	35.0434	32.14
4	19.7809	6.283	28	30.631	16.974
5	22.4044	6.52	29	28.1736	10.163
6	24.0206	7.71	30	26.4282	7.437
7	25.8175	9.365	31	25.4712	7.114
8	27.1188	9.532	32	25.6455	6.963
9	28.5932	9.698	33	25.9198	7.184
10	29.8345	10.542	34	25.7174	7.739
11	29.6207	9.854	35	24.2444	7.888
12	28.897	8.895	36	21.6372	7.056
13	29.3244	9.081	37	19.013	5.382
14	30.5428	9.963	38	17.341	4.771
15	30.7373	10.148	39	16.9903	4.868
16	29.4235	8.897	40	19.3905	7.292
17	26.5548	6.691	41	20.613	8.264
18	24.8538	6.066	42	21.9722	9.029
19	23.6454	6.295	43	20.5639	7.664
20	23.0726	6.313	44	19.85	7.199
21	22.5719	6.584	45	18.8334	6.535
22	24.1142	10.653	46	17.5373	5.451
23	31.8623	30.628	47	16.6788	4.904
24	56.6734	117.676	48	16.149	4.474

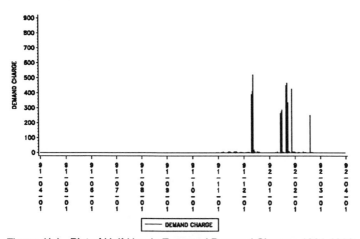

Figure 4(a). Plot of Half-Hourly Expected Demand Charges 1991-1992

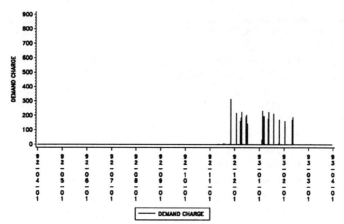

Figure 4(b). Plot of Half-Hourly Expected Demand Charges 1992-1993

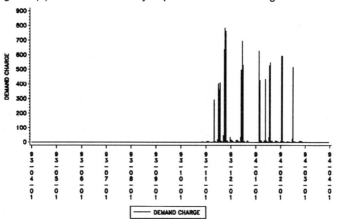

Figure 4(c). Plot of Half-Hourly Expected Demand Charges 1993-1994

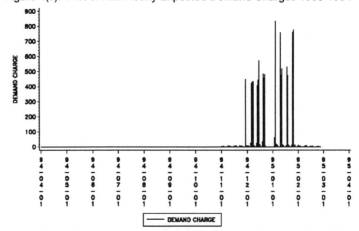

Figure 4(d). Plot of Half-Hourly Expected Demand Charges 1994-1995

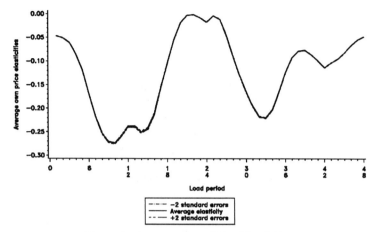

Figure 5. Average Own Price Elasticities
BIC 17000: Water Supply Industry

the expected price is more than three times the value of mean, which indicates the potential for an enormous amount of variability in prices for the same load period across days.

Figure 6 presents a 3-dimensional plot of the sample mean of the cross-price elasticities. To facilitate the interpretability of this cross-price elasticity plot, the own-price elasticities are excluded from the plot. The peaks in the plots on both sides of diagonal indicate that most of the substitutability in electricity consumption within the day comes from substitution across adjacent load periods. This industry exhibits the type of within-day substitution patterns that would enable a REC serving these customers predictably to demand-side bid significant amounts of

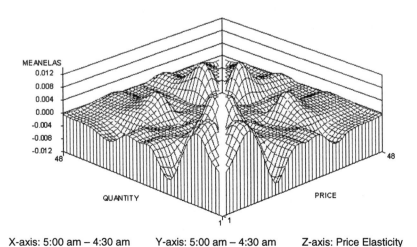

X-axis: 5:00 am – 4:30 am   Y-axis: 5:00 am – 4:30 am   Z-axis: Price Elasticity

Figure 6. Mean Cross-Price Elasticities
Customers with BIC = 17000, Water Supply

capacity when the *PSP* increases dramatically between one day to the next or the probability of a triad charge substantially increases across two adjacent days.

6. Use of Model Results

These demand system estimates enable the measurement of the effects of alternative time-varying and consumption-dependent pricing structures on customer-level electricity loads and the resulting effects on the electricity supplier's revenue and customer's benefits.   There are many examples we could present illustrating various uses of the model, but, for conciseness, we restrict ourselves to two in this section and discuss additional uses in the conclusions of this chapter. First we present examples comparing alternative vectors of energy price and demand (triad) charge changes.   We then present an example where we use this procedure to develop demand-side bids derived from changes in the real-time pricing (PPC) customers' demands as a result of price changes. See Patrick and Wolak (1997a,b) for additional detail and the procedures used in constructing the following examples.

We first use the model to predict the demand response to changes in various components of the expected prices—the sum of expected *PSP* and the expected demand charge. Figure 7 considers two changes in the expected *PSP*. The baseline scenario is the pattern of consumption for a representative weekday evaluated at the sample mean of the observed expected prices. The first scenario is a 50 percent increase in all 48 half-hourly expected *PSPs* holding the expected demand charges constant. Consistent with the own-price elasticities, we find significant reductions in demand relative to baseline scenario in load periods early in the day and later in day with only a small reduction in demand during the high priced periods of the day.   The second scenario decreases the expected *PSPs* in load periods 30-34 by 50%. Significant increases in the electricity consumption are predicted in these load periods, with very small reductions in consumption predicted in the immediately adjacent periods.

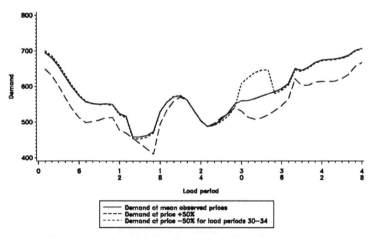

Figure 7. Price Responses: BIC 17000 Water Supply

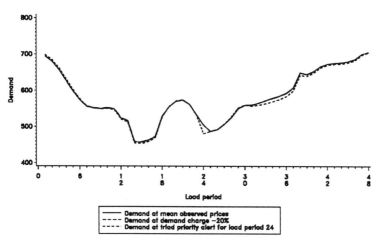

Figure 8. Price Responses: BIC 17000 Water Supply

The second two scenarios, which are given in figure 8, consider the impact of changes in components of the expected demand charge on the pattern of within-day electricity consumption. The first considers a 20% decrease in the demand charge. The representative day selected for this scenario did not have a triad priority alert in any of the load periods, so the probability of a demand charge was uniformly small for all load periods in the day. As a consequence, this reduction in the demand charge had no discernable predicted impact on the pattern of electricity consumption. The second scenario assumed that a triad priority alert was in fact issued for load period 24, so using the estimated probability function given in Patrick and Wolak (1997a,b) the probability of a demand charge in period 24 went from close to zero to approximately 0.12. As a result of issuing this triad priority alert, a significant demand reduction is predicted to occur in load period 24. There is also predicted to be a slight reduction in electricity demand in load periods 31 to 36.

These examples illustrate some of the types of predicted price responses that can be computed using these parameter estimates. Given this information on price responses and the standard errors around these responses, the electricity supplier or REC can then estimate the effect of alternative prices on customer load, customer benefits, and supplier revenues as well as compute the associated uncertainty in these estimates.

We next provide an example of how our demand system estimates can be used to formulate demand-side bids by electricity suppliers (RECs in the United Kingdom) serving customers on real-time prices (or the PPC). As discussed above, the existence of a substantial price response in the aggregate demand that sets the market clearing price will also reduce the variability of these prices over the course the of day. Substantial amounts of demand-side bidding by suppliers can result in half-hourly demands which imply significant reductions in the amount demanded as the price of electricity increases. Figure 9 illustrates the effects of demand-side bidding in the E&W price-determination process. TSL is the perfectly price inelastic forecasted demand used along with generator bids to supply electricity to

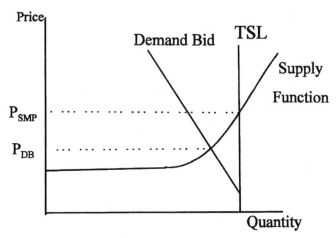

Figure 9. Impact of Demand-Side Bidding on Market-Clearing SMP

determine the half-hour's *SMP* (labeled P_{SMP}). Demand-side bidding effectively introduces elasticity into the demand-side in the price determination process, leading to the half-hour's *SMP* of P_{DB}, which is lower than the *SMP* set by an inelastic demand. Recall that this analysis assumes no change in bidding behavior by generators in response to demand-side bidding. This behavior seems unlikely given that they now face (under demand-side bidding) the likelihood not being called on to generate as a result of bidding too high of a price into the pool and should therefore bid more aggressively, resulting in an even lower *SMP*.

We now consider the impact of changing a single half-hourly price within the day on the demand in that load period and all other load periods during the day. We assume that the base period pattern of prices is the sample mean of the vector of load period-level expected prices given in table 4. We assume that the REC has ten customers from BIC 17000 (which is the approximate number of water supply customers on the REC's PPC in 1994-95). We assume that the price in load period 27, P_{27d}, increases from its sample mean of 35 £/MWh to 100 £/MWh, a large but not unheard of change in prices. The own-price response is a reduction in demand in load period 27 of 41.13 kWh per customer, or a total of 411.3 KWh for ten customers. Computing the demand change for each load period in the day except load period 27 and multiplying by 10 yields the demand schedule plotted in figure 10, which indicates where portions of the 411.3 kWh that are predicted no longer to be consumed in load period 27 are predicted to be consumed during the other load periods during the day.

Proceeding in this manner for a variety of prospective prices, given the mix of customers on the PPC, the REC can determine the magnitudes of price responses it can expect from various changes in the expected prices aggregated over all of its customers. Coupled with information on the standard errors of the these predicted price responses, the REC can then formulate demand-side bid functions which account for the aggregate estimated price response of all of the REC's PPC customers and the uncertainty associated with these responses.

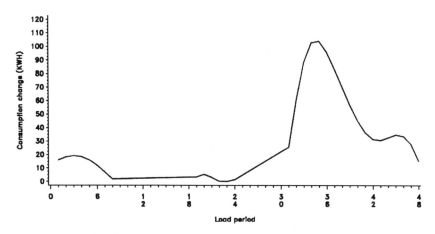

Figure 10. Price Response of Demand to Change in PE_{27d}
Price Responses: BIC 17000 Water Supply

6. Directions for Future Research

The demand model discussed in this chapter provides essential input into the successful design of market-based strategies for enhancing customer and utility benefits in increasingly competitive electricity markets. The most successful electricity supply companies will be those that offer a menu of pricing options. Such pricing options would be designed to attract and maintain a portfolio of customers that simultaneously yield sufficient revenues to the supplier to cover total production costs and a time-path of aggregate customer-level demands that can be produced in a least-cost manner given generation, transmission, and distribution capacities.

This movement toward attracting and maintaining a profitable portfolio of customers will change the market structure of electricity supply and expand the array pricing and marketing strategies used, and create incentives for the development of nonlinear pricing options for electricity. Nonlinear pricing allows the price charged for each unit consumed to vary along dimensions such as time of day, week, month or year electricity consumed, quantity consumed during day, week, month or year. These kinds of pricing policies can also vary depending on the degree of price stability and/or certainty over day, week, month or year, and reliability of supply over day, week, month or year.

References

Brough, Martin, and Seumas Lobban. 1995. *Guide to the Economic Regulation of the Electricity Industry*. Oxford, U.K.: OXERA Press.

Electricity Association. 1995. *UK Electricity*. London: Electricity Association Services Limited.

Energy Information Administration. 1996. *The Changing Structure of the Electric Power Industry: An Update*. DOE/EIA-0562(96), U.S Department of Energy, Washington, DC.

Government Statistical Service. 1980. *Standard Industrial Classification Revised 1980.* Central Statistical Office, Her Majesty's Stationary Office Publications Centre, London, U.K.

Government Statistical Service. 1991-95. *Business Monitor: MM22 Producer Price Indices.* Central Statistical Office, HMSO Publications Centre, London, U.K.

Patrick, Robert H., and Frank A. Wolak. 1997a. "Estimating the Customer-Level Demand for Electricity Under Real-Time Market Pricing." Mimeo.

Patrick, Robert H., and Frank A. Wolak . 1997b. *Customer Load Response to Spot Prices in England: Implications for Retail Service Design.* TR-109143, Electric Power Research Institute, Palo Alto, CA.

Phelps, A.K. 1994. "A Study of Real Time Pricing in the UK: The Midlands Electricity Experience." Midlands Electricity plc, Halesowen, United Kingdom. Mimeo.

Stewart, Thomas A. 1997. "When Change is Total, Exciting and Scary." *Fortune* (March 3): 169-170

Wilson, Robert. 1993. *Nonlinear Pricing.* Oxford University Press.

Wolak, Frank A., and Robert H. Patrick. 1997. "The Impact of Market Rules and Market Structure on the Price Determination Process in the England and Wales Electricity Market." Mimeo.

Wolak, Frank A., and Robert H. Patrick. 1996a. "Industry Structure and Regulation in the England and Wales Electricity Market." In *Pricing and Regulatory Innovations Under Increasing Competition*, edited by M.A. Crew. Boston, MA: Kluwer Academic Publishers.

Wolak, Frank A., and Robert H. Patrick. 1996b. "The Time Series Behavior of Market Prices and Output in the England and Wales Electricity Market." Mimeo.